German Foreign Policy, 1918–1945
A Guide to Research and Research Materials

Guides to European Diplomatic History
Research and Research Materials

Series Editor
Christoph M. Kimmich
Brooklyn College
The City University of New York

British Foreign Policy, 1918-1945
Revised Edition
By Sidney Aster
ISBN: 0-8420-2310-0

European International Economic Relations, 1918-1945
By Harold James and Diane B. Kunz
ISBN: 0-8420-2370-4

French Foreign Policy, 1918-1945
Revised Edition
By Robert J. Young
ISBN: 0-8420-2308-9

German Foreign Policy, 1918-1945
Revised Edition
By Christoph M. Kimmich
ISBN: 0-8420-2311-9

International Organizations, 1918-1945
Revised Edition
By George W. Baer
ISBN: 0-8420-2309-7

Italian Foreign Policy, 1918-1945
Revised Edition
By Alan Cassels
ISBN: 0-8420-2307-0

Soviet Foreign Policy, 1918-1945
By Robert H. Johnston
ISBN: 0-8420-2312-7

Available from Scholarly Resources Inc.
Wilmington, Delaware

German Foreign Policy
1918–1945

A Guide to Research and Research Materials

Compiled and Edited
by
Christoph M. Kimmich

Revised Edition

SR *Scholarly Resources Inc.*
Wilmington, Delaware

The paper used in this publication meets the minimum requirements of the American National Standard for permanence of paper for printed library materials, Z39.48, 1984.

Scholarly Resources Inc.
104 Greenhill Avenue
Wilmington, DE 19805-1897

Library of Congress Cataloging-in-Publication Data

Kimmich, Christoph M.
    German foreign policy, 1918–1945: a guide to research and research materials / compiled and edited by Christoph M. Kimmich. — Rev. ed.
        p.   cm. — (Guides to European diplomatic history research and research materials)
    Includes bibliographical references and index.
    ISBN 0-8420-2311-9
    1. Germany—Foreign relations—1918–1933—Library resources. 2. Germany—Foreign relations—1933–1945—Library resources. 3. Germany—Foreign relations—1918–1933—Archival resources. 4. Germany—Foreign relations—1933–1945—Archival resources. 5. Germany—Foreign relations—1918–1933—Bibliography. 6. Germany—Foreign relations—1933–1945—Bibliography. I. Title. II. Series.
Z6465.G4K54 1990
[DD240]
026'.32743—dc20
                                   90-31141
                                         CIP

ABOUT THE EDITOR

Christoph M. Kimmich is professor of history and provost at Brooklyn College, The City University of New York. He was educated at Haverford College and Oxford University and has been a Guggenheim Fellow; an International Affairs Fellow at the Council on Foreign Relations, New York; and a Visitor at the Institute for Advanced Study, Princeton. He is the author of The Free City: Danzig and German Foreign Policy, 1919–1934 (1968) and Germany and the League of Nations (1976).

INTRODUCTION TO THE SERIES

The reception accorded this series when it first appeared confirmed the editors in their belief that these research guides would meet a genuine need. It seems appropriate, therefore, since new material, published and unpublished, has become available over the last decade, that the series be brought up to date. A second edition is also an opportunity to add further volumes to the series. The series now consists of revised volumes on France, Germany, Great Britain, Italy, and International Organizations, and new volumes on the Soviet Union and on International Economic Relations.

The series is intended for scholars doing research for seminar papers, dissertations, and books dealing with European diplomatic history between 1918 and 1945. It provides information to assist them in their researches and to guide them on their visits to libraries and archives. It will enable them to find their way quickly and efficiently through the voluminous research and research materials that have become available in recent years and will point them toward solutions to the problems they will encounter in the course of their work.

The individual handbooks in this series are organized to serve the researcher's needs. Each has its own distinctive features, for the archival holdings and the research based on these holdings vary considerably. They are, however, meant to be complementary. They focus on materials relevant to different subject areas and, within the limits set by the history of international relations, avoid unnecessary repetition. They are organized along similar lines, and researchers who need to consult several volumes will have no trouble finding their way.

The first chapter will help the reader understand the nature and significance of the sources and allow him to determine where to concentrate his research, how to allot research time, and, not least, how best to approach the materials in the archives. It describes how foreign policy was made--how the foreign ministry was organized and how it functioned, how it affected the conduct of foreign affairs and diplomacy, and how it was influenced by bureaucratic politics, domestic developments, and public opinion.

The second chapter brings together the most current information on public and private archives, libraries, research institutes, and newspaper collections. It indicates what work can be undertaken on this side of the Atlantic and what has to be left for a visit to Europe, and further, what repository will be most useful and rewarding.

The remainder of the volume is bibliography. Sections on general and bibliographical reference works are followed by a survey of the literature in the field, ranging from documentary series to memoirs to significant secondary sources. Arranged topically within a broadly chronological framework, largely annotated, this bibliography permits ready reference to specific books and articles, historical personalities, and diplomatic events. Together with the archival information, the bibliography will suggest areas for further research or reassessment.

Each volume is edited by an authority in the field. Each reflects experience gained on the spot in archives and libraries as well as knowledge shared by colleagues, archivists, and librarians. The volumes therefore are as current and reliable as possible. They will be valuable companions to all who are interested in international affairs and diplomacy.

Christoph M. Kimmich
Series Editor

CONTENTS

I. INTRODUCTION

The student of German foreign policy between 1918 and 1945 is confronted with masses of material—archival and published sources, books and articles, newspapers and serials. This material is dispersed in repositories in Europe and North America, classified and catalogued in different ways. Archival records are not always where one would expect them to be, since some collections were broken up after the war, while others were filmed and duplicated. The quantity and variety of scholarly publications is such that one can barely keep up with them and determine whether they are relevant to one's work.

The student of German foreign policy is confronted also with certain unique conditions that will govern research on the subject. First, the depredations of the war and its aftermath tore sizable holes in the records accumulated by German ministries and offices. There is no assurance that documentation will be complete on any one subject or period, or that sufficient materials will be located in other collections to offset such losses. Second, and particularly characteristic of the Nazi period, the decline of the foreign ministry and the rise of rival agencies and organizations, each with its own purposes and priorities, created a profusion of foreign policies, of competing and overlapping jurisdictions. Researchers must therefore turn to the records not only of the foreign ministry but also of party plenipotentiaries, party agencies and offices, the adjutant or staff secretariats of the major players, and assorted maverick groups. And, finally, it should be noted that, in a period defined first by the terms of the peace treaty and then by the ambitions of a system driven to conquest, foreign policy was so deeply interwoven and interrelated with economic and financial policy, with military and rearmament policy that it is difficult to speak of foreign policy as such.

This handbook tells you about the various repositories and their holdings, their rules and regulations, and their facilities for research. It indicates the nature and extent of the gaps and losses in the materials that have survived. It guides you through the literature on the subject, making sources of information and of research available at a glance. And it describes how foreign policy was made and how it was implemented, so that you can decide what materials are pertinent and how they should be assessed.

The first chapter deals with the foreign ministry and foreign policy. It outlines the ministry's functions and organization and shows how these changed between 1918 and 1945. It describes the ministry's foreign missions, its agents, and its subterfuges, and traces the role of tradition and personality within the foreign service. And it explains how the ministry kept and stored its records. The chapter also touches on the ways in which policy was affected by constitutional provisions, parliamentary politics and partisan rivalries, public and private interests, and by changes in the style and scope of international

1

relations, for research that confines itself to the diplomats and their activity cannot comprehend the dynamics of foreign policy. An appendix to the chapter provides biographical data on the leading figures in Germany's foreign affairs and lists the major foreign diplomats stationed in Berlin.

The second chapter deals with archives, libraries, and research institutes in different countries. It describes the scope and arrangement of their holdings, and cites the published guides and inventories. It provides information on location, facilities, and hours, explains the formal procedures for gaining admission, and offers some practical advice. You will be able to plan your research trip ahead of time and, once you are on the road, to change plans without having to search elaborately through schedules and catalogues. The chapter also indicates what materials survived the war and where they can now be found, so that you can undertake preliminary research before you leave for Germany and spend what may be limited travel time more efficiently and productively on materials that can only be examined abroad. This second chapter is closely aligned with the first. It lists and describes the records of institutions and of many individuals mentioned earlier, not only those officially charged with the conduct of diplomacy but also those who shaped and pursued policy on their own. Questions concerning these external influences clearly require different sources and different archives.

The section on bibliography is the largest. It lists all published documents, regardless of whether they were published for scholarly or for propaganda purposes. It lists appropriate bibliographies and works of reference, significant contemporary works, memoirs and diaries. And it lists those secondary sources that may be said to have contributed to scholarship, were published recently (and in Western languages), and are readily available. Books and articles are annotated whenever they seemed obscure or problematical or important. The bibliography indicates that much has been done on German foreign policy and diplomatic history; it also suggests that much remains to be done.

The table of contents is quite detailed, so that you can find what you need without delay. The index lists authors, collections of documents, and important diplomatic events and personalities.

II. THE FOREIGN MINISTRY AND FOREIGN POLICY

For most of the period between 1918 and 1945, the foreign ministry held a key position in the conduct of foreign affairs. It controlled the flow of information from the diplomats in the field; it analyzed and assessed that information; it defined issues, outlined choices, and advised the foreign minister on all matters of policy. It carried out policy decisions, acting through its envoys in foreign capitals or at international conferences, who made and solicited proposals, engaged in negotiations, and concluded agreements. It consulted with other government ministries, with representatives of the German states, and with parliamentarians, academic specialists, and members of the business community whenever their views had some bearing on policy. And it dealt with the foreign diplomats accredited in Berlin, who came with inquiries or messages and negotiated on behalf of their governments. In all these activities, the ministry was able to exercise its judgment, and this judgment, reflecting the corporate view of the institution as well as the attitudes of its members, influenced foreign policy.

The ministry was considered primus inter pares among the ministries in Berlin. Though it was not above criticism, it enjoyed a high degree of respect, both within the government and outside, at least until the late thirties. It commanded some degree of priority in the government's budgetary decisions, and it routinely attracted well-educated and well-connected candidates to its openings. In some ways, its direct influence was probably greatest in the early twenties, when cabinets lasted only a few months, and the ministry was headed either by professional diplomats or by politicians whose modest familiarity with foreign affairs obliged them to rely heavily on their staff. But that influence was compromised by the fact that in such central issues as reparations and disarmament, the ministry was often kept on the periphery of decision making, yielding the field to outside experts, to representatives from other agencies, and to the military and the cabinet, which in turn was subject to a wide range of outside pressures. The consolidation of the ministry under the administrative leadership of Carl von Schubert, who was state secretary from 1924 to 1930, engendered a broad-based institutional self-confidence and effectiveness that contributed significantly to the shape and success of Germany's foreign policy. Even Stresemann and Brüning, who were highly aware of the eminence of their position, were not altogether immune to bureaucratic routine and professional opinion.

The Nazi regime had a profound effect on the workings of the ministry. Though it hardly touched the ministry directly, at least in the early years, it promoted internal divisions by encouraging, later even mandating, party membership; more importantly, it provided a context and a setting for the emergence of rivals who invaded the diplomatic preserve. Caught up in a

3

clutter of agencies with conflicting and competing claims, unaccustomed to the unorthodox style that characterized Hitler's rule, the foreign service was gradually stifled and ignored, and ultimately subjected to crippling restraints.[1]

A. ORGANIZATION

How the ministry exercised its duties was closely related to how it was organized. Its internal organization established a hierarchy of authority, prescribed lines of command and communication, and defined the functions and responsibilities of each member of the staff. Its filing system--which remains in effect in the archives today--was geared to the organization of the departments it served. In general, files were arranged by country or region and, within these categories, by subject, but since departments differed in how they allocated their work load, individual files or documents are not always where one would expect them to be. It is not very difficult, however, to discover which offices received copies of what documents, and where these would be filed.[2]

The ministry underwent reorganization twice between the wars--in 1919-20 and again in 1936. The first reform abolished a nineteenth-century system; the second restored much of what had been abolished. Under the prewar system, the ministry was divided into three sections--political, legal, and commercial--and each was under a director virtually independent of the others. The political division predominated. It exercised exclusive control over "high policy" and was staffed by diplomats, most of whom were aristocrats. The other two divisions were less prestigious. They were considered technical and collateral and were run by consular officials. The entire ministry was headed by a foreign secretary, who was appointed by the chancellor and in effect served as the chancellor's assistant in foreign affairs.

The war made this system obsolete and reduced the status and size of the ministry. The armistice and peace negotiations produced further disarray. A reform movement, led by Edmund Schüler, an official in the personnel department, undertook to modernize the ministry--to adapt it to a world in which international politics was shaped increasingly by social and economic pressures and was conducted by new elites. The reformers proposed to eliminate the separation of political and economic issues (and thus the dominance of the political division and the invidious distinction between consular and diplomatic careers), and to recruit talented outsiders who moved with ease in areas unfamiliar or suspect to old-line diplomats. They sought to create an organization that was rational, efficient, well ordered, and run according to professional, businesslike principles. While the reforms led to a decline in administrative coherence and coordination in the first few years, to the detriment, occasionally, of the conduct of policy, many of the principles thus established remained in place.[3]

Schüler's reform movement combined with the constitutional reforms adopted after the war. The system that emerged in March 1920, modified slightly until 1923, was to remain substantially unchanged until 1936. The ministry was now headed by a full-fledged foreign minister, responsible to cabinet and parliament, and more independent and more powerful than the former foreign secretary. Immediately under him was the state secretary (Staatssekretär), a career diplomat, who put the technical apparatus of the ministry at the minister's disposal and served as his deputy and principal adviser. (Until 1922, there were actually two state secretaries, one responsible for political, the other for economic, affairs.) Since the state secretary was the link between the minister and the ministry, the files of his personal secretariat (Büro Staatssekretär) rank with those of the minister's secretariat (Büro Reichsminister or, later, Büro RAM) as the most valuable to research on foreign policy. The ministry itself was divided into six departments (Abteilungen) and some special sections (Sonderreferate). Each of the departments was headed by a Ministerialdirektor and, beginning in 1921, by a deputy (sometimes by two), the Ministerialdirigent. Since the work of each department flowed through the hands of its director, his working files (Handakten) and sometimes his personal papers (Nachlass) are of interest. To maintain coordination within the ministry and to minimize duplications and delays, the minister held a conference in his office every morning (irreverently termed "Morgenandacht"), in which he and the state secretary met with the directors and their deputies, occasionally joined by the head of the press department and officials from the special sections.

Of the six departments, three were organized along regional, three along functional lines, and all but one were concerned with policy. Each consisted of six to eight sections (Referate), staffed by senior officials and young attachés. The individual Referate did the basic work of the ministry, and their files tend to be the most extensive on any issue (and, if they dealt with matters of particular importance, were usually kept as secret files or Geheimakten). The composition of the departments remained fixed, though it might change if a new director happened to have expert knowledge of a certain area of the world. By the mid-twenties, the departments were organized as follows:

Abteilung I
General administration, personnel and budget; technical services.
Abteilung II
Western and Southern Europe; Vatican; Occupied territories and the Saar; Disarmament Questions.
Abteilung III
Britain and the Dominions; the Americas; the Near East; Colonial Affairs; War Guilt Questions.
Abteilung IV
Russia, Poland, and Danzig; the Baltic states; Scandinavia; the Far East.
Abteilung V
Legal affairs; legal counsel on all questions of policy; international law; treaties and agreements.
Abteilung VI
Cultural affairs, ranging from the support of German cultural activities abroad (schools, churches, the press) to the problems of German ethnic minorities.

The ad hoc sections, which were set up as the need arose and later either dismantled or absorbed by departments, enjoyed a certain autonomy. Subject directly to the state secretary, they tended to be small (two to four officials), and each maintained its own files. Among the more important were

Friedensabteilung (originating in the Friedenskommission of 1918-19), which dealt with questions arising from the peace treaty;

Sonderreferat Deutschland (1919-31, 1933-40), which maintained liaison with parliament, the political parties, and the German states, and in general followed political developments at home; Sonderreferat Wirtschafts- und Reparationspolitik (later Abteilung Wirtschaft, 1920-36), which was concerned with reparations issues, economic negotiations, and trade relations; Sonderreferat Völkerbund (1923-29), which looked after League of Nations affairs.

There was also a press department (Presse Abteilung), operated jointly by the ministry and the chancellery. It kept track of the press and wire services, prepared news digests for the ministry as well as the chancellery and the president's office, served as spokesman on official policy, and saw to public relations. It was closely associated with WTB (Wolff's Telegraphisches Büro) and the Deutsche Allgemeine Zeitung, which for some years was owned by the government, and it subsidized news agencies such as Ostexpress, which specialized in news from abroad. One of its subsidiaries--the Reichszentrale für Heimatdienst--was used mainly to explain policy at home and to marshal public support.

The reorganization of 1936, the outcome of deliberations that had begun in 1931, was designed to increase centralized control. It fused the three regional departments (II, III, IV) and Abteilung Wirtschaft into a Political and a Commercial Department. The new Political Department became predominant. It was larger than the Commercial Department and administered by a director for whom the prewar title of under state secretary was revived in 1938. The rest--minister, state secretary, functional departments--were left unchanged. Where necessary, the filing system was adapted to the new structure.[4]

Ribbentrop became foreign minister in 1938, but it was only after the outbreak of war that he introduced structural changes. In September 1939, he and his staff became mobile, in order to be close to Hitler's shifting field headquarters. They first attached themselves to Himmler's entourage, and then they acquired their own train, Sonderzug Westfalen. This pocket foreign ministry, dominated by the Adjutantur Ribbentrop and the Persönlicher Stab Ribbentrop, marked the ascendancy of the party amateurs. They took over planning, made decisions, and sent out instructions, keeping in touch with Berlin and the diplomatic missions, occasionally summoning officials for brief consultations. Through Walther Hewel, Ribbentrop's liaison at headquarters, they kept track of Hitler's views and of the interviews that Hitler, alone or with Ribbentrop, had with foreign statesmen. Often they were better informed than the ministry.

Ribbentrop also tried to take advantage of the opportunities created by the war. He set up new departments, staffed them with outsiders from the party, and entrusted them with functions from the old departments. In 1939 he established an Information and a Radio Department, which competed with both the intelligence services and the propaganda ministry in conducting propaganda campaigns abroad. In 1940 he established Abteilung Deutschland as a link to the rapidly expanding domain of the SS. Headed by Martin Luther, a close associate, this department was virtually independent of the ministry and enjoyed broad discretionary powers. It was responsible for matters of particular interest to the party--negotiations to arrange the deportation of Jews from vassal states, efforts to recruit foreign volunteers for the armed units of the SS, or plans for the assassination of political leaders in other countries. As these activities grew in importance, the Abteilung and its ambitious chief assumed an important place among the other departments. Early in 1943, when Luther tried to engineer Ribbentrop's removal, Ribbentrop struck back by reorganizing the ministry and purging its staff. He dissolved Luther's department and its offices, and transferred its duties to other departments and to a completely new office, Inland I and Inland II, which reported to him directly. He merged the cultural and information departments into a new Kulturpolitische Abteilung and in general redefined functions and reassigned responsibilities among the traditional departments. He set up ad hoc offices, such as the America Committee, the Europe Committee, and nearly a dozen similar bodies, which were charged with mapping out plans for the postwar future. He relieved members of the senior staff of their duties and recalled many of the diplomats from abroad. Steengracht von Moyland, a member of his secretariat, became state secretary, and party associates were put in charge of departments. By the end of 1943, the ministry's organization had lost its last shred of rationality, and many of its tasks resembled traditional diplomacy only remotely.[5]

B. DIPLOMATS IN THE FIELD

During the Weimar years, Germany was represented abroad by nine embassies--Ankara, London, Madrid, Moscow, Paris, Rome, Tokyo, Vatican, Washington; which, after 1933, were increased by seven--Brussels, Buenos Aires, Peking/Nanking, Rio de Janeiro, Santiago de Chile, Vienna, and Warsaw. There were some forty legations, and over one hundred consular offices. These posts differed in diplomatic importance and prestige. The embassies were clearly in a class by themselves, but some legations and even some consulates were accorded special significance. The legation at Berne was for a long time the prime observer of events at the League; that at Warsaw was a key element in the uneasy relationship with Poland. Among the consulates, those at Danzig and Geneva covered areas of particular interest to Germany. Some of the larger embassies had press attachés, labor attachés, and trade or commercial attachés on their staff. Military and naval attachés were prohibited under the peace treaty and withdrawn in March 1920, but they returned soon after 1933.[6]

During the Weimar period, a good many foreign missions were in the charge of men drawn from outside the foreign service. By 1923 eight of the 26 diplomatic posts in Europe were held by outsiders. The appointments of such outsiders had been part of the Schüler reforms, but it had also become necessary when some of the former enemy states refused to treat with prewar diplomats. By the mid-twenties, however, this practice fell into disuse, and the Nazis, at least between 1933 and 1939, resorted to it only in a few cases (of which Papen in Vienna and Ribbentrop in London are the most notable). During the war Ribbentrop took to staffing diplomatic posts with party loyalists. Thus, in 1940-41, he appointed SA officers to head the legations in Rumania, Hungary, Slovakia, Yugoslavia, and Bulgaria.

The diplomats in the field were kept informed on matters relating to their posts, and they were generally consulted on policy. On issues of particular importance, they were recalled to Berlin for direct consultation. On occasion, diplomats who disagreed with policy tried to come to Berlin to press their case personally, but since they had to obtain permission to leave their post, the ministry was usually able to restrain such independence.

At first Hitler continued to rely on his diplomats abroad, reading the official correspondence, especially from London, Paris, and Rome, and consulting some of his ambassadors personally, most frequently, Papen and Hassell. In time, however, he relied less on diplomatic dispatches than on irregular, often obscure sources of information, such as Göring's Forschungsamt, which tapped telephones and intercepted diplomatic cables, and his interviews with his ambassadors became perfunctory.[7] He now made use of special emissaries, whom he sent abroad to pursue policies more in keeping with Nazi ideology. These plenipotentiaries, whose role in Nazi policy is still poorly understood, seem in many cases to have exercised the most immediate kind of influence on policy and events. Under instructions from Hitler personally, they took soundings, conducted negotiations, and concluded agreements, bypassing the ministry and the diplomats in the field. Göring pursued economic policy in the Balkans and laid claim to dealing with Poland and Italy; Ribbentrop negotiated with Britain and Japan; Wilhelm Keppler, an economic adviser and specialist in annexation, worked in Austria and Czechoslovakia. By the late thirties, the regular chiefs of mission were often left in the dark, ordered to remain neutral in diplomatic crises, or even recalled from their posts for months on end. And during the war much diplomatic business was turned over to "ambassadors on special assignment" (Gaus, Rintelen, Ritter) or to roving emissaries (Altenburg, Neubacher, Rahn, Veesenmayer), who took orders from Hitler or Ribbentrop and were not integrated into the workings of the ministry.

The files of many of the diplomatic missions have survived. They are useful for indicating how the mission arrived at policy recommendations and how it implemented policy, and since they often contain copies of telegrams and reports from other missions as well as important memoranda from the ministry, they can help fill gaps in the ministry's records. Similarly, the surviving files of some of the special envoys and liaisons, now incorporated into the foreign ministry archives, can fill in on matters, especially for the war years, on which the ministry was kept in ignorance.

C. UNOFFICIAL AND INFORMAL AGENTS

The ministry subsidized ostensibly private organizations and used them to support Germany's policies outside official channels. They disseminated propaganda, sponsored sympathetic causes, and conveyed money to German minorities abroad. Some of these front organizations, such as those affiliated with the Arbeitsausschuss deutscher Verbände, focused their efforts broadly on the revision of the peace terms. Others were more specialized, addressing themselves to the concerns of German enclaves around the world (Auslandsdeutschtum) or in Germany's border regions (Grenzdeutschtum). Its leading members were the Verein für das Deutschtum im Ausland, in Berlin, the Deutsches Auslandsinstitut in Stuttgart, and the Deutscher Schutzbund für das Grenz- und Auslandsdeutschtum, a federation of various agencies of this kind. Funds that went to support German cultural activities, farmers and small businessmen, schools and churches in foreign countries were distributed through the Deutsche Stiftung (founded in 1920 and headed by Erich Krahmer-Möllenberg) and the Ossa Vermittlungs- und Handelsgesellschaft (founded in

1926, headed by Max Winkler), both seemingly autonomous but controlled by the ministry and funded by the government. Indeed, the ministry was elaborately inventive in finding and using front organizations for these purposes, and the Deutsche Stiftung and Ossa are only the most prominent. (After 1933, these programs and organizations were among the first to be taken over by the Nazis.)[8]

The ministry also made use of Germany's academic establishment, at universities and research centers, which were given funds to offer lecture series and conferences and to sponsor various publications that would document Germany's views and advance her programs. Prominent among the research centers was the Institut für Auswärtige Politik in Hamburg. In the 1920s, its director, Albrecht Mendelssohn-Bartholdy, was close to Stresemann; in the 1930s, his successor, Fritz Berber, was virtually Ribbentrop's mouthpiece. The Institut edited the Grosse Politik and published Europäische Gespräche (later Monatshefte für Auswärtige Politik), a respected journal, as well as numerous studies. Other such centers were the Deutsche Institut für Aussenpolitische Forschung in Berlin, known particularly for its political yearbooks and for its prolific publications on German policy during the war years, and the Deutsches Auslandswissenschaftliches Institut, also in Berlin, which, like its earlier incarnation, Hochschule für Politik, published yearbooks, bibliographies, journals, and various monograph series.[9]

Of course, the ministry also employed individual agents. Such agents were often given diplomatic titles, though they were not members of the foreign service. They served in capacities that did not bind or commit the ministry--as go-betweens, as observers, as semi-official representatives. Count Harry Kessler, a man with wide connections, was sent on special missions to London and Geneva; Moritz Schlesinger, an expert on trade and financial relations with the Soviet Union, was an intermediary between Berlin and Moscow. At no time, however, did such agents play the kind of role that Hitler's personal emissaries assumed in Nazi foreign policy.

D. IMPACT OF TRADITION AND PERSONALITY

Functional responsibilities and organizational structure cannot account fully for the constellations of power and influence in the German foreign service. Force of tradition and personality also played a major role in the formulation and execution of German foreign policy.

The Schüler reforms did not break the power of the old-line professionals or eradicate traditional ways and attitudes. After a few years, the old guard resumed control of the ministry. It eliminated what it considered the most objectionable innovations, such as the position of state secretary for economic affairs and the Aussenhandelsstelle, or bureau of foreign trade, both of which had been designed to link politics and economics more closely but were, in truth, somewhat cumbersome. Less formally, the diplomats of the old guard pushed out some of the new appointments (in part for reasons simply of quality) and sought to restore the predominance of the prewar political division by having the deputy directors, all career officials, report directly to the state secretary. Until 1939 the personnel department was in the hands of career diplomats, and these tended to favor candidates of the traditional sort. For promotion to the higher ranks, aristocratic origin was no longer mandatory, but an upper-class background, conservative outlook, family connections and old diplomatic names, university fraternities and military service still mattered. It is telling that, of the 20 outsiders on the senior staff, only one--Erich Wallroth, the director of Abteilung IV, 1923-28--reached and maintained a position of importance in the ministry, though some others made good careers abroad--Friedrich Sthamer in London, Adolf Müller in Berne, and Ulrich Rauscher in Warsaw. Stresemann tried to introduce new blood, but none of his protégés had more than a headstart by the time he died. Neurath was able to shield the ministry against nazification, and few seem initially to have joined the party, various pressures notwithstanding (though their ability to retain their posts to the end suggests that most were able to adapt readily enough). Under Ribbentrop, the senior officials were obliged to become members of the party (and often also of the SS), but Nazi influence on recruitment and promotion was limited largely to the middle and lower echelons. In fact, Ribbentrop's habit of appointing party emissaries and staffing his offices with his own men indicates that he never entirely trusted the traditionalists.[10]

The impact of personality is a more elusive matter. In the exercise of its functions, the ministry was obviously affected both by the strong personality of certain individuals and by various personal configurations, whether old loyalties or temporary alliances, friendship or kinship, cabals or intrigues. For example, Maltzan, Bülow, and later Weizsäcker enjoyed wide respect within the foreign service; others, such as the prickly Nadolny, were little liked. Some men were consulted on matters of general policy, even if they were not directly involved or were out in the field--Brockdorff-Rantzau, Hoesch, and Rauscher in the 1920s, Hassell in the 1930s. The ministry dropped in competence and morale in 1935-36, when it lost its entire senior staff and its ambassadors in London and Paris, and installed replacements who did not measure up in quality or in courage. After 1938, when Ribbentrop was foreign minister, state secretary Weizsäcker became a center of influence because he controlled a network of career officials who kept watch on the Nazi intruders.

Personal influence can be gauged by tracing the development of individual careers. The so-called high flyers, men who enjoyed extraordinarily rapid career advancement, helped shape policies and priorities and were instrumental in setting the institutional tone. Schubert, who became deputy director of Abteilung III at 38, its director at 39, and state secretary at 42, put his stamp on the policy line of the 1920s. Gaus, whose formidable legal skills made him a participant in all major negotiations, headed the legal department for over twenty years. Ritter parlayed his economic expertise into a career as trade negotiator, department head, high-level troubleshooter, and ambassador at large, serving from the early 1920s down to 1945. Bülow rose rapidly through the ranks and was made state secretary in 1930 (at age 45), ahead of men more senior and more experienced. His rise afforded opportunities to likeminded others, among them Dieckhoff, Köster, and Weizsäcker. Assignments to embassies and to legations are also suggestive. In the Weimar years, for example, diplomats out of favor in Berlin were posted to southern or southeastern Europe.

Interesting information on these matters can be found in the extensive and candid correspondence of Bülow with his colleagues, and, dispersed through the files, in the semi-private, semi-official letters of the gossipy Köpke. Personal papers and diaries, many still in private hands, as well as the records of oral history should be consulted. Some of the diplomatic memoirs are also revealing, often inadvertently, though generalizations based on individual experience must be treated with caution.[11]

E. EXTERNAL CONSTRAINTS

Foreign policy was influenced by politics, of course. In Weimar Germany, as elsewhere, public opinion played an important role. The international shift to conference diplomacy gave rise to a corps of amateur diplomats, mostly heads of state or political leaders, who measured the effectiveness of policy by the effect it had on the public. To the extent that such conference diplomacy could be used to stabilize domestic affairs, it was subject to ideology, manipulation, and pressure. Policy decisions often reflected what was politically prudent rather than what was diplomatically appropriate. In consequence, the professional diplomats lost the initiative on many issues. They found that their advice carried less weight, that it might even be disregarded.

Political influence was brought to bear also in a narrower, more technical way than simply through the effect of public opinion. Under the Weimar constitution, the conduct of foreign affairs became explicitly subject to political influence. The executive and the legislative branches of government shared responsibility for policy, and these branches were vulnerable to the importunings of special interest groups. Though no one has yet assessed the relative power of these groups, or measured it against that of the foreign ministry, it is clear that their activities imposed constraints on the ministry. The Reichstag, for example, could set conditions for negotiations, delay the ratification of agreements, and worst, use foreign policy issues to bring down the government. The interest groups, representing a broad spectrum of opinion, applied pressure directly or through party tactics and newspaper campaigns. Their petitions fill the files of the president's office, the chancellery, and the foreign ministry. No minister could afford to ignore such pressures, and members of the foreign ministry met regularly with parliament and parliamentary committees, with various formal and informal lobbies. Indeed, one of the reasons for the practice of using journalists, parliamentarians, trade unionists, lawyers, and the like in delegations at international conferences was to secure political support. Stresemann's success in defending his policies was largely the result of his influence in the government coalition and his skill in party politics.[12]

The professional diplomats, accustomed to more traditional patterns of diplomacy, resented this interference. They claimed that parliamentary debates, press conferences, and newspaper campaigns undercut their effectiveness, preventing them from advancing the policies they considered necessary and from taking advantage of favorable diplomatic opportunities. Such claims were exaggerated, for at least until the mid-thirties the ministry's role in making policy was never seriously challenged. The very complexity of policy and of the conduct of policy ensured the influence and power of the career diplomats.

The Nazi regime relieved the ministry of some of these formal constraints. It suspended the constitution, eliminating the provision for consultation and ratification in the legislative bodies. It centralized power by combining the offices of chancellor and president, putting an end to a source of conflict. And it turned the cabinet, which during the Weimar period debated policy and reached decisions collectively, into a place where Hitler informed his ministers of measures he had taken or was about to take, and dropped it altogether in 1938.

F. ROLE OF THE CHANCELLOR AND THE CABINET

The constitution made the foreign minister responsible for the administration of foreign affairs. He was to advise the government on policy and see to the execution of policy decisions. But the constitution limited his power by making him subject both to the authority of the chancellor, who determined the principles and priorities of policy (Richtlinien), and to the approval of the cabinet (arts. 56, 57).

In practice, of course, policy as well as approval were arrived at in discussion among the ministers, but the chancellor carried considerable weight in these deliberations, and it was therefore important to have his goodwill and support. The foreign minister and his senior staff kept in close touch with the chancellor or his state secretary, and the ministry routinely supplied the chancellery with copies of dispatches and memoranda. For meetings of the cabinet, the ministry prepared extensive material for the chancellery's staff, which in turn made its own assessment of the issues and offered suitable commentary. If the issues were controversial or unusually important, the foreign minister consulted informally with his colleagues before the meeting, and in the meeting itself he worked on occasion with a group of like-minded ministers, whose joint influence would be decisive. The chancellery files, which include the cabinet minutes, contain much that is interesting both on foreign policy and on the politics of policymaking.[13]

Since many of the draft bills introduced by the foreign ministry touched upon the competence of other ministries, the foreign ministry was obliged to consult with them and solicit their cooperation. For instance, on reparations and foreign loans, the ministry worked with the Finance Ministry; on trade policy and tariffs, with the Economics Ministry; on disarmament and rearmament questions, with the Reichswehr Ministry; on the occupied Rhineland, with the Ministry for Occupied Territories (1923-30). Whenever policy affected former Prussian provinces, such as Upper Silesia, Posen, or Danzig, the Prussian ministries of finance and of the interior were brought in. Since these ministries had their own expert staffs, which often participated in negotiations and conferences, their files have much material on foreign policy.

These ministries had their own loyalties and purposes, and each was intent on expressing its particular views and furthering its particular concerns. They tried to influence policy while it was being planned, as it was being decided, and even when it was being implemented. Conflicts would take the form of disputes over the composition of diplomatic delegations, the chairmanship of negotiation teams, the role and number of participating experts. Every so often, one or the other ministry would exceed its competence, as when the army dealt independently with the Soviet Union in the 1920s. Since the foreign ministry insisted on having exclusive control over external affairs, the relations between the diplomats and officials from other ministries (particularly with the finance ministry and, more so, with the Reichswehr ministry) were not always smooth. In cases where prestige was heavily committed on both sides and differences of opinion could not be ironed out, settlements were generally reached only at the ministerial level, at a Ministerbesprechung or Chefbesprechung.

Specifically on questions of trade and tariff policy, the foreign ministry worked with the Handelspolitischer Ausschuss (commercial policy committee) and the Reichswirtschaftsrat (economic council). The Handelspolitischer Ausschuss was a standing committee of ministerial representatives set up in the spring of 1925, when the restrictive trade conditions imposed by the peace treaty fell away. Composed originally of the state secretaries of the foreign ministry and of the ministries of economics, finance, and food and agriculture, in the 1930s it became something of an empire for Karl Ritter, and was enlarged by representatives from the Four-Year Plan, the High Command, and the Reichsbank. It prepared policy, coordinated trade negotiations, and, during the war, helped plan the economic annexation of the conquered European countries. Almost from the start, its meetings were kept secret, even from other government agencies, but references to its proceedings turn up in various files. The Reichswirtschaftsrat was constitutionally entitled to be consulted on all economic and social policy (art. 165). It was cumbersome and unwieldy, with over three hundred members, and it never evolved beyond provisional status (and was abolished in 1934). Its committee hearings, however, offered a forum in which the foreign minister could explain policy, solicit support, and, not least, respond to requests and proposals. In this respect, the council was simply a more formal setting for the extensive collaboration the foreign ministry developed with industrialists, businessmen, and bankers, whose services as foreign investors, informal intermediaries, and conference delegates usually benefited both sides. During World War II, many of the larger German companies took part in the economic exploitation of areas controlled by the German army. Here the files of individual firms and of chambers of commerce are of interest.[14]

G. ROLE OF THE PRESIDENT

The constitution also gave the president certain prerogatives in foreign affairs. He officially represented Germany in her relations with other states, concluded treaties and alliances, accredited and received ambassadors (art. 45), though his orders and decrees had to be countersigned by the chancellor or the appropriate minister (art. 50). His power was therefore less on the constitutional than on the political and personal level. He could engage his prestige to influence policy, directly or indirectly, in public speeches, private conversations, and meetings with German and foreign diplomats. Both Ebert and Hindenburg were interested in foreign affairs and both guarded their prerogatives zealously. They insisted on being briefed regularly, receiving copies of telegrams and dispatches, and interviewing diplomats returning from the field. When they had reservations or recommendations (which in Hindenburg's case often reflected the views of his former military associates or of conservative politicians), their state secretary, Otto Meissner, relayed these to the chancellor or the foreign minister and attended the sessions of the cabinet at which they were discussed. In general, they had little impact, though on occasion they made for some difference in detail or timing.[15]

H. REICHSTAG AND REICHSRAT

The Reichstag had the right to advise and consent. It could remove the chancellor and his cabinet, or a minister independent of the cabinet as a whole, by a vote of no confidence (art. 54). It held the chancellor and his ministers accountable for their actions, and the foreign minister regularly addressed the plenum on his policies.

It took opportunity to debate foreign policy (or the minister's personnel and administrative policy) during the annual budget hearings or when, as stipulated by the constitution, it was asked to ratify treaties (art. 45). Often quite critical, though generally more about means than ends, these debates show fairly clearly the differences among the political parties.

The constitution emphasized the Reichstag's special interest in foreign policy by providing for a standing Committee on Foreign Affairs (Auswärtiger Ausschuss). Consisting of twenty-eight members, representing the major parties in the Reichstag, the committee remained in session even while parliament was in recess or after it had been dissolved (art. 35). It could summon officials, examine official documents, and take testimony under oath, and it usually met the foreign minister (or his deputy) in closed session to be informed and consulted. Only rarely were such sessions very candid, however, for the committee could not guarantee confidentiality, and partisan rivalries inhibited discussion. On major policy initiatives and sensitive issues, selected committee members and party experts were briefed in camera. Information on policy, and especially on the ministry's varied (and often secret) expenditures, was also available to the Reichstag's budget committee (Haushaltsausschuss), a committee similar to the other both in format and procedure.

The Reichsrat, through which the individual German states had a voice in federal affairs, had less influence. According to the constitution, the Reichsrat could oblige the cabinet to keep it informed and to seek its consent before submitting a bill to parliament, and it could oblige parliament to reconsider a vote (arts. 67, 69, 74). In actual fact, however, it could not prevent any action from taking place. It therefore exerted influence more by political than constitutional means--by withholding approval and cooperation or by exerting pressure through the parties in the state legislatures and the Reichstag.

Throughout the Weimar period, the Reichsrat expressed strong interest in cases where policy could affect state interests directly, such as the occupied Rhineland. It set up its own foreign affairs committee (composed of Prussia, Bavaria, Saxony, Württemberg, Baden, Thuringia, Hessen, Hamburg, and Braunschweig), which discussed policy with senior members of the foreign ministry. The ministry also met privately with the state representatives (all of whom carried the diplomatic title of Gesandter), and provided them routinely with copies of the confidential reports that circulated internally, the Wochenberichte and Politische Berichte. On unusually important issues, such as the Locarno negotiations, the ministry bypassed the Reichsrat and met with the state prime ministers themselves, in so-called Ministerkonferenzen, to hear their views and enlist their cooperation.[16]

I. THE FOREIGN MINISTRY UNDER HITLER

Hitler took a hand in policy from the beginning. He reserved the major decisions to himself, and he often determined the timing and chose the instruments. He adopted a style that resembled the style he favored in domestic politics, unsystematic and flexible, given to improvisation when opportunity arose. Because he had no personal experience in foreign affairs, however, and because he lacked qualified advisers within the party, the ministry retained a decisive voice. The foreign minister stayed in office, as did the state secretary,

14

and apart from a few outsiders and a handful of resignations and dismissals, the staff remained the same. By and large, the ministry continued to follow its established course. It prepared and justified the diplomatic moves of those years, and it occasionally resorted to quiet diplomacy to moderate impulsive actions.

Yet at the same time, the ministry was increasingly challenged by other ministries and by organs of the party. Its files alone, therefore, will not suffice for tracing the sources of policy and the ways in which policy was implemented after 1933. The armed forces, for example, prompted by Hitler's interest in rearmament and strategic planning, took on a much larger role in determining policy. With Göring's support, they often acted independently of the ministry. So did the ministries of finance and of economics, which, together with the Reichsbank, pursued an aggressive foreign trade policy, especially in southeastern Europe, in concert with a number of industries and businesses. The propaganda ministry encroached on the foreign ministry by taking charge both of German propaganda abroad and of relations with the foreign press (using such agencies as Terramare and Transocean Dienst), and tried to assume responsibility for cultural relations with other countries. From within the party, agencies of the Hitler Youth and the NS-Studentenbund, the Reichsarbeitsdienst, and the Reichsnährstand, as well as a number of Gauleiters pursued foreign policies of their own--though much of their time was wasted on bureaucratic infighting. Of a different format, of course, were Hitler's special emissaries, such as Göring, Goebbels, and Ribbentrop, who scored some successes, notably the naval agreement with Britain in 1935, but were also to blame for the fiasco in Austria in 1934.

The turning point came in 1936-37, when Hitler moved toward an expansionist policy. More confident of his powers, he became less dependent on the professional diplomats and drew less and less on the ministry's resources and services. In laying down general lines of policy, he gradually dispensed with Neurath's advice and turned more to men closer to him. In time, he also abandoned the habit of having Neurath join him whenever important foreign visitors were received at the chancellery, and the ministry was often not told what had taken place. While he did not renounce the ministry's counsel, he stopped consulting it regularly on initiatives and strategy, and he ignored its warnings and dismissed its drafts. Ribbentrop managed to recapture some lost ground when he took over in 1938, though he did not restore the ministry's independence. He installed members of his private retinue (Dienststelle Ribbentrop) and various pro-Nazi diplomats in important positions, and created extraordinary positions, such as state secretary on special assignment, to accommodate people who would carry out his policies. He obliged all senior officials to join the party, even the SS, and he directed the diplomats in the field to spread Nazi propaganda. He also linked the ministry more closely with Himmler's intelligence services, providing subsidies for undercover work, placing agents at embassies and legations, and promoting contacts for the Gestapo in Italy and elsewhere. The professional diplomats were deeply implicated in the diplomatic initiatives of that period, all of which departed from their traditional policy and their diplomatic style. They advised caution and warned against war. They were ignored, for Ribbentrop, no less than Hitler, was determined to press a policy of blackmail and intimidation. They acquiesced--and negotiated and drafted the terms of pacts and alliances.

As the ministry declined, the chancellery, restyled Neue Reichskanzlei, took on new significance. Where once it had coordinated government business and mediated between chancellor and ministers, it now controlled access to Hitler, determining, as the files show, what reached him and in what form, and it became the conduit through which Hitler transmitted decisions on matters of state. Its state secretary, Hans Heinrich Lammers, thus held a pivotal position until Bormann outmaneuvered him during the war.[17]

J. RIVAL ORGANIZATIONS

The ministry also had to contend with various organizations that infringed on its functions or tried to displace it altogether. These organizations were the creations of ambitious party leaders, who sought a place for themselves in the new state, and they had few qualifications and no experience in foreign affairs. They engaged the ministry in constant jurisdictional disputes, and their activities, consisting in large measure of propaganda and subversion, burdened Germany's diplomatic relations, especially with the United States and Latin America.

The Aussenpolitisches Amt der NSDAP (APA), set up by Alfred Rosenberg in April 1933, was prominent in the first years. Rosenberg, the party's ideologue on foreign affairs, apparently believed that he was the future foreign minister and that the APA was the future foreign ministry. He therefore contested Neurath's authority and began to push his own programs. But his very first diplomatic ventures proved so embarrassing that Neurath had little difficulty discrediting him. Thereafter, the APA was active mainly in areas toward which the ministry was indifferent. It disseminated Nazi doctrine abroad, seeking to promote understanding and support, and established contact with sympathetic groups and individuals. It also prepared the way for Nazi expansion by building ideological alliances against bolshevism and drafting blueprints for the dismemberment of Russia. Not least, it devoted itself to training a generation of diplomats suited to the tasks of Nazi policy. Because Rosenberg retained Hitler's favor, he was able to arrange interviews for foreign visitors to Germany, prominent politicians or fascist leaders, among whom Vidkun Quisling was probably his greatest discovery.

Several agencies competed with the ministry for the control of Volkstumspolitik--policy toward Germans living abroad. The first to appear was the Auslandsorganisation der NSDAP (AO), which emerged in 1934 as the final incarnation of a series of earlier party offices. Headed by Ernst Bohle, a protégé of Rudolf Hess, Hitler's deputy, the AO evolved within two or three years from an insignificant office in Hamburg into a sizable agency with branches throughout the world. It was the liaison with party members outside of Germany, and, working through a network of Landesgruppenleiter, it tried to organize and indoctrinate German nationals abroad. The ministry succeeded in curtailing these efforts, which were regarded abroad as evidence of subversion, and it resisted Bohle's attempt to manipulate German minorities in eastern and southeastern Europe. In 1936, the AO served briefly as a direct link between Hitler and Franco, but that was its only foray into high-level diplomacy. The following year it moved to Berlin and was incorporated into the ministry. Bohle was given the title of state secretary, which in rank if not in fact put him on a level with the existing state secretary. He was to gain some influence over appointments, but as the files show, his role was never more than marginal, and in 1941 he was eased out by Ribbentrop.

The Volksdeutsche Mittelstelle (VM or Vomi), established in 1937 and nominally under Ribbentrop's jurisdiction, marked the first incursion of the SS into foreign policy. VM was the successor of the Volksdeutsche Rat (1933-35) and the Büro von Kursell (1935-37), and it assumed direction of all political and financial relations with German minorities abroad. Unlike its predecessors, however, VM was concerned less with aiding the Volksdeutsche and their activities than with activating them for National Socialism. Under the leadership of Werner Lorenz, an officer in the SS, it imposed its ideological stamp on Volkstumspolitik and nazified both the Volksdeutsche organizations abroad and the various Volkstum agencies at home. It soon developed into a formidable rival, and became active in policy (among the Sudeten Germans and in Slovakia) within the year. Its relationship with the foreign ministry was openly opportunistic: the two struggled over control of policy but joined forces to keep others out of the field.[18]

K. THE FOREIGN MINISTRY AND THE WAR

When Germany went to war, the foreign ministry entered decline. Diplomatic activity gave way to military operations, and as the war widened, diplomacy declined correspondingly. By 1942 all but twenty-two countries had broken off diplomatic relations, and the neutral governments had lost their value as sources of information. Conquest and occupation brought new opportunities, but the ministry did not benefit, for in the struggle for power Ribbentrop and his representatives were outclassed. He tried to adjust the ministry to the new order, repeatedly changing the organization and the personnel, but this only led to confusion and encouraged camarillas and intrigue. Major decisions were made and executed elsewhere, and the diplomats lost their influence on events. The researcher in this period will have to disentangle the array of offices, agencies, commissions, and plenipotentiaries, each of which claimed authority in external affairs, and will have to consult the most diverse sources.

As long as Ribbentrop remained in Hitler's favor, he retained influence. In the first two years of the war, he engaged in negotiations with the Soviet Union, Italy, and Japan, trying to concert action and work out future spheres of influence, and he offered Hitler various plans for conducting and ending the war. He joined Hitler in meetings with representatives of the allied and vassal states, and he participated in situation conferences and planning sessions. But he was generally excluded from the important discussions of grand strategy, which were attended by Hitler's military and naval advisers (who recorded them in their official or private diaries) and by those in Hitler's confidence (Göring, Rosenberg, Lammers, Bormann). He was not among the small number of intimates who gathered around Hitler and listened to his monologues in the early hours of the morning.

The ministry was left with a greatly diminished range of activity. It continued to receive and evaluate reports from its diplomatic missions, it organized student exchanges and subsidized visitors from abroad, it sought out dissidents and potential collaborators in foreign countries. With the allied states, it negotiated about the conduct and extension of the war, drawing up military conventions and economic aid agreements. It maintained contact with the military, giving advice on the diplomatic and legal implications of the war--

the transit of German troops through friendly countries, the rights of prisoners of war, maritime commercial warfare, and the like. It took part in the armistice negotiations with France and was represented on the armistice commission that remained in France. On its own, and in deep secret, it worked through intermediaries to explore possibilities of peace. Indicative of the morale in the ministry is the obvious decline in personal initiative: the diplomats became messengers, carrying out Ribbentrop's directives, and their memoranda and reports became cautious and noncommittal.[19]

L. OTHER AGENCIES

In the tangle of offices and agents that made policy in Hitler's Europe, power accrued to the most tenacious and ruthless. By 1942-43 Ribbentrop and his ministry had obviously been relegated to an ancillary role. Thus, Ribbentrop insisted on having his say in occupation policy, but with the exception of France and Denmark, where he installed plenipotentiaries (Otto Abetz in France; Cecil von Renthe-Fink and, after November 1942, Werner Best in Denmark), he had to content himself with attaching liaison officers to the various occupation authorities--Zivilverwaltung, Militärbefehlshaber, Reichskommissar, and Gauleiters. In the struggle for control over the economy in the conquered territories, the diplomats were pushed aside not only by different ministries (arms and munitions, economics, finance, food and agriculture) but also by military and state agencies, such as the Four-Year Plan and the commissioner for labor recruitment, and even by private industry. They were excluded altogether from dealings in Czechoslovakia, Poland, and most notably, Russia and the Baltic states, where Ribbentrop's old rival Rosenberg exercised power through a Ministry of Occupied Eastern Territories (Ministerium für die besetzten Ostgebiete).

The most troublesome rival was the SS, which implemented Nazi policy in the occupied areas but extended it also to foreign countries. The Volksdeutsche Mittelstelle, swollen to great size, opened branch offices abroad, maintained representatives in Croatia and Rumania, negotiated with minority leaders in the Near East, sponsored trips by SS officers to other countries and by foreign delegations to Germany--all without informing the ministry. It collaborated with the Reichskommissariat für die Festigung Deutschen Volkstums (RKFDV), which repatriated ethnic Germans or resettled them in the occupied areas. RKFDV in turn coordinated its activities with other SS units, with the military, and with various ministries, but with the foreign ministry only in cases that involved Germans still in foreign countries. The Sicherheitsdienst (SD), the SS intelligence service, also usurped the prerogatives of the professional diplomats. Its agents, attached to embassies and legations as "police attachés," spied on the diplomatic staff, and their reports on conditions and events often superseded those from the chief of mission. It also sent agents on secret trips to South America, Spain, and Rumania, and, in time, engaged in negotiations with foreign diplomats both abroad and at home (right down to 1945, when Himmler sent out private peace feelers).[20]

M. THE MINISTRY IN DISSOLUTION

By 1943 Ribbentrop had lost Hitler's favor. Seeking to reinstate himself, he battled his rivals in carrying out policies for the extermination of the Jews, and he extended half-hearted overtures toward the Russians and, later, toward the western powers. He discharged or pensioned off a large number of career diplomats, and turned more and more to his special envoys, who represented his interests.

As the air raids on Berlin increased, the ministry began to evacuate the city. It moved all but the current files, and stored them variously in eastern and western Germany. It then moved them again, trying to keep them from falling into Soviet hands. Ribbentrop remained in Berlin until April 1945. Then, giving orders that the files be destroyed, he left quietly and went into hiding. His successor, Count Schwerin-Krosigk, who was Dönitz's foreign minister, was in charge of a foreign ministry not worthy of the name.[21]

N. APPENDIX

1. German Diplomats, 1918-45

This list includes those German diplomats who, by virtue of their positions, exercised influence on foreign policy.

Abetz, Otto (b. 1903). Reichsjugendführung, 1933; Dienststelle Ribbentrop (specialist on French affairs), 1934-38; ambassador, Paris, and political adviser to the military government in France, 1940-44. Memoirs.

Albrecht, Erich (b. 1902). Joined foreign service, 1928; deputy director, Rechtsabteilung, 1938-43; director, Rechtsabteilung, 1943-45. Applications for NSDAP membership rejected 1939, 1941, 1943.

Altenburg, Günther (b. 1894). Joined foreign service, 1920; Embassy Rome, 1925; legation, Vienna, 1933-34; foreign ministry, Abteilung II (specialist on southern and southeastern Europe), 1934-38; deputy chief, Informations Abteilung, 1939; plenipotentiary with military government in Greece, 1941-43; Dienststelle Altenburg, Vienna, 1944-45. Joined NSDAP, 1935.

Aschmann, Gottfried (b. 1884). Consul general, Geneva, 1923-28; counselor of embassy, Ankara, 1928-32; deputy director, Presse Abteilung, 1932-33; director, Presse Abteilung, 1933-39; employed on special duties (political warfare), The Hague and Brussels, 1939-40.

Bergen, Diego von (b. 1872). Joined foreign service, 1895; chief, Political Division, 1919; ambassador, Holy See, 1920-43.

Bismarck, Otto von (b. 1897). Reichstag deputy (DNVP), 1923-27; joined foreign service, 1927; counselor of embassy, London, 1928-36; deputy director, Politische Abteilung, 1937-40; embassy, Rome, 1940-43; foreign ministry, 1943-44. Joined NSDAP, 1933.

Bohle, Ernst Wilhelm (b. 1903). Joined NSDAP 1932; Auslandsabteilung der NSDAP, 1931; Gauinspekteur, Gau Ausland, 1932; chief, Auslandsorganisation der NSDAP (AO), 1933-45; Gauleiter, Ausland, 1934; chief, Auslandsorganisation im Auswärtigen Amt (with the title of state secretary), 1937-41. Nachlass, Politisches Archiv, Bonn.

Brockdorff-Rantzau, Ulrich von (b. 1869). Joined foreign service, 1894; minister, Copenhagen, 1912-18; foreign secretary, Dec. 1918-Feb. 1919; foreign minister, Feb.-June 1919; ambassador, Moscow, 1922-28. Nachlass, Politisches Archiv, Bonn.

Bülow, Bernhard Wilhelm von (b. 1885). Joined foreign service, 1911; at Brest-Litovsk and Versailles, 1918, 1919; extended leave of absence, 1919-23; chief, Sonderreferat Völkerbund, 1923-28; deputy director, Abteilung II (specialist on Western Europe), 1925-30; state secretary, June 1930-June 1936. Personal correspondence, Politisches Archiv, Bonn.

Clodius, Carl August (b. 1897). Joined foreign service, 1921; stationed abroad (Paris, Vienna, Sofia), 1921-34; foreign ministry, Wirtschaftsabteilung, 1934-38; deputy director, Commercial Department, 1938-44; director, Commercial Department, 1944-45. Handakten, Politisches Archiv, Bonn.

Dieckhoff, Hans Heinrich (b. 1884). Joined foreign service, 1912; counselor of embassy, Washington, 1922-26; counselor of embassy, London, 1926-30; director, Abteilung III, 1930-36; acting state secretary, Aug. 1936-Apr. 1937; ambassador, Washington, 1937-41 (recalled Nov. 1938); chief, Amerika Komitee, 1940-43; ambassador, Madrid, 1943-44. Nachlass, Politisches Archiv, Bonn.

Dirksen, Herbert von (b. 1882). Joined foreign service, 1917; chargé d'affaires, Warsaw, 1920-21; foreign ministry, Abteilung IV, 1921-22; consul general, Danzig, 1923-25; deputy director, Abteilung IV, 1925-28; director, Abteilung IV, Mar.-Nov. 1928; ambassador, Moscow, 1928-33; ambassador, Tokyo, 1933-38; ambassador, London, 1938-39. Memoirs. Handakten, Politisches Archiv, Bonn; Nachlass, Zentrales Staatsarchiv, Potsdam.

Dufour von Feronce, Albert (b. 1868). Joined foreign service, 1919; counselor of embassy, London, 1920-24; minister, embassy, London, 1924-26; under secretary general, League of Nations, 1926-32; minister, Belgrade, 1932-33.

Eisenlohr, Ernst (b. 1882). Joined foreign service, 1911; counselor of embassy, London, 1920-22; counselor of embassy, Belgrade, 1923-25; foreign ministry, Sonderreferat Wirtschaft, 1926-31; minister, Athens, 1931-36; minister, Prague, 1936-39 (recalled Sept. 1938); chief, Sonderkommission für Wirtschaftsfragen, Prague, 1939-40; foreign ministry, on Ritter's staff, 1940-43. Handakten, Politisches Archiv, Bonn.

Erdmannsdorff, Otto von (b. 1888). Counselor of legation, Mexico, 1920-23; foreign ministry and president's office, 1923-28; counselor of embassy, Peking, 1928-33; deputy director, Abteilung IV, 1934-37; minister, Budapest, 1937-41; deputy director, Politische Abteilung, 1941-43.

Etzdorff, Hasso von (b. 1900). Joined foreign service, 1928; secretary of legation, embassy, Tokyo, 1931-34; foreign ministry, minister's secretariat, 1934-37; embassy, Rome, 1937-38; foreign ministry, 1938-39; representative of foreign ministry, army high command, 1939-44; consul general, Genoa, 1945. Joined NSDAP, 1933. Handakten, Politisches Archiv, Bonn.

Freytag, Hans Wilhelm (b. 1869). Joined foreign service, 1903; chargé d'affaires, then minister, Bucharest, 1921-26; director, Abteilung VI, 1926-32; minister, Lisbon, 1933.

Frohwein, Hans (b. 1887). Joined foreign service, 1921; consulate, New York and Seattle, 1924-26; foreign ministry, Rechtsabteilung, then Abteilung II (disarmament), 1926-36; minister, Reval, 1936-40. Handakten, Politisches Archiv, Bonn.

Gaus, Friedrich Wilhelm Otto (b. 1881). Joined foreign service, 1907; at Brest-Litovsk and Versailles, 1918, 1919; deputy director, Rechtsabteilung, 1921-23; director, Rechtsabteilung, 1923-43 (at Genoa, 1922; London, 1924; Locarno, 1925; League of Nations, 1926); ambassador on special assignment, 1943-45. Handakten, Politisches Archiv, Bonn.

Haas, Walter de (b. 1864). Joined foreign service, 1903; foreign ministry, Sonderreferat Wirtschaft, 1922-23; deputy director, Abteilung III, 1923-26; director, Abteilung III, 1926-30.

Haniel von Haimhausen, Edgar Karl (b. 1870). Joined foreign service, 1900; representative of foreign ministry in armistice commission, 1918-19; secretary general, German peace delegation, June-July 1919; under state secretary, 1919-20; state secretary, 1920-22; minister, Munich, 1922-30. Nachlass, Politisches Archiv, Bonn.

Hassell, Ulrich von (b. 1881). Joined foreign service, 1909; counselor of embassy, Rome, 1919-21; consul general, Barcelona, 1921-26; minister, Copenhagen, 1926-30; minister, Belgrade, 1930-32; ambassador, Rome, 1932-38. Joined NSDAP, 1933. Diary.

Heilbron, Friedrich Gottlieb (b. 1872). Joined foreign service, 1902; director, Presse Abteilung, 1920-21, 1923-26; consul general, Zurich, 1926-31.

Hencke, Andor (b. 1895). Joined foreign service, 1922; embassy, Moscow, 1922-29; foreign ministry, Abteilung VI, 1929-33; consul, Kiev, 1933-35; foreign ministry, Abteilung II, 1935-36; counselor of legation, Prague, 1936-39; chargé d'affaires, Prague, Sept. 1938-Mar. 1939; representative of foreign ministry, Protectorate of Bohemia and Moravia, 1939; chief, Deutsch-Sowjetische Kommission, Oct. 1939; liaison to the Danish foreign ministry, 1940; representative of the foreign ministry, Franco-German armistice negotiations, 1940-41; counselor of embassy, Madrid, 1943; director, Politische Abteilung, 1943-45. Memoirs. Handakten, Politisches Archiv, Bonn.

Hewel, Walther (b. 1904). Hitler Putsch, 1923; Landsberg prison, 1924-25; plantation manager, Java, 1927-34; Auslandsorganisation der NSDAP (specialist on East Asia), 1933-37; Dienststelle Ribbentrop (specialist on England), 1937-38; foreign ministry, Persönlicher Stab Ribbentrop, 1938-39; Ribbentrop's representative at Hitler's headquarters, 1940-45; ambassador on special assignment, 1943-45. Handakten, Politisches Archiv, Bonn.

Hoesch, Leopold von (b. 1881). Joined foreign service, 1907; counselor of embassy, Paris, 1921-23; chargé d'affaires, Paris, 1923-24; ambassador, Paris, 1924-32; ambassador, London, 1932-36.

Keller, August Friedrich von (b. 1873). Joined foreign service, 1901; minister, Belgrade, 1921-24; minister, Brussels, 1924-28; minister, Buenos Aires, 1928-32; permanent representative to the League, Jan.-Oct. 1933; ambassador, Ankara, 1935-38.

Keppler, Wilhelm Karl (b. 1882). Engineer and manager, chemical industry; economic adviser to Hitler, 1932; plenipotentiary for economic questions, chancellery, 1933-36; Four-Year Plan, 1936-38; state secretary on special assignment, foreign ministry, Mar. 1938-45; plenipotentiary, Vienna, Mar.-July 1938. Joined NSDAP, 1927.

Koch, Walter (b. 1870). Saxon representative, Reichsrat, 1920-21; minister, Prague, 1921-35.

Köpke, Gerhard (b. 1873). Joined foreign service, 1902; director, Rechtsabteilung, 1921-23; director, Abteilung II, 1923-35. Handakten, Politisches Archiv, Bonn.

Kordt, Erich (b. 1903). Joined foreign service, 1928; member, delegation at the disarmament conference, 1932; legation, Berne, 1933-34; foreign ministry, Abteilung II (specialist on disarmament), 1935-36; liaison to Dienststelle Ribbentrop, 1934-36; counselor of embassy, London, 1936-38; chief, Büro RAM, 1938-41; embassy, Tokyo, 1941-42; embassy, Nanking, 1943-44; Shanghai, 1944-45. Memoirs. Nachlass, Institut für Zeitgeschichte, Munich.

Köster, Roland (b. 1883). Legation, Brussels, 1920-21; legation, Prague, 1922-25; foreign ministry, chief of protocol, 1925-29; minister, Oslo, 1929-30; foreign ministry, director of Abteilung I, then of Presse Abteilung, 1930-32; ambassador, Paris, 1932-35.

Krauel, Wolfgang (b. 1888). Joined foreign service, 1922; foreign ministry, Abteilung II, 1922-25; legation, Rio de Janeiro, 1925-28; consul general (acting), Geneva, 1928; foreign ministry, Referat Völkerbund, 1929-32; consul general, Geneva, 1932-45.

Langwerth von Simmern, Ernst (b. 1865). Foreign ministry, under state secretary, Jan.-June 1919; ambassador, Madrid, 1920-25.

Lerchenfeld, Hugo von (b. 1871). Joined foreign service, 1919; minister, Darmstadt, 1920-21; Bavarian prime minister, 1921-22; Reichstag deputy (BVP), 1924-26; minister, Vienna, 1926-31; minister, Brussels, 1931-33. Nachlass, Politisches Archiv, Bonn.

Lorenz, Werner (b. 1891). Landowner in Danzig; officer in SS, 1931-37; chief, Volksdeutsche Mittelstelle, 1937-45. Joined SS, 1930; NSDAP, 1931.

Luther, Martin Franz Julius (b. 1895). Businessman (export business); Dienststelle Ribbentrop, 1936-38; joined foreign service, 1938; foreign ministry, director, Parteireferat, 1938-40; director, Abteilung Deutschland, 1940-43 (participant in Wannsee conference). Joined NSDAP, 1932. Handakten, Politisches Archiv, Bonn.

Mackensen, Hans Georg von (b. 1883). Joined foreign service, 1919; service abroad (Copenhagen, Rome, Brussels, Tirana), 1919-29; foreign ministry, Abteilung II (disarmament) 1929-31; embassy, Madrid, 1931-33; minister, Budapest, 1933-36; state secretary, Mar. 1937-Feb. 1938; ambassador, Rome, 1938-44. Neurath's son-in-law. Joined NSDAP, 1934. Nachlass, Politisches Archiv, Bonn.

Maltzan, Adolf Georg Otto (Ago) von (b. 1877). Joined foreign service, 1907; director, Abteilung IV, 1921-22; state secretary, Dec. 1922-Dec. 1924; ambassador, Washington, 1925-27. Nachlass, Politisches Archiv, Bonn.

Meyer, Richard (b. 1883). Joined foreign service, 1913; foreign ministry, 1920-23; counselor of embassy, Holy See, 1923-25; chargé d'affaires, Asunción, 1926-27; deputy director, Abteilung II, 1930-31; director, Abteilung IV, 1931-35. Handakten, Politisches Archiv, Bonn.

Moltke, Hans-Adolf von (b. 1884). Joined foreign service, 1913; representative of foreign ministry, plebiscite commission in Upper Silesia, 1920; member, mixed commission in Upper Silesia, 1922; counselor of embassy, Constantinople, 1924-28; deputy director, Abteilung IV, 1928-31; minister, Warsaw, 1931-39; foreign ministry, compiler of German White Books, 1939-43; ambassador, Madrid, 1943. Handakten, Politisches Archiv, Bonn.

Müller, Adolf (b. 1865). Deputy, Bavarian Landtag (SPD), 1899-1918; minister, Berne, 1919-33.

Nadolny, Rudolf (b. 1873). Joined foreign service, 1902; foreign ministry, Politische Abteilung, 1917-19; chief, president's office, 1919; minister, Stockholm, 1920-24; ambassador, Ankara, 1924-33; chief, disarmament delegation, 1932-33; ambassador, Moscow, 1933-34. Memoirs.

Neubacher, Hermann (b. 1893). Deputy mayor, Vienna, 1938-39; plenipotentiary for economic questions, Rumania, 1941; plenipotentiary for economic questions, Greece, 1942; representative of foreign ministry in Balkans, 1943-44. Memoirs.

Neurath, Constantin von (b. 1873). Joined foreign service, 1901; minister, Copenhagen, 1919-21; ambassador, Rome, 1921-30; ambassador, London, 1930-32; foreign minister, 1932-38; Reichsprotektor, Böhmen und Mähren, 1939-43 (on leave after Sept. 1941). Joined NSDAP, 1937. Nachlass, Bundesarchiv, Koblenz; Handakten, Zentrales Staatsarchiv, Potsdam.

Ott, Eugen (b. 1889). Reichswehr Ministry, 1931-33; attached to Japanese army, 1933; military attaché, 1934-38; ambassador, Tokyo, 1938-42. Nachlass, Institut für Zeitgeschichte, Munich.

Papen, Franz von (b. 1879). Deputy, Prussian Landtag (Center Party), 1920-28, 1930-32; chancellor, June-Dec. 1932; vice-chancellor, 1933-34; plenipotentiary for the Saar, 1933-34; minister, then ambassador, Vienna, 1934-38; ambassador, Ankara, 1939-44. Memoirs.

Prittwitz und Gaffron, Friedrich Wilhelm von (b. 1884). Foreign ministry, Referat Deutschland, 1919-20; counselor of embassy, Rome, 1921-27; ambassador, Washington, 1927-33. Memoirs.

Rahn, Rudolf Hermann (b. 1900). Joined foreign service, 1928; embassy, Ankara, 1930-34; foreign ministry, Abteilung III, 1934-38; counselor of embassy, Lisbon, 1938-39; foreign ministry, 1939-40; counselor, embassy Paris, 1940-43 (special missions to Syria, 1941, and to Tunis, 1942-43); ambassador, Rome, 1943-45. Memoirs. Handakten, Politisches Archiv, Bonn.

Rauscher, Ulrich (b. 1884). Government spokesman, 1918-20; minister, Tiflis, 1920-21; minister, Warsaw, 1922-30.

Renthe-Fink, Cecil von (b. 1864). Joined foreign service, 1913; foreign ministry, 1919-22; embassy, Paris, 1922-23; secretary general, Elbekommission, 1923; member of the political section, League of Nations secretariat, 1926-33; foreign ministry, Abteilung II, 1933-36; minister, Copenhagen, 1936-40; plenipotentiary, Copenhagen, 1940-42; plenipotentiary, Vichy, 1943. Joined NSDAP, 1939. Nachlass, Politisches Archiv, Bonn.

Ribbentrop, Joachim von (b. 1893). Special envoy, Paris and London, 1933-34; special commissioner for disarmament questions, 1934; ambassador extraordinary and plenipotentiary on special missions, 1935-36; ambassador, London, Aug. 1936-Feb. 1938; foreign minister, 1938-45.

Rintelen, Emil von (b. 1897). Joined foreign service, 1921; foreign ministry, 1921-23; posted abroad (Paris, Warsaw), 1923-32; foreign ministry, Abteilung II, 1932-36; foreign ministry, Politische Abteilung, 1936-41; deputy director, Politische Abteilung, 1941; Persönlicher Stab Ribbentrop, 1941-43; ambassador on special assignment, 1943-45. Joined NSDAP, 1940.

Ritter, Karl (b. 1883). Joined foreign service, 1921; deputy director, then director, Wirtschaftsabteilung, 1922-37; ambassador, Rio de Janeiro, 1937-

38; ambassador on special assignment, 1939-45; liaison to chief, armed forces high command, 1940-44. Handakten, Politisches Archiv, Bonn.

Rosenberg, Frederic Hans von (b. 1874). Joined foreign service, 1903; minister, Vienna, 1920-22; minister, Copenhagen, 1922; foreign minister, Nov. 1922-Aug. 1923; minister, Stockholm, 1924-33; chief, German delegation, League assembly, Sept. 1932; ambassador, Ankara, 1933-35.

Schmidt, Paul Otto Gustav (b. 1899). Joined foreign service, 1923; chief interpreter, 1923-45; director, Nachrichten- und Presse Abteilung, 1940. Memoirs. Handakten, Politisches Archiv, Bonn.

Schubert, Carl Theodor von (b. 1882). Joined foreign service, 1906; counselor of embassy, London, 1920; director, Abteilung III, 1921-24; state secretary, Dec. 1924-June 1930; ambassador, Rome, 1930-32. Handakten, Politisches Archiv, Bonn.

Schulenburg, Friedrich-Werner von (b. 1875). Joined foreign service, 1901; minister, Teheran, 1922-31; minister, Bucharest, 1931-34; ambassador, Moscow, 1934-41. Joined NSDAP, 1936. Nachlass, Zentrales Staatsarchiv, Potsdam.

Simons, Walther (b. 1861). Joined foreign service, 1911; director, Rechtsabteilung, 1918-19; German peace delegation, Apr.-June 1919; foreign minister, 1920-21. Handakten, Politisches Archiv, Bonn.

Solf, Wilhelm (b. 1862). Foreign secretary, Oct.-Dec. 1918; ambassador, Tokyo, 1920-28. Nachlass, Politisches Archiv, Bonn.

Steengracht von Moyland, Gustav Adolf (b. 1902). Kreisbauernführer, 1934-36; Dienststelle Ribbentrop, 1936-38; joined foreign service, 1938; Persönlicher Stab Ribbentrop, 1940-43; state secretary, 1943-45. Joined NSDAP, 1933.

Sthamer, Friedrich (b. 1856). Mayor, Hamburg, 1920; chargé d'affaires, London, 1920; ambassador, London, 1920-30. Nachlass, Staatsarchiv, Hamburg.

Stohrer, Eberhard von (b. 1883). Joined foreign service, 1909; deputy director, Presse Abteilung, 1922-24; director, Abteilung I, 1924-27; minister, Cairo, 1927-35; minister, Bucharest, 1935-37; ambassador, Madrid, 1937-43.

Thermann, Edmund von (b. 1884). Joined foreign service, 1913; counselor of legation, Budapest, 1919-21; counselor of embassy, Washington, 1921-23; consul general, Danzig, 1925-33; minister, then ambassador, Buenos Aires, 1933-41. Joined NSDAP, 1933.

Trautmann, Oskar (b. 1877). Joined foreign service, 1904; consul general, Kobe, 1921; counselor of embassy, Tokyo, 1922-25; deputy director, Abteilung IV, 1925-28; director, Abteilung IV, 1928-31; minister, Peking/Nanking, 1931-35; ambassador, Peking/Nanking, 1935-41 (on leave after June 1938). Handakten, Politisches Archiv, Bonn.

Veesenmayer, Edmund (b. 1904). Verbindungsstab der NSDAP (economic adviser), 1933; assistant to Wilhelm Keppler, 1933-44; staff member, plenipotentiary for Austria, 1938; minister and plenipotentiary, Budapest, 1944-45. Joined NSDAP, 1932.

Wallroth, Erich (b. 1876). Joined foreign service, 1920; chargé d'affaires, Helsingfors, 1920-21; minister, Riga, 1921-23; director, Abteilung IV, 1923-28; minister, Oslo, 1928-29. Handakten and Nachlass, Politisches Archiv, Bonn.

Weizsäcker, Ernst von (b. 1882). Joined foreign service, 1920; consul, Basel, 1921-25; counselor of embassy, Copenhagen, 1925-26; foreign ministry,

Abteilung II (disarmament, League affairs), 1927-31; minister, Oslo, 1931-33; delegate, disarmament conference, 1932-33; minister, Berne, 1933-36; director, Politische Abteilung, 1936-38; state secretary, Mar. 1938-May 1943; ambassador, Holy See, 1943-45. Joined NSDAP, 1938. Memoirs. Nachlass, Bundesarchiv, Koblenz (microfilm).

Welczeck, Johannes von (b. 1878). Joined foreign service, 1905; extended leave, 1919-23; minister, Budapest, 1923-26; ambassador, Madrid, 1926-36; ambassador, Paris, 1936-39.

Wiehl, Emil Karl Josef (b. 1886). Joined foreign service, 1920; secretary of legation, London, 1920-23; counselor of embassy, Washington, 1925-28; foreign ministry, Wirtschafts Abteilung, 1928-33; consul general, Pretoria, 1933-34; minister, Pretoria, 1933-37; director, Commercial Department, 1937-44. Joined NSDAP, 1934. Handakten, Politisches Archiv, Bonn.

Woermann, Ernst (b. 1888). Joined foreign service, 1918; foreign ministry, 1928-30; legation, Vienna, 1930-33; foreign ministry, Rechtsabteilung, 1933-36; counselor of embassy, London, 1936-38; director, Politische Abteilung, 1938-43; ambassador, Nanking, 1943-45. Joined NSDAP, 1938. Handakten, Politisches Archiv, Bonn.

Zechlin, Walter (b. 1879). Joined foreign service, 1903; foreign ministry, Presse Abteilung, 1919-24; deputy director, Presse Abteilung, 1924-26; director, Presse Abteilung, 1926-32; minister, Mexico, 1933-34.

2. Foreign Diplomats in Berlin, 1918-45

This list is limited to the representatives of the states which had significant dealings with Germany.

Austria
   Hartmann, Ludo, Nov. 1918-20
   Riedl, Richard, July 1921-25
   Frank, Felix, June 1925-33
   Tauschitz, Stephan, Mar. 1933-38

Belgium
   Kerchove de Denterghem, André de, 1920
   Faille de Leverghem, Georges della, July 1920-25
   Everts, Robert, Mar. 1925-32
   Kerchove de Denterghem, André de, Feb. 1932-35
   Graeffe, Egbert (chargé d'affaires), 1936
   Davignon, Jacques, Apr. 1936-40

Czechoslovakia
   Kobr, Milos, 1920
   Korner, Eduard, 1920
   Tusar, Vlastimil, Mar. 1921-24
   Krofta, Kamil, May 1924-27
   Chvalkovsky, Frantisek, Mar. 1927-32
   Mastny, Vojtech, July 1932-39

France
   Chassain de Marcilly, E.H.A., 1920

Laurent, Charles, July 1920-22
Margerie, Pierre de, Dec. 1922-31
François-Poncet, André, Sept. 1931-38
Coulondre, Robert, Nov. 1938-39

Great Britain
Lord Kilmarnock (chargé d'affaires), 1920
Lord D'Abernon, July 1920-26
Lindsay, Ronald, Nov. 1926-28
Rumbold, Horace, Aug. 1928-33
Phipps, Eric, May 1933-37
Henderson, Nevile, May 1937-39

Hungary
Emich de Emoke, Gustav, Sept. 1920-25
Kánya, Kolomon von, Nov. 1925-33
Masirevich, Constantin de, Aug. 1933-35
Sztójay, Döme, Dec. 1935-44

Italy
Aldrovandi-Marescotti, Luigi, Dec. 1919-20
Frassati, Alfredo, Jan. 1921-22
Bosdari, Alessandro de, Dec. 1922-26
Aldrovandi-Marescotti, Luigi, Mar. 1926-29
Orsini-Baroni, Luca, Dec. 1929-32
Cerruti, Vittorio, Oct. 1932-35
Attolico, Bernardo, Sept. 1935-40
Alfieri, Dino, May 1940-43
Anfuso, Filippo, Oct. 1943-45

Japan
Debuchi, K. (chargé d'affaires), Mar. 1920-21
Hioki, E., Jan. 1921-24
Honda, Kumataro, Feb. 1924-26
Nagaoka, Harukazu, Aug. 1926-31
Torikitchi, Obata, Apr. 1931-33
Matsuzo, Magai, Apr. 1933-35
Mushakoje, Kintomo, Feb. 1935-38
Oshima, Hiroshi, Nov. 1938-39
Kurusu, Saburo, Dec. 1939-41
Oshima, Hiroshi, Feb. 1941-45

Poland
Szebeko, Ignace (chargé d'affaires), Mar. 1920-21
Madejski, Georg de, Oct. 1921-23
Olszowski, Kazimierz, June 1923-28
Knoll, Roman, July 1928-31
Wysocki, Alfred, Feb. 1931-33
Lipski, Józef, Sept. 1933-39

Rumania
Nano, Constantin G., Feb. 1921-32
Petrescu-Comnène, Nicolae, June 1932-38
Djuvara, Radu T., Apr. 1938-39
Crutescu, Radu, Mar. 1939-41
Bossy, Raoul, Mar. 1941-43
Gheorghe, Ion, June 1943-45

Soviet Union
Joffe, Adolph, Apr.-Nov. 1918
Kopp, Victor, Nov. 1919-21
Krestinsky, Nicolai, July 1922-30
Khinchuk, Leo, Dec. 1930-34
Suritz, Jacob, Oct. 1934-37
Jurenjew, Konstantin, July 1937-38
Merekalov, Alexei, July 1938-39
Shkvarzev, Alexander, Sept. 1939-40
Dekanosov, Vladimir, 1940-41

Spain
Soler y Guardiola, Pablo, Aug. 1920-27
Espinosa de los Monteros, Fernando, May 1927-31
Castro, Américo, May 1931-33
Zulueta, Luis de, Aug. 1933-35
Agramonte y Cortijo, Francesco, Mar. 1935-37
Magáz, Antonio, Aug. 1937-40
Espinosa de los Monteros, Fernando, Sept. 1940-41
Finat y Escriva de Romani, José, Nov. 1941-42
Vidal y Saura, Ginés, Dec. 1942-45

United States
Dresel, Ellis L. (chargé d'affaires), 1920
Houghton, Alanson B., Apr. 1922-25
Schurman, Jacob Gould, June 1925-30
Sackett, Frederick M., Feb. 1930-33
Dodd, William E., July 1933-37
Wilson, Hugh, Mar. 1938-40
Kirk, Alexander C. (chargé d'affaires), 1938-40

Vatican (Papal Nuncio)
Pacelli, Eugenio, Mar. 1920-29
Orsenigo, Cesare, May 1930-45

END NOTES

1. General overviews are in Heinz G. Sasse and E. Eickhoff, 100 Jahre Auswärtiges Amt, 1870-1970 (Bonn, 1970), and in Kurt Doss, "The History of the German Foreign Office," in The Times Survey of Foreign Ministries of the World, edited by Zara Steiner (London, 1982), pp. 225-57. For the Weimar period, see Herbert von Hindenburg, Das Auswärtige Amt im Wandel

der Zeiten (Frankfurt/M., 1932), a popular account; for the Nazi period, see Hill (no. 648), Jacobsen (no. 651), and Seabury (no. 660). 2. On office routine and filing systems, see Introduction to George O. Kent, A Catalog of Files and Microfilms of the German Foreign Ministry Archives, 1920-1945, 4 vols. (Stanford, 1962-73). An analysis of the files themselves is in the appendix of Documents on German Foreign Policy, 1918-1945, Series D (Washington, 1949-64). 3. Recent accounts are in Lamar Cecil, The German Diplomatic Service, 1871-1914 (Princeton, 1976); Doss (no. 304); Paul Gordon Lauren, Diplomats and Bureaucrats: The First International Responses to Twentieth-Century Diplomacy in France and Germany (Stanford, 1976); and Klaus Schwabe, ed., Das Diplomatische Korps, 1871-1945 (Boppard, 1985). Older but still useful is Schifferdecker (no. 99). For contemporary criticisms of the reforms, see [Julius Adolf] von Griesinger, "Aufbau, Neubau, und Abbau des Auswärtigen Amtes," Deutsche Revue, 1 (1922); R.R. von Scheller-Steinwartz, "Reform des Auswärtigen Amts," Handbuch der Politik, 3d ed. (Berlin, 1921), 351-55; and Kuno Tiemann, Das Auswärtige Amt und die Notwendigkeit seiner Reform (Berlin, 1920). 4. On organization, see Henry K. Norton, "Foreign Office Organization," The Annals of the American Academy, vol. 143, supplement (Philadelphia, 1929); Frederick L. Schuman, "The Conduct of German Foreign Affairs," ibid., vol. 176 (Philadelphia, 1934), 187-221; Kraske (no. 97); and Kraus (no. 97). Information on the ministry's cultural policies and agencies is in Kurt Düwell, Deutschlands auswärtige Kulturpolitik, 1918-1932 (Cologne, 1976); Kurt Düwell and Werner Link, eds., Deutsche auswärtige Kulturpolitik seit 1871 (Cologne, 1981); Kurt Koszyk, Deutsche Presse, 1914-1945, Pt. 3 (Berlin, 1972); Johannes Richter, Die Reichszentrale für Heimatdienst (Berlin, 1963); and Markus Schöneberger, Diplomatie im Dialog: Ein Jahrhundert Informationspolitik des Auswärtigen Amtes (Munich, 1981). 5. Paul Seabury, "Ribbentrop and the German Foreign Office," Political Science Quarterly, 66 (1951), 532-55; Christopher R. Browning (no. 1098); by the same author, "Unterstaatssekretär Martin Luther and the Ribbentrop Foreign Office," Journal of Contemporary History 12 (1977), 313-44; Döscher (no. 641); Saxton Bradford, "Deutsche Auslandspropaganda," Department of State Bulletin, 14 (1946), 278-81, 311-16, 365-69. 6. In general, see Alfred Vagts, The Military Attaché (Princeton, 1967), and Manfred Kehrig, Die Wiedereinrichtung des deutschen militärischen Attachédienstes nach dem Ersten Weltkrieg (Boppard, 1966). On diplomats in the field, the best guide is Auswärtiges Amt, Verzeichnis der deutschen diplomatischen und konsularischen Vertretungen im Ausland, and Verzeichnis der Mitglieder des diplomatischen Korps in Berlin, which appeared irregularly but at least once a year. Another useful directory is the Almanach de Gotha (no. 34). On German ambassadors in London, Heinz G. Sasse, 100 Jahre Botschaft in London (Bonn, 1963), and in Washington, Frank Lambach, Our Men in Washington (Cologne, 1976). 7. For the history of the Forschungsamt, see David Irving, Breach of Security (London, 1968). 8. Hans Draeger, ed., Der Arbeitsausschuss Deutscher Verbände, 1921-1931 (Berlin, 1931), is a contemporary account. Scholarly studies of the subject are cited below, nos. 373-385, 696-718. 9. On this, see the memoirs of Margarete Gärtner (no. 118); Evans and Baylen (no. 470); and Frauendienst (no. 471). The files of the Kulturabteilung are illuminating on the relationship between the ministry and private scholars and publicists, institutes, publishers, interest groups, and such. For the role of the various research institutes, see Klaus Jürgen Gantzel, ed., Kolonialrechtswissenschaft, Kriegsursachenforschung, Internationale Angelegenheiten (Baden Baden, 1983), and Wissenschaftliche Verantwortung und politische Macht (Berlin, 1986). See also Manfred Messerschmidt, "Revision, Neue Ordnung, Krieg: Akzente der Völkerrechtswissenschaft in Deutschland, 1933-1945," Militärgeschichtliche Mitteilungen, 9 (1971), 61-95.

10. Krüger (no. 315), and, for information on social backgrounds, family connections, and party membership, Döscher (no. 641). Hans von Herwarth, "Der deutsche Diplomat: Ausbildung und Rolle in Vergangenheit und Gegenwart," in Karl Braunias and Gerald Stourzh, eds., Diplomatie unserer Zeit (Graz, 1959), pp. 227-45; Heinz G. Sasse, "Das Problem des diplomatischen Nachwuchses im Dritten Reich," in Richard Dietrich and Gerhard Oestreich, eds., Forschungen zu Staat und Verfassung (Berlin, 1958), pp. 367-83.

11. See Jacobsen (no. 651), Krüger (no. 653), the essays by Craig, Holborn, and Schorske in Gordon A. Craig and Felix Gilbert, eds., The Diplomats, 1919-1939 (Princeton, 1953), and Werner-Otto von Hentig, "Erfahrungen im auswärtigen Dienst, " Frankfurter Hefte (1955), 117-22, 294-98.

12. Pohl (no. 98); Ernst Wolgast, "Die auswärtige Gewalt des Deutschen Reiches unter besonderer Berücksichtigung des Auswärtigen Amtes," Archiv des öffentlichen Rechts, 5 (1923), 1-112.

13. On the chancellery and its functions, see the introductory comments in K.H. Harbeck (no. 62) and the memoirs of Pünder (no. 149) and of Max von Stockhausen (Sechs Jahre Reichskanzlei [Bonn, 1954]).

14. Grupp and Jardin (no. 310); Dr. Hauschild, Der vorläufige Reichswirtschaftsrat, 1920-1926 (Berlin, 1926); Radkau (no. 737); and Friedrich Facius, Wirtschaft und Staat (Boppard, 1959).

15. Andreas Dorpalen, Hindenburg and the Weimar Republic (Princeton, 1964); Peter Haungs, Reichspräsident und parlamentarische Kabinettsbildung (Cologne, 1968); Walther Hubatsch, Hindenburg und der Staat (Göttingen, 1966).

16. See note 12 above and Wahl (no. 101). The Reich government maintained legations in Munich and Darmstadt; its representatives were accredited to the respective state governments and reported to the chancellery (with carbon copies to Referat Deutschland in the foreign ministry). See Hans-Joachim Schreckenbach, "Innerdeutsche Gesandtschaften, 1867-1945," in Archivar und Historiker (Berlin, 1956), and Friedrich P. Kahlenberg, ed., Die Berichte Eduard Davids als Reichsvertreter in Hessen, 1921-1927 (Wiesbaden, 1970).

17. Martin Broszat, Der Staat Hitlers, 10th ed. (Munich, 1983); Jost Düllfer, "Zum 'decision-making process' in der deutschen Aussenpolitik, 1933-1939," in Funke (no. 643); H.C. Frend, "Hitler and his Foreign Ministry, 1937-1939," History, 42 (1957), 118-29; Heineman (no. 683).

18. Emil Ehrich, Die Auslands-Organisation der NSDAP (Berlin, 1937), is an official tract. See Hans-Adolf Jacobsen, "Die Gründung der Auslandsabteilung der NSDAP (1931-1933)," in Ernst Schulin, ed., Gedenkschrift Martin Göhring (Wiesbaden, 1968), pp. 353-68, and the charts in Jacobsen's "Zur Struktur der NS-Aussenpolitik, 1933-1945," in Funke (no. 643), pp. 137-85.

19. The best account is still in Seabury, note 1 above. See also Martin (no. 1193); Walter Petwaidic, Die autoritäre Anarchie (Hamburg, 1946); and Hans G. von Studnitz, Als Berlin brannte: Diarium der Jahre 1943-1945 (Stuttgart, 1963).

20. For occupation and annexation policies, see Stuckart (no. 100), the legal journals Deutsches Recht (1943-45) and Deutsche Verwaltung (1923-45), the annual Jahrbuch für Auswärtige Politik (no. 96), and Franz Neumann's Behemoth (New York, 1944). On the implementation of these policies, see Ruth Bettina Birn, Die Höheren SS- und Polizeiführer: Himmlers Vertreter im Reich und in den besetzten Gebieten (Düsseldorf, 1986); Peter R. Black, Ernst Kaltenbrunner: Ideological Soldier of the Third Reich (Princeton, 1984); and Broszat, note 17 above.

21. On the destruction of the ministry's files, see the appendix in Documents on German Foreign Policy, 1918-1945, note 2 above; on the fate of the files that survived and fell into Allied hands, see Robert Wolfe, ed., Captured German and Related Records (Athens, OH, 1974).

III. ARCHIVES AND LIBRARIES

The sources for the history of German foreign policy in the twentieth century are scattered through various collections, each with its own system of organization and with its own rules on access and use. The archival sources are almost all in archives in the two German states. The records of the government and its branches and agencies are in public archives, as are those of political parties and pressure groups, of corporations and of individuals who have played historic roles. They are accessible to all who meet certain formal conditions (though visitors from abroad may find themselves barred if their country fails to extend the same courtesies). The records of business and industry are in private archives, which are usually affiliated with the institutions whose records they hold. They tend to be less important than the public archives, though on particular issues they may be indispensable. Each has its own rules and regulations, and access is by no means assured. Personal records, consisting of correspondence, diaries, reminiscences, and sometimes official documents will be found in private collections or family archives. Such collections have much that is significant and valuable. Access depends entirely on the decision of the family.

Some of these archival sources are available on microfilm. The films are held by repositories outside of Germany, and they can usually be acquired by purchase. Microfilms are no substitute for actual research in the archives, but they can make such research less laborious and more productive.

The records of the Nuremberg war crimes trials are a unique source. They consist of the thousands of documents gathered as evidence by the prosecution and the defense, and of the transcripts of pre-trial interrogations and trial testimony. This material was translated into the languages of the court and was reproduced in numerous copies. After the trials, it ended up in various collections, and some of it was published in several voluminous series.

The published records of German policy, parliamentary proceedings, memoirs, and secondary sources are in research institutes and research libraries. Many of these institutes and libraries specialize in international affairs or have special collections (often including oral history transcripts). Some of them also have small archives or Handschriftensammlungen.

Newspaper libraries have lost some of their importance as newspapers have been put on microfilm and made available through interlibrary loan. Nonetheless, the larger newspaper libraries are still worth visiting, for their often highly diverse holdings will contain material not on film. It goes without saying that perusing the originals is far easier than scanning microfilm.

Many of the archives and libraries have finding aids--printed guides, catalogues, and inventories. The most important of these are listed and described at the end of this chapter.

31

A. ARCHIVES IN GERMANY

The largest accumulation of materials on German foreign policy is in the Federal Republic, which has fallen heir to the documentary collections captured by the western armies in 1945. The Democratic Republic has a few collections of importance but otherwise holds only fragments of collections largely in the West.

Both states have national and regional archives (though those in the Democratic Republic, unlike those in the Federal Republic, are highly centralized). The archives organize their holdings in much the same way, keeping the records of individual institutions together as single collections and usually in the form in which they were first assembled. Records dating from before May 1945 are generally available to legitimate researchers, though archives in both states put restrictions on material they consider sensitive. The Democratic Republic has party and military archives that are virtually inaccessible. In the Federal Republic, some of the regional archives require special permission on materials less than fifty years old, and of course many of the private and family archives limit access to their holdings.

The facilities for research are reasonably uniform. The archives provide reading rooms, generally equipped with microfilm readers and reader-copiers, and with a small reference library of handbooks, directories, and works based on the documents in the archives. They have photocopying and microfilming services or can arrange for such services, though they are reluctant to film whole record series. They are open on weekdays, sometimes also on Saturdays, throughout the year. They are busiest in summer, when researchers arrive in droves, and cannot always accommodate everyone. And they all have house rules on how to request archival records and how to use them, and on what may be copied and published and in what form. These rules are set forth in writing, and you will be asked to sign a statement indicating that you have read them. You will also be asked to sign a statement that you assume all responsibility for the possible infringement of personal rights in using or publishing documents.

You can save yourself time and annoyance if you prepare your visit before you go. Acquaint yourself with the appropriate finding aids and with the regulations on access and use; archivists have little time for elementary questions about their holdings and inventories. Write to the archives if you need information, and talk to researchers just back from the field, for they will know about recent or contemplated changes. You will find most archivists knowledgeable about other archives and willing to share what they know.

If you want to track down private papers (Nachlässe), consult the published guides by Mommsen and Denecke and by Friedrichs (see below, pp. 64-65) as well as the staff of the Bundesarchiv and of the Institut für Zeitgeschichte. Some of the Nachlässe in the archives are available only with permission of the family or the estate; ask the archivists to help you secure permission. For Nachlässe in private collections, address yourself directly to the family. Describe your project and your interest, and inquire whether and when the papers are available.

The addresses of public and private archives in Germany, together with listings of their regulations and facilities, and an overview of their holdings, are in Minerva Handbücher, Archive: Archive im deutschsprachigen Raum (2d ed., Berlin, 1974).

ARCHIVES AND LIBRARIES

1. Federal Republic of Germany

The welcome you get in the archives here will depend entirely on what you do to pave the way. All archives prefer advance notice of your visit. They would like to know the nature of your research and the sorts of documentation you think you will need. This will enable them to prepare the material and to check their holdings for other things that might have some bearing on your work. They would also like to know when you plan to arrive and how long you expect to stay, so that they can reserve space in the reading room. Your letter (preferably in German) should be addressed to the head of the archive--the Leiter or Direktor. He will route it to the archivist most familiar with your archival material, who will correspond with you and serve as your contact when you arrive.

Upon your arrival, you must show identification: your passport and, if you are a graduate student, a letter of introduction from your thesis adviser. The archives at Bonn and Koblenz require that visitors from abroad also have a letter of introduction from the cultural attaché of their embassy in Bonn. You can apply for such a letter, either directly or in writing, enclosing a copy of a letter from your home institution or thesis adviser.

In Germany, unlike Britain or the United States, the records of the foreign ministry are preserved at the ministry itself and not at a central repository. For the diplomatic documents you must therefore go to Bonn:

Politisches Archiv des
Auswärtigen Amts
Adenauerallee 99-103
5300 Bonn 1

(Open Mon.-Thur., 8:15-4:30,
Fri., 8:15-3:30; closed weekends
and holidays)

With the exception of some wartime losses and some material held at the Zentrales Staatsarchiv in Potsdam, the records are complete and, with the exception of the personnel files, open to research. They consist of the original copies of the Akten produced by the ministry and the diplomatic missions, as well as the working files and personal papers (Handakten and Nachlässe) of individual diplomats. Among the latter, the papers of Stresemann are particularly important for the Weimar years, those of Ritter, Clodius, Wiehl, and Gaus for the Nazi years. The collection is divided into three parts (1867-1920, 1920-36, 1936-45), in keeping with the organizational changes in the ministry. The most severe losses are in the third category: for 1940-43, some files are badly depleted and others are missing altogether; for 1943-45, only fragments survive. The secret files of the legal department are gone, as are many of the secret files of the political and commercial departments and of the embassies at London and Paris. The files of Ribbentrop's Büro RAM were burned on Ribbentrop's orders, but many of the more important documents have survived on microfilm (the so-called Loesch films). Some of the Handakten and embassy files, however, partly offset these losses.

The holdings are inventoried in two catalogues, one edited by the American Historical Association's Committee for the Study of War Documents, the other by George O. Kent (see below, p. 66). The catalogues indicate what part of the

33

material has been filmed and is therefore available elsewhere, and what has to be seen in the original at Bonn. Since they are used, with some emendations, as inventories at the Politisches Archiv, you should refer to them when you compile the list of files you wish to see, For some record groups, the archive has put together more detailed inventories. These can be examined in the reading room or in the offices of the archivists; you should ask for them.

A selection of documents from this archive has been published in the series Akten zur deutschen auswärtigen Politik, 1918-1945 and, in translation, in Documents on German Foreign Policy, 1918-1945. Each document is printed with a reference to the file it came from; footnotes and appendices draw attention to related documents or to documents that are missing. The various volumes in the series are therefore a guide to the important files, and you should look at them before you launch a search in the archive.

The other major archive you will want to visit is near Bonn, at Koblenz:

Bundesarchiv
Potsdamerstrasse 1
5400 Koblenz 1

(Open Mon.-Thur., 8:00 a.m.-8:45 p.m.,
Fri., 8:00-7:00; closed weekends
and holidays)

The archive, established in 1952, serves as the repository of all noncurrent records of the government (except those of the foreign ministry) and of private institutions and individuals. Its holdings are catalogued in a massive published guide (see below, p. 66); individual record groups are catalogued in detailed repertories or Findbücher at the archive. Some of its materials have been or are being microfilmed and are available for purchase. As the main national archive, the Bundesarchiv has become something of a broker of information on developments and holdings in other archives, and you will find the archivists have answers to most of your questions. There is also a central file on Nachlässe in Germany and elsewhere, the Nachlasskartei.

For the diplomatic historian, the most important records are those of the Reichskanzlei, almost complete for the period 1919-45, supplemented by those of Ministerbüro Lammers. This collection, which includes the cabinet minutes, contains substantial material on policy and policymaking in the Weimar years. The records of the ministry of finance, another sizable collection, furnish information on the implementation of the peace terms, on reparations and secret subsidies, and on wartime occupation policies. Relevant material can also be found in the records of the ministries of justice, of reparations, of the interior, and of propaganda, all of which were involved in foreign affairs. There are special collections related to Volkstumspolitik (RKFDV, Vomi, DAI) and to the activities of the SS (Himmler's personal staff, policy in occupied territories) as well as some files of the APA, of two of Hitler's special emissaries (Papen, Wiedemann), and of the Reichstag (budget committee, 1924-33). The propaganda ministry's daily briefings of the German press, which provide much insight into Nazi policy, are in Sammlung Brammer. Not least important, there are the papers of corporations, trade and industrial associations, and of individuals who have deposited their records, or portions of their records, in the archive.

34

German military records are held at a branch of the Bundesarchiv in Freiburg:

> Bundesarchiv
> Abteilung Militärarchiv
> Wiesentalstrasse 10
> 7800 Freiburg i.B.

> (Open Mon.-Tues., 7:30-4:00;
> Wed.-Thur., 7:30-3:30; Fri., 7:30-2:30;
> closed weekends and holidays)

These records, originally housed in the Militärgeschichtliches Forschungsamt in Freiburg, were transferred to the Militärarchiv in 1968. They consist of the surviving records of the Reichswehrministerium (later Kriegsministerium) and of the armed forces. Among them are various war diaries, that is, daily logs kept by staff officers at headquarters, which contain much important political and diplomatic information. There are also files of military and naval attachés, of commanders in occupied countries, and of the armistice commission in France (1940-44), as well as a number of Nachlässe. The army files hold copies of documents from the foreign ministry, dating from as late as December 1944, which are not in the archive at Bonn.

Documentary materials on the Nazi party are at the Berlin Document Center, in Berlin-Zehlendorf, Wasserkäfersteig 1. The BDC was established to provide government agencies with information on Nazis and Nazi organizations, and it originally held material on a broad range of Nazi activity. Much of the material has since been transferred to Koblenz (and is available on microfilm, see below, pp. 42-43). What remains are biographic collections: the membership files of the Nazi party and its affiliates, containing some 22 million names and filled with information on the party, on politics, and often also on specific events. These (along with some diplomatic personnel records available on film) are the only personnel files open to researchers for the period 1918-45.

The BDC is under the authority of the United States Department of State, and application for a visit should be made to:

> Director
> Berlin Document Center
> U.S. Mission Berlin
> APO, New York 09742

Your application should describe the nature and purpose of your research, and should indicate as precisely as possible what material, or what type of material, you wish to see. Requests for microfilm of specific records may be made from abroad (but since there are no published inventories, this is difficult).

The records of the Prussian government after 1918 are not directly relevant to Germany's diplomatic history, but some material of interest can be found at the

> Geheimes Staatsarchiv
> Preussischer Kulturbesitz
> Archivstrasse 12-14
> 1000 Berlin 33

(Open Mon., Wed.-Fri., 8:00-3:45,
Tues., 8:00-7:45; closed weekends
and holidays)

Among these records are those of the Preussische Staatsministerium (Alsace-Lorraine, 1918-24, Stabsamt Göring, 1933-44), the Prussian ministry of interior, which took part in executing the terms of the peace treaty, the Preussische Staatsbank (Seehandlung), which had a hand in financial negotiations and settlements with foreign countries, and both the Saxon representative to the Reichsrat (1918-32) and the East Prussian representative in Berlin (1920-32), who were kept informed on matters of foreign policy. Among the Nachlässe, the most important is that of Otto Braun, prime minister of Prussia from 1920 to 1932.

Until 1979, the Stiftung Preussischer Kulturbesitz had a branch in Göttingen--the Staatliches Archivlager. This archive had among his holdings material from the Memel Landtag (1926-39) and various Nachlässe (Oskar Hergt, August Winnig); there was also a major collection of Nuremberg war crimes records. In 1979, most of the holdings were transferred to the Geheime Staatsarchiv in Berlin, the rest going to the Bundesarchiv in Koblenz. The Nuremberg trials records went to the university library in Göttingen.

Researchers should not overlook Germany's regional archives as a source of material on the history of German foreign policy. These archives hold the records of the various state governments, and these were involved in the conduct of foreign affairs through the Reichsrat. Among the materials in the archives are copies of foreign ministry documents (including the weekly digest of events and the confidential print of important ambassadorial dispatches), correspondence between the state governments and their representatives in Berlin, and voluminous material pertaining to the meetings of the foreign affairs committees of the Reichstag and the Reichsrat. There is also interesting material in the files of the state ministries of commerce and of economics, which were usually consulted on foreign economic relations, as well as a number of Nachlässe.

Among the more important of these archives (with their relevant holdings listed in parentheses) are:

Generallandesarchiv Karlsruhe
7500 Karlsruhe 1, Nördl. Hildapromenade 2

(Staatsministerium: Verhältnis zum Ausland,
Kriegssachen; Badische Gesandtschaft in Berlin,
1918-33; Nachlass Willy Hellpach)

Bayerisches Hauptstaatsarchiv
  Abt. Geheimes Staatsarchiv
8000 München 22, Schönfeldstrasse 5-11

(Bayr. Staatsministerium des Äussern; Bayerische
Gesandtschaft in Berlin, 1918-33)

Niedersächsisches Staatsarchiv
3340 Wolfenbüttel, Forstweg 2

(Braunschweigisches Staatsministerium;
Braunschweigische Vertretung beim Reich, 1918-34)

Staatsarchiv Bremen
2800 Bremen 1, Am Staatsarchiv 1

(Senatskommission für auswärtige Angelegenheiten;
Bremische Gesandtschaft, 1920-37)

Staatsarchiv Hamburg
2000 Hamburg 36, ABC-Strasse 19A

(Senatskommission für Reichs- und auswärtige
Angelegenheiten, 1919-33; Hamburgische
Gesandtschaft, 1918-32; German representative on
German-American reparations commission, 1922-34;
Nachlässe Friedrich Sthamer, Carl Petersen)

Nordrhein-Westfälisches Staatsarchiv
4930 Detmold, Willi-Hofmann-Strasse 2

(Lippisches Staatsministerium: Auswärtige
Angelegenheiten; Landesvertretung Lippe, 1918-32)

Archiv der Hansestadt Lübeck
2400 Lübeck 1, Mühlendamm 1-3

(Lübeckische Vertretung; Nordische Gesellschaft)

Niedersächsisches Staatsarchiv
2900 Oldenburg, Damm 43

(Oldenburgische Vertretung im Reichsrat, 1918-34)

Niedersächsisches Staatsarchiv
4967 Bückeburg, Schloss (Ostflügel)

(Bestand Schaumburg-Lippe: Angelegenheiten des
Reichs; Bevollmächtigter des Freistaats Schaumburg-
Lippe zum Reichsrat, 1918-34)

Hauptstaatsarchiv Stuttgart
7000 Stuttgart 1, Konrad-Adenauer-Str. 4

(Württ. Staatsministerium: Auswärtige
Angelegenheiten, 1918-38; Württ. Gesandtschaft in
Berlin, 1918-25; Württ. Gesandtschaft in München;
Nachlass Conrad Haussmann)

Significant materials are also held by the private archives of business and
industrial corporations, banks, and chambers of commerce and industry. Their
collections of company records, correspondence files, and personal papers

relate to such matters as reparations, international cartelization and industrial cooperation, rearmament and economic mobilization, the exploitation of resources in occupied countries, and, in general, shed light on the convoluted linkages between foreign policy and economic interest.

The records of the most important trade associations of the Weimar years, such as the Reichsverband der Deutschen Industrie or the Centralverband des Deutschen Bank- und Bankiergewerbes, survive only in fragments. Thus, of the various Fachgruppen of the RDI, the records of only one (Bergbau) are available; of the Fachverbände, only those of the Verein deutscher Eisen- und Stahlindustrieller and the Verein deutscher Eisenhüttenleute. The records of chambers of commerce and industry fared somewhat better. Many are still with their home institutions (as in Munich, Hamburg, and Bremen) or have been transferred to local municipal archives (as in Frankfurt/M. and Mannheim) or to the regional economic archives in Cologne and Dortmund. The records of the Deutsche Industrie- und Handelstag, the national association of these chambers, are in the Bundesarchiv. The losses in organizational records of course enhance the value of the personal papers of men who played leading roles in these organizations. There are many of these, often held as the mainstay of a private archive.

There are about 400 private archives in the Federal Republic (see below, pp. 66-67). Many of them are open to legitimate research, though they are under no obligation to provide access or to render assistance and service. You should try to get a firm commitment on access in advance of your visit. Moreover, unlike public archives, the private archives organize their holdings for the purpose and use of the institutions they serve, not for historical research. They therefore presume some knowledge about the hierarchy and organization of the institution whose records you want to examine.

Among the more important private archives (with some of the significant holdings listed in parentheses) are:

Historisches Archiv, Fried. Krupp GmbH
4300 Essen 1, Villa Hügel

(F. Krupp, O. Wiedfeldt papers)

Firmenarchiv der Thyssen A.G.
4100 Duisburg 11, Kaiser-Wilhelm-Str. 100

(A. Thyssen, F. Thyssen papers)

Historisches Archiv der Gutehoffnungshütte
4200 Oberhausen 1, Essener Strasse 55

(P. Reusch, K. Haniel papers)

Bayer Werksarchiv
5090 Leverkusen, Bayerwerk

(C. Duisberg papers)

Historisches Archiv, Hapag-Lloyd A.G.
2000 Hamburg 1, Ballindamm 25

(Hamburg-Amerika Linie files; W. Cuno papers)

Werner-von-Siemens Institut für
Geschichte des Hauses Siemens
8000 München 2, Prannerstrasse 10

(Siemens A.G. files; C.F. von Siemens papers)

Firmenarchiv M.M. Warburg-Brinckmann,
Wirtz & Co.
2000 Hamburg 1, Ferdinandstrasse 75

(M. Warburg, C. Melchior papers)

Historisches Archiv, Deutsche Bank
6000 Frankfurt/M., Goetheplatz 1-3

(Deutsche Bank, Disconto Gesellschaft Berlin,
Deutsche Überseeische Bank Berlin files)

Mannesmann-Archiv
4000 Düsseldorf, Mannesmann-Ufer 2

(Mannesmann, Poensgen Werke, Phoenix A.G. files;
E. Poensgen, H.W. Beukenberg papers)

Historisches Archiv der Salzgitter A.G.
3320 Salzgitter 41, Postfach 411129

(P. Pleiger papers; Reichswerke Hermann Göring)

There are also two excellent regional economic archives, whose holdings include materials from individual firms, trade associations, chambers of commerce and industry, as well as private papers and documents from the Nuremberg war crimes trials:

Rheinisch-Westfälisches
Wirtschaftsarchiv zu Köln e.V.
Unter Sachsenhausen 10-26
5000 Köln 1

(Open Mon.-Thurs., 9:30-4:30,
Fri., 9:30-12:00; closed weekends
and holidays)

Westfälisches Wirtschaftsarchiv
Märkische Strasse 120
4600 Dortmund 1

(Open Mon.-Thurs., 9:00-4:00;
Fri., 9:00-3:00; closed weekends
and holidays)

39

Several of the collections in these archives were among those captured at the end of the war. The more important (Dresdner Bank, Flick A.G., IG Farben, Krupp, Reichswerke Hermann Göring) were microfilmed in the United States before they were returned to the original owners. Individual documents were used at Nuremberg and found their way into the trial records. For more on this, see below, pp. 50-54.

2. German Democratic Republic

The archives in the Democratic Republic are not closed to western scholars, but permission to visit them is not granted automatically to all applicants. According to the official <u>Taschenbuch: Archivwesen der DDR</u> (below, p. 67), permission may be denied if the projected research is inconsistent with "national interests," or when the material that is being requested is required for purposes of the state or is in no condition to be used. Permission is generally granted for research deemed congenial to the interests of the state. The recent political changes taking place in the German Democratic Republic will undoubtedly affect policies governing access to the archives. However, until such policies are officially announced, researchers should follow the guidelines in this chapter.

Prior written application is absolutely essential. Inquiries and applications for access to both the national and the regional archives should be addressed to

> Ministerrat der
> Deutschen Demokratischen Republik
> Ministerium des Innern
> Staatliche Archivverwaltung
> Berliner Strasse 98-101
> 1500 Potsdam

The application, which should be filled out carefully, must include certain specific information. (1) Personal information: your full name; date and place of birth; nationality or citizenship; permanent address; anticipated address in the Democratic Republic (if known); previous address in the Democratic Republic (if any); profession or position, and place of employment; number of passport, and city where it was issued; point where you expect to cross the border. (2) Professional information: for whom are you doing the research (yourself, a thesis adviser, or an institution); what is the purpose of your research (dissertation, book, or article; and if it is to be published, where will it appear); what is your topic and what period will it cover; when will you conduct your research, and how long do you expect it to take. It is advisable to be as specific as possible in defining the research subject and in describing the records you want to consult.

The Archivverwaltung will respond within two to four months. If the reply is favorable, you should notify the archives of your date of arrival, so that they can reserve a place for you. If in the course of your work in the achive, you find that you need to extend your researches in ways you did not foresee when you submitted your application, you can make an appropriate request to the archive. Such requests are usually handled fairly promptly. You may order microfilms of documents you have examined; you may also order them directly from the inventories. In either case, you will have to wait two to three months before you get them. In general, rules on the use and the publication of material, as well as on what may be copied, tend to be more stringent than in the Federal Republic. They should be strictly observed.

For diplomatic historians, the most important records are at the national archive in Potsdam:

> Zentrales Staatsarchiv
> Historische Abteilung I
> Berliner Strasse 98-101
> 1561 Potsdam
>
> (Open Mon., 9:00-4:00, Tues.-Thur.,
> 8:00-6:30, Fri., 8:00-4:00;
> closed weekends and holidays)

This archive, formerly known as the Deutsches Zentralarchiv, holds assorted records of the German government between 1871 and 1945, many of which fell into Soviet hands at the end of the war. Some of these come from the foreign ministry. Predominant among them are economic files, from individual departments between 1920 and 1936 and from the Commercial Department after 1936. Other extensive collections are those of the armistice commission of 1918-19, the embassy at Moscow and the Nachlässe of the German ambassadors at Moscow (Schulenburg, Dirksen), the legations at Peking and Kabul, and the Deutsche Stiftung. There are some stray files from the legal department, the press department, the AO and APA, and the Ministerbüro Reichsminister (with some Neurath Handakten), 1928-44.

The files of the Büro Reichspräsident (later, Präsidialkanzlei), 1919-45, are useful for tracing the presidents' interest and role in policymaking. Those of the ministries of economics, of occupied territories (1923-30), and of occupied eastern territories (1941-45) have good material. There are sizable holdings of material from the Vorläufige Reichswirtschaftsrat and from the Reichsrat and the Reichstag (including complete committee files), and some smaller holdings of various conservative parties and organizations (Deutscher Schutzbund, Alldeutscher Verband, DNVP, DVP) and of business firms and banks (IG Farben, Reichsbank, Handakten R. Havenstein).

A branch of the national archive, virtually the counterpart of the Geheimes Staatsarchiv in West Berlin, is at Merseburg:

> Zentrales Staatsarchiv
> Historische Abteilung II
> Weisse Mauer 48
> 4200 Merseburg

It holds the bulk of the records of the Prussian government. Of these, those of the ministries of finance and of trade have things of interest.

Some of the regional archives, like those in the Federal Republic, hold the files of the state representatives in Berlin as well as copies of the documents circulated among the state governments by the foreign ministry. The most extensive of such holdings is at the Staatsarchiv Dresden, Archivstrasse 14, 8060 Dresden N6.

Communist and Socialist party records are at the Institut für Marxismus-Leninismus, Abt. Zentrales Parteiarchiv, in East Berlin. Military records, including material on secret rearmament between the wars, are at the Deutsches Militärarchiv in Potsdam. This is the archive of the Nationale Volksarmee and not subject to the Staatliche Archivverwaltung. Neither of these archives appears to be readily accessible.

B. OTHER ARCHIVES

After Germany's defeat in 1945, the Western powers came into possession of great quantities of German material. They exploited it first for purposes of intelligence and the war crimes trials, and then shipped it to Britain and the United States for further study. Most of it was ultimately turned over to the Federal Republic, but not before much of it had been microfilmed. The microfilm, which is now available in archives in different countries, consists of several important collections:

(1) German records filmed at Whaddon Hall in England as part of the project that led to the publication of <u>Documents on German Foreign Policy, 1918-1945</u>. They consist of the major files of the foreign ministry and of the chancellery, 1867-1945. The foreign ministry files include those of the foreign minister and the state secretary, various departments and offices, key officials, and some few diplomatic missions. Those of the chancellery are related to political and diplomatic affairs and include the cabinet minutes. All are catalogued in the American Historical Association and the Kent catalogues, cited below, pp. 65-66.

(2) German records filmed at Alexandria, Va., under the auspices of the American Historical Association and the National Achives. They consist of files from central, regional, and local government authorities, various military echelons (including the OKW, OKH, OKM), Nazi party formations and affiliated organizations, and the papers of private institutions and individuals, dating mainly from the period 1920-45. Also included are the records of some German diplomatic missions that happened to be separated from the foreign ministry holdings. The material is inventoried in a number of mimeographed guides, which have been microfilmed. These guides contain data sheets giving a summary description of each document (content, date, provenance), and its film numbers. The individual guides have no indexes, and since they often contain more than their titles suggest, it is prudent to examine the entire volume thoroughly. Those relevant to Germany's diplomatic history are listed and annotated below, pp. 68-70.

(3) The records of the German navy, commonly called the Tambach archive, filmed by the United States Navy and, to some extent, jointly by the universities of Cambridge and Michigan. This is an enormous collection. It includes records on the armistice and peace treaty, on naval disarmament and rearmament; Hitler directives and conferences on naval matters, the personal papers of Raeder and other admirals, naval attaché files, naval intelligence reports; and the voluminous war diary of the war operations staff (Seekriegsleitung), a very important source on diplomatic, military, and political affairs (and slated for publication in the 1990s). Finding aids are on National Archives microfilm (microcopy T1022, reels 1, 2), and in a two-volume catalogue edited by F.H. Hinsley and H.M. Ehrmann (see below, p. 70).

(4) The Berlin Document Center collection of "non-biographic" materials. This includes records from the party chancellery, the ministries of economics

and of propaganda, the SS and RKFDV, and certain industries (Flick AG., Reichswerke Hermann Göring). There is no published guide, but data sheets exist on microfilm (National Archives microcopy T580, reel 999, and T611, reel 1).

(5) The Nuremberg war crimes trials records, of which more will be said below, pp. 50-54.

There are literally thousands of reels of microfilm, but they contain only a part of the captured material. Some files were filmed totally, others only selectively. Excluded were routine office correspondence, carbon copies, and newspaper clippings. Some important documents may have escaped filming and will have to be examined in the original either at Bonn or at Koblenz. (Since German ministries generally reproduced documents in great number, it is entirely possible that a document missing in one file will turn up in another.)

Every record group or series filmed was assigned a serial number; every page of a document was stamped with a frame number. Individual documents are best identified by their serial and frame numbers, rather than by the number of the individual reel or reel container, for these vary by repository. The contents of the files in each serial are described on data sheets. Most of these were microfilmed and are affixed as a first frame or frames at the beginning of a serial.

The microfilms, which have around 800-900 frames on the average reel, are available for purchase (from the National Archives in Washington or from the Foreign Office Library and the Public Record Office in London). Over the years, research institutes and libraries in North America and Europe have acquired collections of their own, some of which may be borrowed through interlibrary loan. There is no general guide to these scattered collections, however, and researchers will have to make their own inquiries. (But see the guides by Conway, below, p. 70.)

There are still some original German records in repositories outside of Germany. They consist, on the one hand, of relatively small batches of documents incorporated into collections in Britain and the United States (or kept under lock and key by military intelligence), and, on the other hand, of the relatively extensive material left behind in various European countries by retreating German occupation forces. Photocopies or microfilms of some of this material is held by archives and research institutes in the Federal Republic, especially the Bundesarchiv and the Institut für Zeitgeschichte.

1. United States

In the United States, researchers can be virtually certain of gaining access to materials on German diplomatic history. There are no general application procedures, and a letter of introduction from your home institution is a courtesy and only rarely a necessity.

The largest and most complete collection of German records, both original and on film, is at the

National Archives
8th Street and Pennsylvania Ave., N.W.
Washington, DC 20408

(Open Mon.-Fri., 8:45 a.m.-10:00 p.m.,
Sat., 8:45-5:15; closed Sundays
and holidays)

The archive makes its holdings available to all researchers. It has ample room, microfilm readers and copying facilities, and excellent reference services. Its microfilm is for sale, in single reels or entire series, and can be ordered (payable in advance) from the Cashier, National Archives and Records Service, address as above.

The microfilmed records are part of the World War II Collection of Seized Enemy Records (Record Group 242). Almost all of the Whaddon Hall films for the period 1918-45 are on microcopy T120, with some smaller series on T136, T290, T292, and T1141. The Alexandria, Va., films are published under many different microcopy numbers, all of which can be determined through the mimeographed series (below, pp. 68–70). The BDC collection is available on microcopy T580 and T611; the Tambach archive on T1022.

There is some interesting material in (1) the Records of the Department of State Special Interrogation Mission to Germany, 1945-46 (Record Group 59; microcopy T679), and (2) the Records of a War Department Historical Commission (Record Group 165; not microfilmed). The State Department mission was headed by DeWitt C. Poole, the War Department Commission by George Shuster, and both of them interviewed former German officers and officials about military and diplomatic affairs during the war. Many of these interviews (with Neurath, Ribbentrop, Moyland von Steengracht, Lammers, Ritter, Dirksen, Hencke, and others) produced good information. Mimeographed inventories of both collections are available at the archive.

Material on Germany's foreign relations can be found also in the records of the Research and Analysis Branch, Office of Strategic Services, 1941-46 (Record Group 226), the Department of State (Record Groups 59, 76, 84), and the War Department (Record Group 165). A selection of documents from Record Groups 59, 165, and 226 is available on film from University Publications of America, 4520 East-West Highway, Bethesda, Maryland 20814.

Studies dealing with diplomacy, wartime alliances, and intelligence services are among the military studies prepared by former German officers for the Historical Division of the United States Army, 1944-59 (Record Group 338; scheduled for microfilming). Some 200 of these have been published as World War II German Military Studies, edited by Donald S. Detwiler (24 vols., New York, 1979). An inventory of the entire set--about 4,500 manuscripts, in English and in German--is at the archive. (These studies are also available at various army libraries--at the Pentagon, the National War College, the Army War College, and others.)

Military intelligence reports on Germany, 1919-44, are extensive (Record Group 165); a selection is available on film from University Publications of America. There are also several series of military intelligence interrogations, conducted in the immediate aftermath of the war. Many of these are still subject to security classifications and are therefore not accessible.

Audiovisual materials in the archives include captured German films and newsreels; films, still pictures, and recordings from the war crimes trials; German tapes and phonograph records (including propaganda speeches, newscasts, wartime broadcasts)--Record Groups 107, 111, 200, 226, 238, 242.

ARCHIVES AND LIBRARIES

The National Archives has eleven regional branches, all conveniently close to the major population centers. These branches hold many of the archive's microcopy publications--various Alexandria, Va., films, the Poole mission records, Nuremberg war crimes trials records. The holdings vary from branch to branch, though they generally do not include any Whaddon Hall films. The microfilms can be examined at the branches themselves, in reading rooms equipped with microfilm readers and reader-copiers, or they may be borrowed through interlibrary loan. Information on these branches can be obtained from the National Archives; individual branches make their inventories available on request.

German records are also held by the Library of Congress in its

Manuscript Division
James Madison Memorial Building
1st Street and Independence Ave., S.E.
Washington, DC 20540

(Open Mon.-Sat., 8:30-5:00;
closed Sundays and holidays)

The Library has an extensive collection of original documents on Nazism, including the papers of Fritz Wiedemann, Hitler's adjutant, as well as many German publications seized after the war and accessioned to the library's holdings. It has copies of microfilmed records available elsewhere, such as the Himmler files (1938-43), DAI, the Rhoden collection of air force records, and miscellaneous Alexandria, Va., films. It also has tape recordings of speeches, broadcasts, and news conferences. And it holds the papers of William E. Dodd, the American ambassador to Germany between 1933 and 1937.

German naval records are available at the Operational Archives of the

Naval Historical Center
Washington Navy Yard
9th and M Streets, S.E.
Washington, DC 20374

and at the Department of Rare Books and Special Collections of the Library of the

University of Michigan
Ann Arbor, MI 48109

The Operational Archives hold microfilmed copies and photostatic enlargements of translated records from the Tambach archives (Hitler directives and conferences, various war diaries), some historical studies by German naval officers, and miscellaneous other documents, also in translation. Its guide, Information for Visitors to the Operational Archives, is available upon request. The Michigan Library has microfilmed records of the top echelons of the navy between 1870 and 1945, inventoried in the Hinsley-Ehrmann catalogue (below, p. 70). The library also has various Whaddon Hall and Alexandria, Va., films, and a very good collection of printed sources on Nazi Germany.

45

GERMAN FOREIGN POLICY, 1918-1945

Some minor holdings of interest are at the

and at the

> Albert F. Simpson
> Historical Research Center
> Building 1405
> Maxwell Air Force Base, AL 36112

> Office of the Chief of Military History
> and the Center of Military History
> Pulaski Building
> 20 Massachusetts Avenue, N.W.
> Washington, DC 20314

The Simpson Research Center holds copies of German air force records (the Rhoden collection, including war diaries, directives, ministerial correspondence) and the so-called Karlsruhe Collection of historical monographs written by former German air force officers. Both the air force records and copies of the Karlsruhe materials are at the Militärarchiv in Freiburg. The Office of the Chief of Military History has some unpublished studies written by army historians, the so-called German R[esearch] Series, which treat technical as well as diplomatic and historical problems during World War II. (Foreign researchers must apply for admission through the military attaché at their embassy in Washington.)

The Presidential Libraries that have been established for a number of American presidents include among their holdings archival documents, microfilms, and oral histories related to Germany and diplomatic relations with Germany. Of particular interest are the Herbert Hoover Library (West Branch, Iowa), the Franklin D. Roosevelt Library (Hyde Park, New York), and the Harry S. Truman Library (Independence, Missouri).

2. Britain and France

In Britain, archival holdings pertaining to Germany's diplomatic history consist chiefly of filmed copies of the foreign ministry and the naval records. They are housed at the Foreign Office Library, the Public Record Office, and at some smaller repositories, and are open to bona fide researchers.

The Whaddon Hall films of 1920-45, in photostatic enlargements, may be examined at the

> Library and Records Department
> The Foreign and Commonwealth Office
> Cornwall House
> Stamford Street
> London, SE1 9NS

> (Open Mon.-Fri., 9:30-4:45;
> closed weekends and holidays)

This is not a regular archive but, in effect, the editorial offices of the British editors of <u>Akten zur deutschen auswärtigen Politik, 1918-1945</u>, whose work is now virtually complete. Space is limited and advance notice is recommended. There are no formal reference services and no facilities for photocopying (though arrangements can be made to purchase microfilm). You can prepare yourself in advance by consulting the Kent catalogue (below, p. 66), and, once you're there, the original data sheets drawn up at Whaddon Hall, which have detailed descriptions of individual files. (This collection is slated to be transferred from Cornwall House to the Public Record Office by 1992.)

The rest of the foreign ministry records, dating mainly from before 1920, and a good many of the naval records are available at the

> Public Record Office
> Ruskin Avenue
> Kew, Richmond
> Surrey, TW9 4DU
>
> (Open Mon.-Fri., 9:30-5:00; closed
> weekends and holidays, and the last
> week of September and first week of
> October)

Admission to the PRO is by reader's ticket, which may be had upon presenting personal identification and a letter from your thesis adviser or home institution. Space is not reserved, and the reading rooms fill up fairly quickly. Here, as elsewhere, the summer months are the most crowded. Reference services, photocopying, and microfilming are available. The pertinent guides are the American Historical Association catalogue and the Hinsley-Ehrmann volumes (below, pp. 65, 70). The PRO also holds the personal papers of Eric Phipps and Nevile Henderson, British ambassadors to Germany in the 1930s, and some of those of Lord D'Abernon, ambassador between 1920 and 1926, the rest of which are at the British Library.

A full set of the German naval records are located at the Naval Historical Branch of the

> Ministry of Defense
> Empress State Building
> Lillie Road
> London, SW6 1TR

and at the University Library at

> Cambridge University
> West Road
> Cambridge, CB3 9DR

The former holds the entire Tambach archive and both repositories have copies of the Cambridge/Michigan films, covering the period between 1870 and 1945, inventoried in the Hinsley-Ehrmann volumes.

There are also some German records among the holdings of the

> Department of Documents
> Imperial War Museum

Lambeth Road
London, SE1 6HZ

(Open Mon. Fri., 10:00-5:00; closed
weekends, holidays, and the last two
weeks in October)

The Department of Documents requires at least 24 hours' notice of an intended visit. It offers good reference services and has the usual photocopying and microfilming facilities. Some of its collection are subject to special restrictions. In keeping with the museum's focus, the German records (mostly on film, with a few original documents) concern warfare and military affairs. Among them are files of the air ministry (heavily technical but with interesting material on high-level conferences), of the Reichswehr ministry and the armed forces high command (campaign files, operational plans, intelligence reports, war diaries), and of the German occupation authorities in France, Norway, and Denmark. Material relating to the German war economy is in the records of the ministries of armaments and war production (Speer) and of economics (1934-45), and of a number of industrial firms, including IG Farben, Messerschmitt, Junkers, Rheinmetall-Borsig, and Krupp. There is also an extensive collection of war crimes trials records and the David Irving Collection of material on Nazi Germany.

Smaller holdings are at the University of London Library, Senate House, London WC1E 7HU (a selection of Alexandria, Va., films) and at St. Antony's College, Oxford OX2 6JF (Whaddon Hall films of 1914-20 and various foreign ministry documents in the Wheeler-Bennett Collection).

In France, archival holdings of German origin relate mainly to the German occupation and to Germany's relations with the Vichy regime. The largest holdings are at the

Archives Nationales
60, rue des Francs-Bourgeois
75141 Paris

(Open Mon.-Sat., 9:30-6:00; closed
Sundays, holidays, and the first
two weeks in July)

They include the records of the military authorities in France and Belgium (1940-45), the German embassy in Brussels (1929-40), the German delegation at the Franco-German armistice commission, and some of the German agencies and organizations in France during the war. The records of the postwar trials of various Vichy leaders are in a separate collection. Access is granted upon presentation of proper credentials--passport and letter of introduction.

Some smaller holdings, pertaining almost exclusively to Germany's policy toward the Jews, both in France and in other European countries, are at the

Centre de Documentation
Juive Contemporaine
17, rue Geoffroy-l'Asnier
75004 Paris

The Centre holds material from the foreign ministry, some diplomatic missions (Paris, Budapest), the army command, the SS and the Gestapo, and various other offices. It has catalogued the material in a number of detailed indexes, which have been published (see below, p. 71). The diplomatic archives at the Ministère des Affaires Étrangères (37, Quai d'Orsay, 75007 Paris) hold the personal papers of several French ambassadors to Germany (Laurent, de Margerie, Coulondre). The trial records of Otto Abetz, Ribbentrop's envoy in wartime France, are at the Archives de la Cour de Justice in Paris.

3. Other European Countries

The national archives of countries that were occupied by German forces between 1939 and 1945 hold materials related to the occupation. These include the records of the military and civil administrations (which often had liaison officers from the foreign ministry attached to them) and of SS and Nazi party functionaries and commands. They also include the records of various postwar trials, which introduced German documents in evidence against German officials and native collaborators. At some archives there are special collections of German documents pertaining to that particular country and drawn from the Whaddon Hall, Alexandria, Va., and war crimes trials material. (Many of the original German documents in these archives have been filmed and incorporated in the holdings of various archives in Germany.)

Access and research facilities vary. In northern Europe, conditions resemble those in Britain and France; in eastern Europe, they tend to be more restrictive. The major archives are the following:

Northern and Western Europe:

> Rigsarkivet
> Rigsdagsgården 9
> 1218 Copenhagen
> Denmark

> Schweizerisches Bundesarchiv
> Archivstrasse 24
> 3003 Bern
> Switzerland

> Riksarkivet
> Folke Bernadottes vei 21
> Oslo 8
> Norway

Southeastern and Eastern Europe:

> Österreichisches Staatsarchiv
> Archiv der Republik
> Nottendorfergasse 2
> 1030 Wien
> Austria

Statni Ustredni Archiv
M. Strana
Thunovska ul. 22
11000 Prague 1
Czechoslovakia

Archiwum Akt Nowych w Warsawie
Aleja Niepodlegloski 162
Warsaw
Poland

Wojewódzkie Archiwum Panstwowe
w Gdansku
Waly Piastowskie 5
Gdansk
Poland

Archiwum Panstwowe Miasta Poznania
i Województwa Poznanskiego
ul. 23 Lutego 41-43
Poznan
Poland

C. NUREMBERG WAR CRIMES TRIAL RECORDS

The International Military Tribunal (IMT) was held at Nuremberg from November 1945 to October 1946. It prosecuted various Nazi leaders and organizations for planning, preparing, initiating, and waging aggressive war, and for committing war crimes and crimes against humanity. The American Military Tribunal (AMT), also held at Nuremberg, between October 1946 and April 1949, prosecuted some 200 defendants for participating in various specific ways in the crimes broadly defined by the IMT. Of particular interest to the diplomatic historian are the AMT trials of the industrialists (Flick, Krupp, Krauch), some of the top generals (Leeb, List), the SS officers (Greifelt, Ohlendorf, Pohl), and the various high ministerial officials (Weizsäcker and others).

The trial materials are essentially of two kinds. First, there is the documentary and photographic evidence introduced at the trials. This evidence was culled from the captured records of government ministries, military authorities, party organizations, industrial and commercial firms. Of some 100,000 documents sent to Nuremberg, about 40,000 were selected, in whole or in part, for use at the trials. These documents were numbered consecutively, and each number was preceded by a symbol, indicating either the place where the document was first processed (PS, R, L, etc.) or, more logically, the trial with which it was connected (NG, NI, NOKW, etc.). Each document was checked for origin and authenticity, and the results were recorded on a staff evidence analysis attached to the document.

Second, there are the materials generated at the trials themselves. These consist, most extensively, of the official transcripts of the court proceedings, including statements by the lawyers for both sides, evidence given by

50

defendants and witnesses, cross-examinations, and the like, but also of some 15,000 pretrial interrogation transcripts and summaries (whose research value has not really been exploited), of court papers and court opinions, and of prosecution briefs and defense exhibits (chiefly affidavits). Where necessary, both documents and proceedings were translated, often somewhat hastily, from German into English, French, and Russian, and much of the material was mimeographed in order to supply copies to everyone concerned. In the process, a good number of the original documents disappeared.

After the trials were over, the full record was deposited in the archives of the International Court of Justice at The Hague, where it is available for research. Copies were retained by the four prosecuting powers, and deposited in their respective national archives. The American copy is at the National Archives in Washington, the British at the Imperial War Museum, the French at the Archives Nationales. At the National Archives, the trials materials constitute Record Group 238 (World War II War Crimes Records). The IMT material consists of the transcripts and of original copies of many of the documents offered in evidence, of duplicate copies of material introduced by other prosecution teams, and of pretrial interrogation reports and court documents. Some documents not found elsewhere are among the records of the Office of the Chief of Counsel for War Crimes, which are part of this collection. The AMT material consists of the original records of the twelve trials as well as of documentary evidence assembled but then not used. Related to these records are documents that found their way into the files of the Judge Advocate Division, Headquarters, United States Army, Europe, and are part of Record Group 338 (Records of the United States Army, Europe, 1942-60).

Mimeographed sets of copies, or partial copies, consisting of both evidentiary documentation and proceedings, were deposited in various research libraries. In the United States, they went to the Library of Congress, the New York Public Library, the Hoover Institution at Stanford, to the law libraries at Chicago, Columbia, Harvard, and Yale, and to other major libraries. In Britain, a copy is at the Institute for Contemporary History/Wiener Library, which has published a guide to its holdings (Guide to the Collection of Nuremberg Documents, London, 1969).

In Germany, an almost complete set of documents, including interrogation files, questionnaires, and some prosecution documents not found elsewhere is at the Staatsarchiv Nürnberg (Archivstrasse 17, 8500 Nürnberg). The materials are open to researchers, subject to the regulations that ordinarily obtain at German archives. Other sizable collections are at the Institut für Zeitgeschichte in Munich and at the library of the University of Göttingen. There are some smaller and more specialized collections in the files of the various German defense lawyers. They contain evidentiary material related to the defense of particular individuals or organizations. Since these are in effect private collections, only the lawyers, or their offices or heirs, can grant access to them.

The use of the Nuremberg materials, which are organized to serve the purposes of a criminal trial and not those of historical research, is considerably facilitated by several indexes. The Institut für Zeitgeschichte, in collaboration with several other institutions, has produced a classified index, by name and subject, to the documentary series of both the IMT and the AMT. Hans-Günter Seraphim has compiled a set of indexes to the AMT trials, and these are available in mimeographed form at various libraries (see below, p. 72).

The National Archives has microfilmed many of the Nuremberg records in its custody. These microfilms can be examined at the National Archives and at some of its regional branches, at research libraries that have purchased them to replace their crumbling mimeographed copies, and, through interlibrary loan, from the Center for Research Libraries in Chicago (see below, p. 62).

Among these microfilms, students of German diplomatic history will find the following of interest:

    (1)   Of the IMT material:

            Hans Frank diary (microcopy T992)
            Prosecution documents (T988)
            Jodl diary and correspondence (T989)

    (2)   Of the AMT material:

            Document Series
              Industrialists (NI) T301
              Armed Forces (NOKW) T1119
              Government (NG) T1139
              Ministries (NM) M936
              Propaganda (NP) M942
              Interrogation Transcripts M1019
              Interrogation Records M1270

    (3)   Complete AMT trials records:

Pohl	(Case 4)	M890
Flick	(Case 5)	M891
Krauch	(Case 6)	M892
List	(Case 7)	M893
Greifelt	(Case 8)	M894
Ohlendorf	(Case 9)	M895
Krupp	(Case 10)	M896
Weizsäcker	(Case 11)	M897
Leeb	(Case 12)	M898

    (4)   German Documents among the War Crimes Records of the Judge Advocate Division, Headquarters, United States Army, Europe, T1021

Each of these films is described in some detail in brochures put out by the National Archives, and they all come with finding aids that summarize the proceedings and list the various documents, witnesses, and so forth.

Much of the Nuremberg material has also been published. There are several multi-volume series, on both the IMT and the AMT trials, and they are found in most major libraries in North America and Europe.

(1) On the IMT, the official and most comprehensive version is the "Blue Series," published by the Secretariat of the International Military Tribunal:

<u>The Trial of the Major War Criminals before the International Military Tribunal, Nuremberg, 14 November 1945-1 October 1946.</u> 42

vols. Nuremberg, 1947-49. (Available on microfilm and microfiche)

This series appeared in American, English, French, German, and Russian editions. It emphasizes the first part of the indictment (planning and waging war) and gives roughly equal space to the various defendants. The volumes, edited with some care, contain the day-to-day proceedings and slightly more than half of the documents offered in evidence by the prosecution and the defense. Volumes 2-22 are the complete trial transcripts; volumes 25-42 are documents or excerpts from documents keyed to the transcripts. The documents are mostly in German, though each document is introduced by a brief description in the language of that particular edition. Volumes 23 and 24 are indexes--volume 23 to the testimony, volume 24 to the documents; neither is particularly satisfactory. (The reprint edition has an excellent introduction by Gerhard L. Weinberg, both on the trials and on the inadequacies of the published record.) Testimony related to German foreign policy is in volumes 9 (Göring), 10 (Ribbentrop, Steengracht, Schmidt), 15, 16 (Seyss-Inquart), 14 (Weizsäcker), and 16, 17 (Neurath). The famous Hossbach memorandum is in vol. 25, pp. 402-13.

(2) The Office of the United States Chief of Counsel published a translation of the transcripts of interrogations, of numerous documents, and of miscellaneous other items in the "Red Series":

Nazi Conspiracy and Aggression. 10 vols. Washington, 1946-48. (Available on microfiche)

To some extent these volumes duplicate the Blue Series, but they also complement it since they include material not put before the court. They contain the documentary evidence prepared by American and British prosecutors, who were responsible for the case against those charged with preparing and waging aggressive war. There are some 2,000 documents--memoranda, reports, letters, diaries, directives, and the like, from military, naval, and diplomatic sources. The documents, not always reliably translated, are classified under appropriate headings (e.g., "aggression against Austria"; "relating to Ribbentrop") and are indexed in volume 8, pp. 783-1090, and in Supplement A, pp. 1329-91. Supplement A contains documents introduced during cross-examination; Supplement B, pretrial interrogations (including those of Neurath and Ribbentrop). There are useful organizational charts in volume 8 and biographical sketches of the defendants and witnesses in volume 2, pp. 1055-77, and in Supplement B, pp. 1679-1713.

(3) The records of the twelve AMT trials are in the "Green Series," edited by the Office of the Judge Advocate General of the Department of the Army:

Trials of War Criminals before the Nuernberg Military Tribunals under Control Council Law No. 10, October 1946-April 1949. 15 vols. Washington, 1949-53. (Available on microfiche)

These volumes contain selected portions of the record in translation, including the most important parts of the testimony and a number of prosecution and defense exhibits (many of which were also used at the IMT trial). Indexes to both testimony and documents appear in most volumes; the translation is carefully done.

Volumes 4 and 5 contain the case against the SS (Greifelt, Ohlendorf, Pohl); volumes 6, 7, 8, and 9 that against the industrialists (Flick, Krauch, Krupp); volumes 10 and 11 that against the military (Leeb, List); and volumes 12, 13, and 14 that against the diplomats and cabinet ministers (Weizsäcker, Lammers, Schwerin-Krosigk, Meissner, and others). Volume 14 also has an abbreviated record of the Röchling trial, held at Rastatt in 1948 by French authorities. This case concerned the exploitation of French economic resources by the Röchling enterprises acting in collaboration with the Nazi regime (pp. 1016-1143). Volume 15 has information on the trial procedures and an explanation of record keeping and archives at the court.

In using these materials, whether published or unpublished, you should remember that they were selected and produced to serve the prosecution or the defense in a series of criminal trials. They were not assembled to satisfy historical truth. They must therefore be treated with due caution.

D. RESEARCH INSTITUTES

Research institutes have a number of virtues. They permit scholars to work close to the sources, for they hold a rich variety of materials in their libraries and archives. They attract and bring together scholars with similar research interests and provide a setting for intellectual exchange. Their directors and staff members, often historians themselves, can offer guidance on related materials and on pertinent holdings elsewhere. Their libraries have copies of useful inventories and catalogues. And many of the institutes publish collections of sources and sponsor scholarly monographs.

Institutes generally have limited space, and a letter in advance, announcing your coming, is advisable. They keep regular weekday schedules, and they are generally equipped with the necessary microfilm readers and copying facilities. Most will respond readily to specific inquiries by letter.

In the Federal Republic, the most prominent institute of this kind is the

> Institut für Zeitgeschichte
> Leonrodstrasse 46b
> 8000 München 20
>
> (Open Mon.-Thur., 8:30-4:30;
> Fri., 8:30-4:00; closed weekends
> and holidays)

Originally founded for the study of Nazism, it has branched out and is now one of the leading research centers on recent German history. Its library has an excellent collection for the period since World War I, especially on Germany. It is known for its strong holdings in reference works, handbooks, and similar research tools, in government and party publications, in newspapers and newspaper clippings. Its archive holds original and photocopied materials from various government agencies and party organizations, collections of private papers (Liebmann Aufzeichnungen; Kordt Nachlass; Schäffer diary; statements, interviews, and reminiscences by Gaus, Heeren, Hentig, Hewel, Kessel, Nesse, Sthamer, Steengracht, Thomsen, Weizsäcker, and others), and the documents and records assembled by David Irving in his researches (Sammlung

Irving). One of its most valuable resources, much cited in the literature, are transcriptions of oral interviews (Zeugenschrifttum) with politicians, diplomats, military officers, civil servants, and party functionaries. Its microfilm holdings are relatively specialized concentrating on the activities of the Nazi regime, especially in the occupied and annexed areas, and consist of some of the Whaddon Hall and Alexandria, Va., films as well as material from archives in the German Democratic Republic, in Eastern Europe, and elsewhere. Its collection of records of various war crimes trials is among the most extensive anywhere and is proficiently indexed. The institute also has a file on individuals and families that retain papers of historical interest from the interwar period. It publishes a quarterly, Vierteljahrshefte für Zeitgeschichte, as well as several series of source materials and monographs.

An institute devoted to military studies, in close proximity to the Militärarchiv, is the

> Militärgeschichtliches Forschungsamt
> der Bundeswehr
> Grünwälderstrasse 10-14
> 7800 Freiburg i.B.
>
> (Open Mon.-Fri., 8:00-5:00; closed
> weekends and holidays)

Staffed by military officers and civilian historians, the Forschungsamt pursues and publishes research on German military history. It has a superb library, with extensive holdings in military publications and reference works. It edits the Militärgeschichtliche Mitteilungen, an excellent source of archival and bibliographical information, and it sponsors a series of books on military affairs.

Well known for its work on Germany's political parties in the nineteenth and twentieth centuries is the

> Kommission für Geschichte des Parlamen-
> tarismus und der Politischen Parteien
> Poppelsdorfer Allee 55
> 5300 Bonn 1

It promotes and sponsors research, and it provides very useful bibliographical services. Its file on archival sources in public and private collections is kept current, and it has very good contacts with archives and archivists. Its bibliographical reference system includes a bio-bibliography on parliamentarians and politicians in Germany since the mid-nineteenth century. The Kommission itself publishes source collections edited by its members, and it brings out the well-known Beiträge zur Geschichte des Parlamentarismus und der Politischen Parteien.

Research on Germany's economy, her industry, commerce, and trade, and her financial and trade policies, is being done at two institutes located quite close to each other:

> HWWA-Institut für Wirtschaftsforschung
> Neuer Jungfernstieg 21
> 2000 Hamburg 36

Institut für Weltwirtschaft
an der Universität Kiel
Düsternbrooker Weg 120-22
2300 Kiel 1

Both institutes were founded before the first World War, and between them they have accumulated the most extensive library on economic affairs in Europe. They have government and trade publications, statistical compilations, annual reports and such, not readily found elsewhere, as well as large collections of newspaper clippings. Archival materials on the role of big business and industry in interwar politics and foreign policy can be found at the

Institut für deutsche Wirtschaft
Oberländer Ufer 84-88
5000 Köln 51

Among these materials are various Nachlässe (J. Herle, C.H. Steinmüller) and the Sammlung Funcke (Reichsverband der deutschen Industrie).

Materials on German foreign policy are also found at institutes known primarily for their interest in other fields. Among such institutes are the

Forschungsstelle für die Geschichte des
Nationalsozialismus in Hamburg
Rothenbaumchaussee 5
2000 Hamburg 13

(its holdings relate mostly to regional party history, but among them are sources on political parties and conservative groups of the Weimar period as well as the Krogmann diary, an excellent source on Nazi policy);

Volkstum Archiv, Ostakademie e.V.
Herderstrasse 1-11
3140 Lüneburg

(it holds materials for the study of Germany's relations with Eastern Europe and of the former German territories in Eastern Europe, including records of the Deutscher Schutzbund, the Deutsch-Baltische Volksgemeinschaft, and of the German occupation during World War II);

Forschungsinstitut der Friedrich-Ebert-
Stiftung, Archiv der sozialen Demokratie
Godesberger Allee 149
5300 Bonn 2

(this is the archive of the Social Democratic Party, and it includes correspondence and party pronouncements on foreign policy as well as the Nachlässe of Hermann Müller and Carl Severing);

Institut für Internationale Angelegenheiten der Universität Hamburg

Rothenbaumchaussee 19
2000 Hamburg 13

(formerly the Institut für Auswärtige Politik, founded in 1923, this has a good library on foreign affairs and contemporary history and a newspaper clipping file dating back to 1921).

In the United States, the foremost research center on Germany is the

Hoover Institution on War, Revolution,
and Peace
Stanford University
Stanford, CA 94305

(Open Mon.-Fri., 8:15-4:45;
closed weekends and holidays)

The superb holdings of the Hoover Institution, which is located on the campus of Stanford University, have given it an international reputation. It has a massive library on the political, social, and economic history of the twentieth century, which it has made accessible through various published catalogues (and through the Research Libraries Information Network [RLIN]). The collection focuses on diplomatic and military affairs, politics and government, ideologies, and related fields, and it contains some special collections of interest--on the Paris peace conference, the reparations commission and negotiations, the Rhineland and Ruhr occupations, and the plebiscites in Silesia and the Saar. Its Collection on Germany, by far the largest of its extensive Western European Collection, has prominent holdings of government documents (parliamentary proceedings, legal publications, occupation decrees) and of handbooks and reference works on Germany. It also has newspapers and newspaper clippings.

Its archive is probably more important for the extent of its contents than for their uniqueness, for most of them are now available elsewhere. It contains some original records (on Himmler, Goebbels and the propaganda ministry, the German occupation of Belgium and Holland), but most of the material is on film (Whaddon Hall, Alexandria, Va., BDC). One of its most famous collections, the NSDAP Hauptarchiv, was returned to the Federal Republic, where it was broken up into its constituent parts. The Hoover Institution, however, retains a copy on microfilm, and this is of interest to researchers. The Hoover Institution is justifiably proud of its reference services and its facilities. Among its publications are special bibliographies, source collections, and a monograph series.

The German Historical Institute in Washington, DC, founded in 1987 and one of eight such institutes outside of Germany, aims to assist researchers on German history by providing guidance and advice.

German Historical Institute
1607 New Hampshire Avenue, N.W.
Washington, DC 20009

The Institute library, consisting predominantly of new books and journals, has a very useful collection of published as well as unpublished inventories and finding aids to German archives. Its staff is both knowledgeable and helpful, ready to provide up-to-date information on the use of archives, regulations and fees, publication series, and the like. Of interest to researchers working on Nazi policy toward the Jews is the

YIVO Institute for Jewish Research
1048 Fifth Avenue
New York, NY 10028

(Open Mon.-Fri., 9:30-5:30; closed
weekends, secular and Jewish holidays)

It is one of the largest repositories of its kind. Though its principal holding is a collection of Jewish sources depicting Jewish life under the Nazis, it also has significant holdings of Nazi records, originals as well as filmed copies. These include material from the Nazi party and the SS, the ministries of propaganda and of occupied eastern territories, the Whaddon Hall and BDC films, and assorted German records kept in archives in Israel and Poland. Unpublished inventories are available at the Institute.

In Britain the best known of the research centers is the

Institute for Contemporary History/
Wiener Library
4 Devonshire Street
London, W1N 2BH

(Open Mon.-Fri., 10:00-5:30;
closed weekends and holidays)

Founded in the 1930s as The Wiener Library, which specialized in material on Nazi Germany, the Institute is now a prominent library-and-archive with holdings on contemporary European history. It retains its interest in Germany, especially Nazism and anti-semitism. Its strength is its library, which has many rare items as well as a large, classified press cuttings collection. Its archive has unpublished memoirs and histories, private papers, government and party records, and an important cache of the Nuremberg materials. The Institute publishes two journals: the Wiener Library Bulletin, a quarterly of brief articles and research notes, has been appearing since 1946, the Journal of Contemporary History, also a quarterly, since 1965.

There are two institutes that focus on the history of World War II, one in France, the other in the Netherlands. Both collect material on the war, especially as it affected their respective countries, with the intent of depositing it all one day in the national archives.

Le Comité français d'histoire de
la deuxième guerre mondiale
32, rue de Leningrad
75008 Paris

Rijksinstituut voor Oorlogsdocumentatie
Herengracht 474
Amsterdam

Both institutes encourage and coordinate the study of the war and occupation, and they are therefore an excellent source of information on archival collections and scholarly research. Their libraries hold material on the German occupation, 1940-45: books, journals, printed ephemera, newspaper clippings, and archival records (e.g., files of the occupation forces, copies of the Whaddon Hall and BDC films, some personal papers). The Comité français brings out the _Revue d'histoire de la deuxième guerre mondiale_ (1950-), which carries regular bibliographical surveys, and has published such things as the records of the French delegation to the Franco-German armistice commission during the war.

E. RESEARCH LIBRARIES

No single library will have all the published materials you will need for your work. The national libraries have the largest holdings but not necessarily the best selection. As depository libraries, they receive all the books published in their respective countries, but they cannot be nearly as complete in their acquisitions from other countries. They regularly publish catalogues of their acquisitions and holdings, and it is easy to establish what they have. Smaller, more specialized collections, which are found either in special libraries that focus on specific subject areas or as separate units within a large library's general collection, can often be more useful. The location of most printed materials can be determined through national union catalogues, union lists of serials, and the published library catalogues that, over the last decade or so, have appeared for most major libraries in North America and Europe.

In the Federal Republic, the national library is the Deutsche Bibliothek (Zeppelinallee 4-8, 6000 Frankfurt/M.). It holds books published in German since 1945, irrespective of place of publication. In the Democratic Republic, the equivalent is the Deutsche Bücherei (Deutscher Platz, 7010 Leipzig), which has vast holdings accumulated since 1913, when it was founded. The collection emerged from the war relatively unscathed. Both these libraries publish bibliographical reference guides to works published in German--the _Deutsche Bibliographie_ and the _Deutsche Nationalbibliographie_, respectively.

Two other German libraries have come to share the function and reputation of a national library:

Bayerische Staatsbibliothek
Ludwigstrasse 16
8000 München 22

Staatsbibliothek
Preussischer Kulturbesitz
Potsdamer Strasse 33
1000 Berlin 30

The Munich library has an unrivaled collection of books and serials (with especially extensive holdings in political and diplomatic history) and some 80,000 volumes of newspapers. The Berlin library, which shares what remains of the old Preussische Staatsbibliothek with the Deutsche Staatsbibliothek in East Berlin, is notable for having the largest collection of government publications of the period before 1945 (including the proceedings of the Reichstag budget committee). It also has published and unpublished dissertations from all German universities.

There are important libraries in the individual German states (Staats- or Landesbibliotheken) and at various universities. Some of the university libraries specialize in certain fields--Cologne in social science, Hamburg in politics--and they often have satellite libraries at departments and institutes on campus (e.g., the Institut für Europäische Geschichte at the University of Mainz). If you are affiliated with a university or institute, you have ready access to these libraries. Without such affiliation, you may be asked for a letter of introduction from someone known to the library, who in effect acts as your sponsor. Stack privileges are rare in German libraries, and you must get to know the standard finding aids to make your way. (See Welsch, below, p. 65.)

The most prominent among the special libraries is the

> Bibliothek für Zeitgeschichte
> (Weltkriegsbücherei)
> Konrad-Adenauer-Strasse 8
> 7000 Stuttgart 1

> (Open Mon.-Fri., 9:00-5:00,
> Sat., 9:00-1:00; closed Sundays
> and holidays)

Founded as a collection center for material on the first World War, this library gradually expanded to cover contemporary history since 1914. Though it suffered some losses during the war, its holdings are exceptionally strong, especially in international relations, military affairs, and the two world wars. It has several rare collections--maps of every kind and description, pamphlet files, photographs, and ephemera (such as propaganda material). It is not parochial; only about half of its collection is in German.

Since 1960 the library has put out an annual Jahresbibliographie, which continues the earlier Bücherschau der Weltkriegsbücherei (1921-59). Each volume offers exhaustive bibliographical surveys on diverse topics as well as a classified list of the library's annual acquisitions (which now run to around 10,000 items). The library also sponsors a series of bibliographical monographs. Called Vierteljahreshefte der Weltkriegsbücherei (then Bibliographien der Weltkriegsbücherei) from 1934 to 1944, it is now Schriften der Bibliothek für Zeitgeschichte.

Important for its holdings on parliamentary affairs and much acclaimed for its excellent research department, Abteilung Wissenschaftliche Dokumentation, is the

Bibliothek des Deutschen Bundestags
Görresstrasse 15
5300 Bonn 1

The library itself dates from 1949, but its holdings, on contemporary history and politics, go back well before that. Its special collections include government publications, parliamentary proceedings and committee records, party and election publications, and newspapers going back to 1900. The most extensive library for Auslandsdeutschtum and Volkstumspolitik is at the

Institut für Auslandsbeziehungen
Charlottenplatz 17
7000 Stuttgart 1

Originally the library of the Deutsches Auslandsinstitut (whose records are at the Bundesarchiv and, on microfilm, at the National Archives), it has much printed and filmed material on German minorities and enclaves abroad and on Germany's relations with them, and is particularly strong in holdings from the Weimar period.

Two libraries dealing more specifically with German minorities and German territories in Eastern Europe, and with the relations between Germany and the countries of Eastern Europe, are the

Bücherei des deutschen Ostens
Berliner Platz 11
Kulturzentrum
4690 Herne 1

and the

Haus des deutschen Ostens
Bismarckstrasse 90
4000 Düsseldorf 1

Their holdings consist almost entirely of printed materials. The Herne library has a printed catalogue available in all major German libraries.

Outside Germany, the national libraries assume the functions of major research centers. In the United States this function is exercised both by the Library of Congress in Washington, which publishes its catalogues at regular intervals, and by the New York Public Library, actually a private library, which issues a whole series of different catalogues. In Britain it is exercised by the British Library in London, formerly the British Museum Library, which has also published its catalogue (General Catalogue of Printed Books), and by the university libraries at Oxford and Cambridge. In France it is exercised by the Bibliothèque Nationale in Paris, which has catalogued its books up through 1959 in a Catalogue général des livres imprimés with regular supplements to cover newer arrivals, and by the Bibliothèque de la Sorbonne (47, rue des Écoles, 75230 Paris), which is almost of equal importance.

Each of these countries also has a library focused specifically on international affairs since 1914. The holdings extend to books and serials, brochures and pamphlets, and press clipping collections.

Council on Foreign Relations
58 East 68th Street
New York, NY 10021

Royal Institute of International Affairs
Chatham House
10, St. James's Square
London, SW1Y 4LE

Bibliothèque de Documentation
internationale contemporaine
2, rue de Rouen
92001 Nanterre

These libraries are accessible to scholars with proper credentials. A letter requesting permission is recommended.

Good holdings in international relations can also be found at the university libraries at Harvard, Columbia, Georgetown, George Washington, and Pittsburgh, and at the Hoover Institution in the United States, at the London School of Economics and Political Science in Britain, and at the United Nations Library at Geneva, Switzerland. The Library at the Department of State (2201 C Street N.W., Washington, DC, 20520) has probably the most comprehensive collection on international politics in the world. Closed to the public, it is accessible to researchers who can make a good case for its use.

Good holdings on Germany are at the Library of Congress and the New York Public Library, both of which accessioned materials seized in Germany at the end of the war, the university libraries at Berkeley, Harvard, Maryland, Michigan, and Wisconsin, and, again, at the Hoover Institution. For holdings on military and naval affairs, the libraries at West Point and at Annapolis are best.

A unique institution, of enormous service to researchers in the United States and Canada, is the

Center for Research Libraries
6050 South Kenwood Avenue
Chicago, IL 60637

It is a library of three million volumes and various special collections, maintained by a number of member institutions, which, by sharing their assets, increase the volume of library materials available at all these institutions. Material held by the Center must be requested through interlibrary loan at one of the member institutions. It arrives within two to four days and may be used on practically the same terms as those that prevail at the requesting library. The Center holds government publications and parliamentary proceedings, newspapers from all countries, German archival records (Whaddon Hall, Alexandria, Va.), a nearly complete set of war crimes trials documents, and probably the largest collection of foreign (not American or Canadian) dissertations in the world. The collections are described in a Handbook, which is kept up to date through loose-leaf additions, and in several specialized catalogues, available in the reference rooms of the member libraries.

F. NEWSPAPER LIBRARIES

Newspapers are held in virtually all libraries and archives, in bound folios, in clipping collections, or on microfilm. Most holdings include the major newspapers of different political opinion: Frankfurter Zeitung and Berliner Tageblatt (moderate), Vossische Zeitung (liberal), Deutsche Allgemeine Zeitung and Kreuzzeitung (conservative), Germania and Kölnische Zeitung (Catholic), the socialist Vorwärts and the Nazi Völkischer Beobachter. They will also have runs of various journals devoted to international affairs.

No German regional or university library is without a collection, though the collections are in various states of completeness. The best holdings are at the Bayerische Staatsbibliothek in Munich, the Institut für Weltwirtschaft an der Universität Kiel, and the Institut für Zeitungsforschung der Stadt Dortmund (Hansaplatz, Haus der Bibliotheken, 4600 Dortmund 1), which has original and microfilmed copies of thousands of newspapers.

The Deutsche Presseforschung, a division of the Universitätsbibliothek in Bremen (Achterstrasse, 2800 Bremen 33), has a Standortkatalog, or location index, of the German press, which is virtually complete. The staff at the Presseforschung is knowledgeable and helpful, and it answers all inquiries about the location of newspapers and journals.

In the United States, newspaper and serial collections are at the Library of Congress, the Hoover Institution at Stanford, and the New York Public Library (which keeps its catalogue at the main library on 5th Avenue and its collection at the newspaper annex at 521 West 43d Street). Of the various newspaper clipping collections, the best is at the Council on Foreign Relations (58 East 68th Street, New York, NY 10021).

In Britain, an excellent collection is at the Newspaper Library of The British Library (Colindale Avenue, London NW9 5HE). The best of the clipping collections is at the Royal Institute for International Affairs (10 St. James's Square, London SW1Y 4LE), which contains material dating back to 1916. The best collections in France are at the Bibliothèque Nationale in Paris and at the Bibliothèque de Documentation internationale contemporaine (2, rue de Rouen, 92001 Nanterre).

These various holdings of original newspapers are gradually being superseded by holdings on microfilm. The Institut für Zeitungsforschung at Dortmund (see above) maintains the Mikrofilmarchiv der deutschsprachigen Presse, an archive that aims eventually to acquire microfilms of all German-language newspapers and serials since 1800 and to make them available for research. It already has an almost complete collection of the important German papers. It also has a location index to microfilm collections in other German libraries.

In the United States, lists of newspapers and serials on microfilm are published regularly by the Library of Congress. One of the largest collections of such microfilms is at the Center for Research Libraries in Chicago and is accessible through interlibrary loan.

Newspapers themselves of course have archives, and many of these are open to visitors. Each archive will hold the full run of its own newspaper, as well as other papers, assorted documents, photographs, and the like, which are used for in-house research. Many of these materials have historical interest. One of the most extensive and best organized of the newspaper archives is that of the Neue Zürcher Zeitung, the NZZ Archiv (Falkenstrasse 11, 8021 Zürich). Other well-known archives are at the Frankfurter Allgemeine Zeitung (Frankfurt/M.), the Süddeutsche Zeitung (Munich), the Spiegel (Hamburg), and at the New York Times, the London Times, and Le Figaro in Paris. Of the three major newspaper publishing houses in interwar Berlin (Mosse, Ullstein, and Scherl), only Ullstein survives, as part of the Springer Verlag (Berlin).

G. GUIDES, CATALOGUES, INVENTORIES

This list of titles, which is keyed to the entries and descriptions in the text of this chapter, includes not only the major reference works and guides but also the more important finding aids and inventories of individual archives and libraries. The annotations will direct researchers to some of the more specialized and often more detailed guides to archival holdings.

1. Archives in Germany

Benz, Wolfgang, ed. Quellen zur Zeitgeschichte. Deutsche Geschichte seit dem ersten Weltkrieg, vol. 3. Stuttgart, 1973.

Both a survey of holdings in German history in archives in Europe, the United States, and Israel, and a classified list of some 3,600 recent and essential works on German history since 1914.

Epstein, Fritz T. "Germany." In The New Guide to the Diplomatic Archives of Western Europe, edited by Daniel H. Thomas and Lynn M. Case. Philadelphia, 1975.

Brief description of the major national and regional archives in Germany with holdings pertinent to diplomatic history. Extensive bibliography of archival guides.

Friedrichs, Heinz F. Familienarchive im öffentlichen und privaten Besitz. Neustadt/Aisch, 1972.

Guide to collections in public and private archives.

Frohn, Axel. Guide to Inventories and Finding Aids of German Archives. Reference Guides of the German Historical Institute, Washington, DC, No. 2. Washington, DC, 1989.

List of the inventories and finding aids of German archives available in the library of the German Historical Institute in Washington, DC.

Haase, Carl, ed. The Records of German History in German and certain other Record Offices, with short notes on Libraries and other Collections. Boppard, 1975.

Lists archives in both German states, in Austria, and in other European countries where relevant material exists; lists German and Austrian libraries, research institutes, newspaper collections.

Mommsen, Wolfgang A., ed. Die Nachlässe in den deutschen Archiven. 2d ed., Boppard, 1983.

Deneke, Ludwig, and Brandis, Tilo, eds. Die Nachlässe in den Bibliotheken der Bundesrepublik Deutschland. 2d rev. ed. Boppard, 1981.

Descriptive guide to papers in various collections with references to material that is missing or has been destroyed. Mommsen's volume covers libraries and archives in the two German states and elsewhere; Denecke's covers only libraries in the Federal Republic.

Ploetz, Gerhard, ed. Bildquellen Handbuch: Der Wegweiser für Bildsuchende. Wiesbaden, 1961.

Lists archives, libraries, museums, newspaper archives, press and wire services where photographs are kept and may be borrowed. Listed alphabetically by country; systematic indexes.

Welsch, Erwin K., ed. Libraries and Archives in Germany. New York, 1984.

On archives and libraries in both Germanies; emphasis on the Federal Republic. Useful description of organization and use of German libraries (see especially, pp. 2-10).

Henke, Josef. "Das Schicksal deutscher zeitgeschichtlicher Quellen in Kriegs- und Nachkriegszeit: Beschlagnahme, Rückführung, Verbleib." Vierteljahrshefte für Zeitgeschichte, 30 (1982), pp. 557-620.

A detailed assessment of the impact of the war and its aftermath on German archival material. See also Gerhard Schmidt, "Die Verluste in den Beständen des ehemaligen Reichsarchivs im zweiten Weltkrieg," in Archivar und Historiker (Berlin, 1956), pp. 176-207; and the article in Der Archivar (1978), 35-46.

2. Federal Republic

A Catalogue of Files and Microfilms of the German Foreign Ministry Archives, 1867-1920, edited by American Historical Association, Committee for the Study of War Documents. Oxford, 1959 (rpt. 1970).

This incorporates and supersedes all earlier guides on the period (see pp. xl-xlii). Of interest are the files of 1918-20.

A Catalog of Files and Microfilms of the German Foreign Ministry Archives, 1920-1945, edited by George O. Kent. 4 vols. Stanford, CA, 1962-73.

A supplement to the AHA Catalogue (above), it lists all files seized by Britain and the United States and indicates which files were filmed.

The first two volumes cover the period 1920-36. Vol. 1 lists Reichs-minister, Staatssekretär, Department II, and secret files; Vol. 2 the various other departments, the chancellery, Handakten and Nachlässe, and some Sonderreferate.

The second two volumes cover 1936-45. Vol. 3 lists the surviving files of Büro RAM, the Staatssekretär and Unterstaatssekretär, the various depart-ments, Dienststelle Ribbentrop, and the Neue Reichskanzlei; Vol. 4 the mission files and consular files.

The Politisches Archiv in Bonn has rearranged some of its holdings, so that these catalogues are no longer quite accurate. Thus, in the first three volumes, the archival registration has been changed for Inland, Chef AO, Dienststelle Ribbentrop. As for the fourth volume, the archive has made a whole series of new inventories in order to remedy what it considered the volume's deficiencies and errors.

The Introduction to the volumes explains office routine, describes the documents, and comments on their importance.

Granier, Gerhard, Henke, Josef, and Oldenhage, Klaus, eds. Das Bundesarchiv und seine Bestände. 3d ed. Boppard, 1977.

A detailed guide to the holdings of the Bundesarchiv in Koblenz and its military archive branch in Freiburg.

Microfilmed holdings available for purchase are listed in separate Findbücher zu Beständen des Bundesarchivs (1970-). The microfilmed holdings include the Chancellery, various ministries, and a number of Nachlässe (e.g., Groener, Schleicher, von Seeckt).

Browder, George C. "Problems and Potentials of the Berlin Document Center." Central European History, 5 (1972), pp. 362-80.

Not an inventory or catalogue but a tidy account of the holdings, practices, and usefulness of the BDC.

Branig, Hans, et al., eds. Übersicht über die Bestände des Geheimen Staatsarchivs in Berlin-Dahlem. Vol. 2. Cologne, 1967.

Quite general, and now somewhat dated. Material not of Prussian origin was transferred to the Bundesarchiv in 1969 (after this catalogue was published).

Eyll, Klara van, et al., eds. Deutsche Wirtschaftsarchive: Nachweis historischer Quellen in Unternehmen, Kammern und Verbänden der Bundesrepublik Deutschland. 2d ed. Stuttgart, 1987.

Information on the content, extent, accessibility of some 400 collections. On the more important economic archives, see the articles in Der Archivar (1960), pp. 291-326, and Archiv und Wirtschaft, 3 (1970), pp. 8-23, and 8 (1975), pp. 19-22.

Trumpp, Thomas, and Köhne, Renate. Archivbestände zur Wirtschafts- und Sozialgeschichte der Weimarer Republik. Boppard, 1979.

A thorough guide, listing the contents, addresses, and terms of access of German archives with holdings in economic and social history (including much material relevant to the study of foreign policy). See also Trumpp's "Quellen zur Wirtschafts- und Sozialgeschichte der Inflationszeit in Archiven der Bundesrepublik Deutschland," in Historische Prozesse der deutschen Inflation 1914 bis 1924, edited by Otto Büsch and Gerald D. Feldman, Berlin, 1978, pp. 21-45.

3. Democratic Republic

Staatliche Archivverwaltung des Ministeriums des Innern der DDR, ed. Taschenbuch: Archivwesen der DDR. Berlin, 1971.

Lists national and regional archives, their addresses and hours, their inventories and publications. Archives policy, pp. 193-94; archives procedures, pp. 206-10.

See also, Staatliche Archivverwaltung des Ministeriums des Innern der DDR, ed., Lexikon Archivwesen der DDR, 2d ed., Berlin, 1979.

Lötzke, Helmut, ed. Übersicht über die Bestände des deutschen Zentralarchivs Potsdam. Berlin, 1957.

Not reissued or revised since publication, but with Lötzke's Deutsches Zentralarchiv, 1946-71 (Berlin, 1971), a pamphlet issued on the 25th anniversary of the archive, the only guide available in print.

See also, Irmtraud Schmid, "Der Bestand des Auswärtigen Amts im Deutschen Zentralarchiv Potsdam," Archivmitteilungen, 12 (1962), pp. 71-79, 123-32, and Willi Boelcke, "Presseabteilung und Pressearchive des Auswärtigen Amtes, 1871-1945," ibid., 9 (1959), pp. 43-49.

Studanski, Rudolf. "Die Bestände des Deutschen Militärarchivs." Zeitschrift für Militärgeschichte, 4 (1965), pp. 594-98.

Most of the holdings described here date from before 1918. Little detail about materials from 1918-45. For the latter period, see Ernst Volker, Anita Kaun, and Hans-Jürgen Zeidler, "Neuerschlossene Bestände im Militärarchiv der DDR (Zeitraum 1920-1945)," Militärgeschichte, 20 (1981), 95-97.

4. United States

National Archives and Records Administration. Guide to the National Archives of the United States. Rev. ed. Washington, 1987.

General guide to the holdings; supersedes earlier guides (1948 and 1974). Lists record groups with brief descriptions, both German and non-German material.

———. Catalog of National Archive Microfilm Publications. Washington, 1974.

Lists all National Archives microfilms now in existence and available for purchase. Kept up to date with new issues.

South, Charles, ed. List of National Archives Microfilm Publications in the Regional Archives Branches. Washington, 1975.

Guide to the 11 branch archives and their holdings of National Archives microfilm (as of 1975). Lists addresses and describes conditions of access and use. See also, Joyce M. Mitchell, National Archives Microfilm: A Union List for Arizona, California, and Nevada (Fullerton, CA, 1975).

University Publications of America. UPA Research Collections. Bethesda, MD. Annual publication.

Current listing of microform collections available from University Publications of America. Includes records of the German Army High Command, 1938-45; MAGIC Documents: Summaries and Transcripts of the Top-Secret Diplomatic Communications of Japan, 1938-45; ULTRA documents (World War II); documents and war diaries of the London office of the OSS (1942-45); and the files of the Allied Powers Reparations Commission.

American Historical Association, Committee for the Study of War Documents, and the National Archives, eds. Guides to the German Records Microfilmed at Alexandria, Va. Washington, 1958-.

Eighty-four volumes of this guide have appeared to date, with more to come. They are microfilmed on National Archives microcopy T733, reels 1ff. (A guide to the entire set and a detailed index to the guides themselves is said to be in the making.)

Of particular importance to the diplomatic historian are the following:

Vol. 1. Records of the Reichs Ministry of Economics (1958). Material on the occupied territories, war industries, foreign trade; Südosteuropagesellschaft. Microcopy T71.

Vol. 2. Office of the Reich Commissioner for the Strengthening of Germandom (1958). T74.

Vols. 3, 77. Records of the National Socialist German Labor Party (1958-80). Files of the APA, AO, Verein für das Deutschtum im Ausland, Stellvertreter des Führers. T81.

Vols. 5, 8, 36. Miscellaneous German Records Collection, I, II, III (1958-62). Goebbels, Blomberg, Halder, Jodl, Groscurth papers; OKW files; military attaché, Belgium, 1935-39; Four-Year Plan; Anschluss. T84.

Vol. 6. Records of Nazi Cultural and Research Institutions and Records Pertaining to Axis Relations and Interests in the Far East (1959). Deutsche Akademie München, Akademie für Deutsches Recht, Institut für deutsche Ostarbeit Krakau; OKW files on China and Japan. T82.

Vols. 7, 17, 18, 19, 78, 80, 84. Records of Headquarters, German Armed Forces High Command, I, II, III, IV, V, VI, VII (1959-85). Führer directives, 1939-45; OKW Abwehr 1933-45; armistice commission in France and relations with Vichy regime; military attachés, 1934-43; Wehrmacht propaganda; correspondence with foreign ministry; Dönitz government, 1945. T77.

Vol. 9. Records of Private German Individuals (1959). Leaders and organizations active in Volkstumspolitik. T253.

Vol. 10. Records of the Reich Ministry on Armaments and War Production (1959). Speer ministry files. T73.

Vol. 15. Records of Former German and Japanese Embassies and Consulates, 1890-1945 (1960). Missions at Tsingtao, Hankow, and Yokohama; material on general policy and economic issues. T179.

Vols. 16, 21. Records of the Deutsches Auslands-Institut, Stuttgart, I, II (1960-61). On German minorities, emigration, relocation and resettlement (Vomi). T81.

Vol. 22. Records of the Reich Ministry for Public Enlightenment and Propaganda (1961). German propaganda at home and abroad, also in occupied countries. T70.

Vol. 23. Records of Private Austrian, Dutch, and German Enterprises, 1917-46 (1961). Including Frick A.G., Reichswerke Hermann Göring, IG Farben, Krupp, Reichsbank, Dresdner Bank. Many of these documents were used at Nuremberg and are also in the IMT and AMT series. T83.

Vol. 28. Records of the Reich Ministry for the Occupied Eastern Territories, 1941-45 (1961). Rosenberg's career, 1921-45; Einsatzstab Reichsleiter Rosenberg, Reichskommissar Ostland; Ministerium für besetzte Ostgebiete. T454.

Vols. 30, 82. Records of Headquarters, German Army High Command, III, IV (1961-82). Disarmament (IMCC); Franco-German relations; military attachés, 1930s and early 1940s; Fremde Heere Ost. T78.

Vol. 31. Records of the Office of the Reich Commissioner for the Baltic States, 1941-45 (1961). Reichskommissar für das Ostland. T459.

Vols. 32, 33, 39, 81. Records of the Reich Leader of the SS and Chief of the German Police, I, II, III, IV (1961-82). Himmler speeches and correspondence; SS policy in occupied Eastern Europe; SD intelligence reports in occupied and annexed areas; contacts with enemy; German Legation Bukarest. T175.

Vol. 37. Records of Headquarters, German Navy High Command (1962). Dönitz government, 1945: negotiations on surrender, capitulation. T608.

Vols. 38, 57. Records of the German Field Commands: Rear Areas, Occupied Territories, and Others, I, II (1963-68). Armistice commission in France; occupation authorities throughout occupied Europe. T501.

Hinsley, F.H., and Ehrmann, H.M., eds. A Catalogue of Selected Files of the German Naval Archives Microfilmed at the Admiralty, London, for the University of Cambridge and the University of Michigan. 2 vols. London, 1959-64.

The naval records (part of the Tambach archives) filmed by Cambridge and Michigan universities.

Weinberg, Gerhard L., ed. Guide to Captured German Documents. Montgomery, AL, 1952.

Annotated listing of materials kept at various American repositories. Though somewhat dated, remains useful. See also, Supplement (1959).

Conway, John S. German Historical Source Material in United States Universities. Pittsburgh, PA, 1973 (mimeographed).

———. "German Historical Material in Canadian Universities." Canadian Journal of History 2 (1967), pp. 113-20.

Holdings of microfilm--Whaddon Hall, Alexandria, Va., Nuremberg war crimes trials, BDC, NSDAP Hauptarchiv.

Department of State, Office of External Research, ed. Foreign Affairs Research: A Directory of Governmental Resources. Washington, 1967.

Research materials at various government repositories; libraries; bibliographies, grants.

Dillon, Kenneth J., ed. Scholars' Guide to Washington, D.C.: Central and East European Studies. Scholars Guide to Washington, D.C., No. 5. Washington, 1980.

A detailed guide to repositories in the Washington area, with information on archival and library holdings, terms of access, addresses, and opening hours, and with tips for visitors and users.

Burton, Dennis A., James B. Rhoads, and Raymond W. Smock, eds. A Guide to Manuscripts in the Presidential Libraries. College Park, MD, 1988.

A description of some 4,600 manuscript collections, alphabetically arranged, with a name and subject index. The guide also includes practical information on each of the libraries (names, addresses, telephone numbers, hours of operation).

5. Britain and France

Imperial War Museum, Foreign Documents Centre, ed. Provisional Reports, No. 1, Great Britain. London, 1966.

Still useful as a guide to German documents in British archives and libraries.

Lenz, Wilhelm, ed. Manuscript Sources for the History of Germany since 1500 in Great Britain. Boppard, 1975.

A survey of source materials in Britain, in more than 250 public and private archives, libraries, and museums. Emphasis on British materials but with references to German materials in British custody.

Hartmann, Peter Claus. Pariser Archive, Bibliotheken und Dokumentationszentren zur Geschichte des 19. und 20. Jahrhunderts. Munich, 1976.

Detailed information on holdings, location, conditions of access, and the like.

See also Stein, Wolfgang Hans, ed., Inventar von Quellen zur deutschen Geschichte in Pariser Archiven und Bibliotheken, Koblenz, 1986.

Billig, Joseph. Alfred Rosenberg dans l'action idéologique, politique et administrative du Reich hitlérien. Paris, 1963.

Steinberg, Lucien. Les autorités allemandes en France occupée. Paris, 1966.

Inventories of the archives of the Centre de Documentation Juive Contemporaine in Paris. Materials from the Rosenberg files, the German embassy in Paris, the military administration of France, and the Gestapo.

6. Other European Countries

Imperial War Museum, Foreign Documents Centre, ed. Provisional Report No. 3, Italy; No. 5, Austria; No. 6, Poland. London, 1967-69.

Compiled with the visiting researcher in mind. Useful addresses, but no longer entirely current.

Lewanski, Richard C. Guide to Polish Libraries and Archives. New York, 1974.

General survey of holdings in Warsaw and in various regional archives and libraries.

Thomas, Daniel H., and Case, Lynn M., eds. The New Guide to the Diplomatic Archives of Western Europe. Philadelphia, 1975.

Includes descriptive essays, with bibliographies, on all the countries of Western Europe as well as international organizations (League, ILO).

7. Nuremberg Trials Records

Brather, Hans-Stephan. "Die Nürnberger Prozessakten als Geschichtsquelle: eine Bibliographie." Jahrbuch für Wirtschaftsgeschichte, 1969, II, pp. 391-416.

Good overall account of the nature and contents of the Nuremberg materials. Bibliography on the trials, their history, and the publications of their records.

Lewis, John R., ed. Uncertain Judgment: A Bibliography of War Crimes Trials. Santa Barbara, CA, 1979.

Over 3,000 titles of books and articles, covering the entire twentieth century but focusing on World War II.

Tutorow, Norman E., ed. War Crimes, War Criminals, and War Crimes Trials. New York, 1986.

Bibliography of some 4,500 titles, many of them annotated, with a useful introduction on the trials themselves, the documentary evidence, the selection and coding of materials, and the like.

Seraphim, Hans-Günther, ed. Indices zu den zwölf Nürnberger US-Militärgerichtsprozessen. Göttingen, 1958- (mimeographed).

1. Sachindex zu den Urteilen.
2. Sachindex zum Verfahren gegen Ernst von Weizsäcker, u.a.
3. Sachindex, Personenindex, und Dokumentenindex zum Verfahren gegen Wilhelm von Leeb, u.a.
4. Personenindex, Sachindex, und Dokumentenindex zum Verfahren gegen Friedrich Flick, u.a.
5. Personenindex, Sach- und Dokumentenindex zum Verfahren gegen Karl Krauch, u.a.
6. Index zum Verfahren gegen Ohlendorf, u.a.

Set of mimeographed volumes, with names, subject, and document indexes, for use with the published and unpublished AMT records.

8. Research Institutes

Hoch, Anton. "Das Archiv des Instituts für Zeitgeschichte." Der Archivar, 26 (1973), pp. 295-308.

A description and assessment of the published and unpublished holdings of the Institut's archive.

Institut für Zeitgeschichte, Bibliothek. Alphabetischer Katalog, Biographischer Katalog, Länderkatalog, Sachkatalog. With supplements, 18 vols. Boston, 1967, 1973.

Catalogues of the Institut's library--some 50,000 volumes covering the period since 1917.

Gersdorff, Ursula von, ed. Geschichte und Militärgeschichte: Wege der Forschung. Frankfurt/M., 1974.

Includes report on the activities and publications of the Militärgeschichtliches Forschungsamt in Freiburg.

Institut für Weltwirtschaft, Kiel. Kataloge der Bibliothek. 207 vols. Boston, 1966-68.

900,000 titles--books, periodicals, newspapers, trade publications, and the like.

Stanford University, The Hoover Institution on War, Revolution, and Peace. The Library Catalogs of the Hoover Institution: Catalog of the Western Language Collections. 63 vols. Boston, 1969.

The first 56 volumes contain alphabetical entries by author, title and subject; the rest cover special collections (e.g., government publications). Books catalogued since 1969 are listed in subsequent Supplements (Boston, 1972, 1977).

Palm, Charles G., and Reed, Dale. Guide to the Hoover Institution Archives. Stanford, 1980.

Description of the archival and manuscript holdings of the Hoover Library, alphabetically arranged.

Peterson, Agnes F., ed. Western Europe: A Survey of Holdings at the Hoover Institution. Stanford, 1970.

Boeninger, Hildegard R., ed. The Hoover Library Collection on Germany. Stanford, 1955.

Heinz, Grete, and Peterson, Agnes F., eds. NSDAP Hauptarchiv: Guide to the Hoover Institution Microfilm Collection. Stanford, 1964.

Three specialized guides to the Hoover collections. Peterson is a good introduction to some of the special collections (armistice, peace conference 1919), Boeninger covers German history and has an appendix on government documents, Heinz and Peterson detail the contents of the microfilmed NSDAP Hauptarchiv, whose original contents have since been broken up into different parts.

The Wiener Library, London. (1) Persecution and Resistance under the Nazis, 2d ed., 1960; (2) From Weimar to Hitler: Germany, 1918-33, 2d ed., 1964.

Early guides to the library holdings of what is now the Institute for Contemporary History. Strong on contemporary works.

9. Research Libraries

Busse, Gisela von, and Ernestus, Horst. Libraries in the Federal Republic of Germany. Rev. ed. Wiesbaden, 1972.

Introduction to the major libraries and the library system (general holdings and special collections, locator files and regional catalogues, interlibrary loans).

Gebhardt, Walther, ed. Spezialbestände in deutschen Bibliotheken. Berlin, 1977.

Detailed description of special collections in German libraries.

Bibliothek für Zeitgeschichte/Weltkriegsbücherei, Stuttgart. Alphabetischer Katalog, Systematischer Katalog. 31 vols. Boston, 1968.

Alphabetic and classified catalogues of the special collections on contemporary history since the first World War.

Young, Margaret L., et al., eds. Subject Directory of Special Libraries and Information Centers. 6th ed. Detroit, 1981.

Alphabetically arranged listing of special collections in libraries in the United States and Canada. Vol. 4 deals with the social sciences and the humanities.

Meckler, Alan M., and McMullin, Ruth, eds. Oral History Collections. New York, 1975.

Annotated listing of some 12,000 taped interviews found in 388 institutions; arranged alphabetically by subject and location.

Smith, Allen. Directory of Oral History Collections. Phoenix, AZ, 1988.

Directory to institutions in the United States, arranged by state. Subject indexes.

Williams, Sam P., ed. Guide to the Research Collections of the New York Public Library. Chicago, 1975.

Summary description of the Library's holdings, classified by subject. Extensive collection of German books on the period 1933-45, of public documents (parliamentary proceedings, white books), and of newspapers. A Dictionary Catalog of the Research Libraries of the NYPL 1911-1971 (800 vols., New York, 1979-83), with supplements for 1972-81, is available.

The New York Public Library, Research Libraries. Catalog of Government Publications. 40 vols. Boston, 1972 (with supplements, 1976-);

———. Dictionary Catalog of the Manuscript Division. 2 vols. Boston, 1967;

———. Subject Catalog of the World War II Collection. 3 vols. Boston, 1977.

Photo-reproduction of the catalogue cards of the Library's various special collections.

Council on Foreign Relations, Inc. Catalog of the Foreign Relations Library. 9 vols. Boston, 1969 (with supplement, 3 vols., 1979).

Guide to books, pamphlets, documentary series on international relations since 1918.

The Center for Research Libraries, Chicago. Handbook: The Center for Research Libraries. Chicago, 1978.

Guide to the scope and contents of the collection, supplemented by detailed catalogues:

———. The Center for Research Libraries Catalog (microform), Chicago, 1982, on monographs and serials;

———. Newspapers. 2d ed., Chicago, 1978, cumulative.

10. Newspaper Collections

Hagelweide, Gert. Deutsche Zeitungsbestände in Bibliotheken und Archiven. Düsseldorf, 1974.

Inventory of over 2,000 German newspapers, from 1700 to 1972, held in repositories in the two Germanies and Western Europe. A meticulous piece of work: lists the exact number of issues of individual newspapers available at different locations.

Hagelweide, Gert, ed. Zeitung und Bibliothek: Ein Wegweiser zu Sammlungen und Literatur. Pullach, 1974.

Describes the big newspaper collections in German-speaking Europe, including such things as the Deutsche Presseforschung and the Mikrofilmarchiv.

The British Library, Newspaper Library, Colindale. Catalogue of the Newspaper Library, Colindale. 8 vols. London, 1975.

Colindale has about 500,000 volumes and parcels of newspapers, from 1801 onward. Vols. 3 and 4 cover countries other than Britain; vols. 5 through 8 list all the titles in the collection.

Royal Institute of International Affairs. Review of the Foreign Press, 1939-1945. Series A, Enemy Countries, Axis-Controlled Europe, October 1939-June 1945. 9 vols. Munich, 1980.

A review of the foreign press compiled by the staff of the British Foreign Office and of the Royal Institute.

Stanford University, The Hoover Institution on War, Revolution, and Peace. Catalogs of the Western Language Serials and Newspaper Collections. 3 vols. Boston, 1969.

Lists some 26,000 titles, including materials from political parties, military offices, propaganda agencies. Arranged alphabetically by language group. Vol. 3 covers newspapers.

Mikrofilmarchiv der deutschsprachigen Presse, e.V. Bestandsverzeichnis. Dortmund, 1973.

Updated at regular intervals. Copies available from the Institut für Zeitungsforschung.

Library of Congress. Newspapers on Microfilm: Foreign Countries, 1948-1972. Washington, 1973-.

Cumulative listing of newspapers on microfilm in American, Canadian, and foreign libraries. Arranged alphabetically by country. Supplemented by Newspapers in Microform (Washington, 1975-), which appears annually and lists both American and foreign newspapers.

IV. BIBLIOGRAPHY

The bibliography is set out in topical chapters. The first ten chapters are devoted to general works, including reference sources, documentary series, and memoirs. The remaining chapters deal with the secondary literature--books and articles arranged in broadly chronological sequence. Within chapters, the titles are listed in alphabetical order; they are numbered consecutively throughout the entire volume. Titles that are pertinent to different topics are cross-referenced to the number of the title. Head notes to each chapter mention relevant bibliographies and, where appropriate, particular circumstances or problems of the works that follow.

Books not available locally can usually be borrowed through interlibrary loan. The same cannot be said of serials, which are on restricted loan even within libraries, but photocopies of specific pages or articles can generally be purchased. In Canada and the United States, books can be located through the National Union Catalog: Pre-1956 Imprints (London, 1968-) and its subsequent editions, published in five-year cumulative sets. Serials can be located through the Union List of Serials (3d ed., New York, 1965), which lists serials published before 1950, and New Serial Titles: A Union List of Serials commencing publication after Dec. 31, 1949 (Washington, 1953-), issued monthly. In the Federal Republic, where there is no equivalent to the National Union Catalog, books can be located through a number of regional Zentralkataloge or Gesamtkataloge, unpublished catalogues of the holdings of German libraries divided by region (seven in all). German serials are listed in the Gesamtverzeichnis deutschsprachiger Zeitschriften und Serien (Munich, 1978), or GDZS, foreign serials in the Gesamtverzeichnis ausländischer Zeitschriften und Serien, 1939-1958 (5 vols., Wiesbaden, 1959-68), or GAZS.

Many books are now also available on microfilm or microfiche. The Guide to Microforms in Print, 1961- (Washington, 1961-77, Westport, CT, 1978-) is a cumulative annual listing of books, official documents, and serials available from micropublishers throughout the world. The National Register of Microfilm Masters, 1965-, edited by the Library of Congress (6 vols., Washington, 1976; annually since 1976), lists the locations of works on microfilm masters, from which copies can be made quickly and cheaply.

Books available as reprints are listed in the International Bibliography of Reprints, edited by Christa Gnirss (2 vols., Munich, 1976-80), which covers publications through 1973, and in the Guide to Reprints, 1967- (Washington, 1967-), an annual cumulative index.

A. GENERAL

1. Bibliographies

Bibliographies come in all shapes and sizes. General bibliographies range over broad topics and are useful for preliminary surveys; subject bibliographies cover narrow topics in great detail. Retrospective bibliographies list titles published before a certain date. Current bibliographies list titles that have just been published or are about to be published; they appear at regular intervals.

The most comprehensive bibliography of bibliographies is Theodore Besterman's A World Bibliography of Bibliographies (4th ed., 5 vols., Lausanne, 1965-66), brought up to date by a two-volume supplement edited by Alice F. Toomey (Totowa, NJ, 1977). It is a classified index, arranged alphabetically by subject, and lists bibliographies that are published separately. The Bibliographic Index (New York, 1938-) complements Besterman. It comes out twice a year and lists bibliographies published separately or as parts of books, periodicals, and review essays. It is useful particularly for smaller, more obscure topics.

General Bibliographies

1. The American Historical Association's Guide to Historical Literature. New York, 1961.

    A selective, annotated bibliography of source materials, reference works, and secondary literature, the starting point for much historical research.

2. Baumgart, Winfried, ed. Bücherverzeichnis zur deutschen Geschichte: Hilfsmittel, Handbücher, Quellen. Frankfurt/M., 1971. (5th ed., Munich, 1982)

    Compiled with the college student in mind, covers German history from the Middle Ages to the present. Limited to bibliographical indexes, handbooks and encyclopedias, sources.

3. Dahlmann-Waitz: Quellenkunde der deutschen Geschichte. Edited by Hermann Heimpel and Herbert Geuss. 10th ed. Vol. 1-. Stuttgart, 1969-.

The standard retrospective bibliography on German history to 1945, listing publications to 1960. The work will comprise five volumes, and sections are published as they are completed. Especially good on the older literature; not annotated.

4.   Jahresberichte für deutsche Geschichte. Edited by Akademie der Wissenschaften der DDR, Zentralinstitut für Geschichte. Vol. 1 (1949-). Berlin, 1952-.

An annual bibliography, but published too slowly to be current. Covers German history from earliest times through 1945. Arranged topically in chronological order; lists titles in all European languages, and is especially good on East European literature.

Continues Albert Brackmann and Fritz Hartung, eds., Jahresberichte für deutsche Geschichte (Leipzig, 1927-42), which had review articles as well as bibliography.

5.   Morgan, Bayard Quincy, ed. A Critical Bibliography of German Literature in English Translation, 1928-1955. New York, 1955.

A guide to German works that have been translated into English; not limited to belles-lettres. Continued by Murray F. Smith, ed. A Critical Bibliography . . . 1956-1960. (Metuchen, NJ, 1972).

6.   Wile, Annadel N., ed. The Combined Retrospective Index Set to Journals in History, 1838-1974. 11 vols. Washington, 1977.

Bibliographical information on some 400,000 articles in over 500 English-language journals in history, political science, sociology. Vols. 1-9 list entries by subject; vols. 10-11 by author. Vol. 3 covers Germany.

Subject Bibliographies

7.   Benz, Wolfgang, ed. Quellen zur Zeitgeschichte. Deutsche Geschichte seit dem ersten Weltkrieg, vol. 3. Stuttgart, 1973.

Classified bibliography of essential works on German history in the twentieth century. No annotations.

8.   Bird, Keith W. German Naval History: A Guide to the Literature. New York, 1985.

Arranged by chapter (Weimar Republic, Nazi Germany, World War II), each with a lengthy review of the literature and comments on research themes.

9.   Bracher, Karl Dietrich, et al., eds. Bibliographie zur Politik in Theorie und Praxis. Rev. ed. Düsseldorf, 1982.

A bibliography on politics, political history, political theory, international relations, and international organizations, emphasizing the publications of the last ten years. Well-organized, with a classified table of contents that makes the volume easy to use.

10. Foreign Affairs Bibliography: A Selected and Annotated List of Books on International Relations, 1919-32, 1932-42, 1942-52, 1952-62, 1962-72. 5 vols. New York, 1935-76.

A good selection of books on international relations between 1919 and 1972. Strong on Europe and especially on the interwar and war years.

A bibliography of important books published between 1920 and 1970, each reviewed at length from today's perspective, is in The Foreign Affairs 50-Year Bibliography, edited by Byron Dexter, New York, 1972.

11. Jahresbibliographie der Bibliothek für Zeitgeschichte (Weltkriegsbücherei), Stuttgart. Vol. 32 (1960)-. Frankfurt/M., 1960-.

Originally published as Bücherschau der Weltkriegsbücherei (1921-59), lists the titles accessioned by the library, now close to 10,000 items a year. The volumes also contain extensive review articles on diverse subjects.

12. Showalter, Dennis E. German Military History, 1648-1982: A Critical Bibliography. New York, 1984.

Introductory section on general works (archival guides, reference works, handbooks, etc.) followed by some 3,000 entries, annotated, arranged in chronological order. About one fourth of these are related to the Nazi period.

13. Toscano, Mario. The History of Treaties and International Politics. Vol. 1. Baltimore, 1966.

Well-informed guide to the diplomatic sources and memoirs on the origins of the world wars.

Guides to Current Literature

14. American Historical Association. Recently Published Articles. Vol. 1-. Washington, 1976-.

An expanded version of the classified bibliography of journal articles that appeared in the back of the American Historical Review until 1976. Entries are drawn from around 2,000 journals, grouped under headings of period and area.

15. Bibliographie zur Zeitgeschichte. Beilage der Vierteljahrshefte für Zeitgeschichte. Vol. 1 (1953)-. Stuttgart, 1953-. Quarterly.

Classified index to reference works, published documents, and secondary sources on history since 1918. Emphasis on Germany and Europe. Appears both as part of the Vierteljahrshefte and as a separate publication; the quarterly bibliographies for the years 1953 to 1980 were reprinted as Bibliographie zur Zeitgeschichte 1953-1980, edited by Thilo Vogelsang and Hellmut Auerbach, 2 vols., Munich, 1982.

A retrospective supplement, covering books that appeared between 1945 and 1950, is Franz Herre and Hellmuth Auerbach, eds., Bibliographie zur Zeitgeschichte und zum Zweiten Weltkrieg für die Jahre 1945-1950 (Munich, 1955).

16. Internationale Bibliographie der Zeitschriftenliteratur (IBZ). 1963/64-. Osnabrück, 1964-. Semi-annual.

A merger and continuation of two earlier serial article indexes (Bibliographie der deutschen Zeitschriftenliteratur [1896-1964] and Bibliographie der fremdsprachigen Zeitschriftenliteratur [1925-64]), it indexes periodical articles in German and non-German journals, newspapers, transactions, etc. Alphabetically arranged under classified subject headings in German, but with English and French equivalents cross-referenced to the German.

For a review index, see Internationale Bibliographie der Rezensionen (Osnabrück, 1971-), a continuation of Bibliographie der Rezensionen und Referate (1900-43), semi-annual. Cites reviews in some 2,500 periodicals worldwide; arranged alphabetically by author of book reviewed under subject headings arranged in German alphabetical order (with English and French subject headings interspersed).

17. Public Affairs Information Service (PAIS). 1915-. New York, 1915-. Semi-monthly.

An index to the literature of the social sciences, focusing on public affairs. Lists books, pamphlets, government publications, yearbooks, selected articles, etc., published in English.

The PAIS Foreign Language Index, 1968- (1972-), a quarterly, indexes a selected number of social science titles in the major European languages other than English. For both indexes, data base is available for computerized literature searches.

18. Social Sciences Citation Index. 1972-. Philadelphia, 1973-. Three times a year.

A broad-gauged index, indexing well over 100,000 articles a year from social science monographs and journals, which identifies related works by collating similar titles and sources. Data base available for computerized literature searches.

Each issue consists of three parts: (1) Source Index, which lists by author the articles that appeared in the period covered, with full bibliographical citations; (2) Citation Index, which lists by author all the published sources cited in the articles listed in the Source Index, and then indicates those articles that cited one or more of these sources; (3) Permuterm Subject Index, which lists every significant word in the titles of the articles listed in the Source Index, then under each such word lists other significant words that appeared with that particular word, and then indicates authors who used that word combination in their articles.

Dissertations

19. Dissertation Abstracts: A Guide to Dissertations and Monographs Available in Microfilm. Ann Arbor, MI, 1938-. Bimonthly. (Published between 1938 and 1951 as Microfilm Abstracts.)

    Appears since 1966 in two sections (The Humanities and the Social Sciences; The Sciences and Engineering), and is supplemented since 1969 by Dissertation Abstracts International, also divided into two sections. Lists North American and (since 1969) European dissertations affiliated with University Microfilms in Ann Arbor. Arranged under principal subject categories; gives full bibliographical reference and abstract of contents. Author and subject index in each volume. Microfilms are available for purchase.

20. Reynolds, Michael M., ed. A Guide to Theses and Dissertations: An International Bibliography of Bibliographies. Rev. ed. Phoenix, AZ, 1985.

    A guide to all the standard bibliographies of dissertations accepted in universities throughout the world. Arranged by subject ("History") and country ("Germany").

2. Works of Reference

Works of reference are indispensable, but in their number and variety often bewildering. Researchers should become familiar with the most important and get to know their uses.

There are two excellent guides to reference works--Eugene P. Sheehy, ed., Guide to Reference Works (10th ed., Chicago, 1986) and A.J. Walford, ed., Guide to Reference Material (4th ed., 2 vols., London, 1980-82, with a third volume to come). Both are international in scope, and both arrange their listings systematically by subject and describe them clearly and succinctly. The German counterpart of these guides is Wilhelm Totok et al., eds., Handbuch der bibliographischen Nachschlagewerke (6th ed., Frankfurt/M., 1984), which emphasizes works in German.

More specialized are Helen J. Poulton, The Historian's Handbook: A Descriptive Guide to Reference Works (Norman, OK, 1972), and John Brown

Mason, ed., <u>Research Resources: Annotated Guide to the Social Sciences</u> (2 vols., Santa Barbara, CA, 1968-71). Poulton covers most of the basic works in history (some 700 different titles), all conveniently arranged and annotated. Mason's approach is interdisciplinary, and he focuses mainly on current events.

Encyclopedias and Dictionaries

21. Bracher, Karl Dietrich, and Fraenkel, Ernst, eds. <u>Internationale Beziehungen</u>. Frankfurt/M., 1969.

Articles on various aspects of international relations (balance of power, diplomacy, nationalism, and the like), by political scientists with a historical bent. An earlier version was entitled <u>Aussenpolitik</u>.

22. <u>Dictionnaire Diplomatique</u>. Edited by Académie Diplomatique Internationale. 8 vols. Paris, 1933-73.

Monumental set of reference volumes on diplomatic history and practice since 1918, written by both diplomats and scholars. Information on states, regions, diplomatic events; appendices list conferences, treaties, mandates, etc. Vol. 5 has biographical sketches of diplomats from the Middle Ages to the 1950s. Later volumes bring earlier volumes up to date. In French.

23. Haensch, Günther, ed. <u>Wörterbuch der Internationalen Beziehungen und der Politik</u>. 2d ed. Munich, 1975.

The basic vocabulary of diplomacy and international law, grouped according to subject matter, in English, French, German, and Spanish.

For the basic vocabulary in politics and economic policy, see the trilingual dictionary (no Spanish) by Hans E. Zahn, ed., <u>Wörterbuch zur Politik und Wirtschaftspolitik</u> (Frankfurt/M., 1975).

24. Plano, Jack C., and Olton, Roy, eds. <u>The International Relations Dictionary</u>. 4th ed. Santa Barbara, CA, 1988.

A general dictionary of words and phrases for students of international politics. The terms are defined and explained in a dozen topical chapters (e.g., diplomacy, military policy, war).

A German counterpart, with short definitions arranged in dictionary-form, is Fritz Bleiber, <u>Handwörterbuch der Diplomatie und Aussenpolitik</u> (Darmstadt, 1959).

25. Rössler, Hellmuth, and Franz, Günther, eds. <u>Sachwörterbuch zur deutschen Geschichte</u>. 2 vols. Munich, 1956-58. (Rpt. Nendeln/Lichtenstein, 1978).

Bosl, Karl, et al., eds. <u>Biographisches Wörterbuch zur deutschen Geschichte</u>. 2d ed. 3 vols. Munich, 1974-75.

Companion volumes, the former emphasizing ideas, events, institutions, the latter historic personalities, from all periods of German history. Arranged alphabetically; bibliographies.

26. Schlochauer, Hans-Jürgen, ed. Wörterbuch des Völkerrechts. 2d ed. 4 vols. Berlin, 1960-62.

The legal side of international politics, as seen by the German-speaking world. Long essays on principles, concepts, purposes, and treaties in international law, written by international lawyers. See also, Alfred von Verdross, Völkerrecht (5th ed., Vienna, 1964; originally 1937), a shorter compendium.

27. Taddey, Gerhard, ed. Lexikon der deutschen Geschichte: Personen, Ereignisse, Institutionen. Stuttgart, 1977.

Short articles on people, events, institutions important in German history. Good on biographical data, also for minor figures.

News Digests and Surveys

28. Horkenbach, Cuno, ed. Das deutsche Reich von 1918 bis Heute. 4 vols. Berlin, 1931-35.

A manual for politicians and journalists. For the main part, a chronicle of events (1918-30, 1931, 1932, 1933), but also a list of government agencies and private organizations (with staff), tables of statistical data, and biographical information on the leading personalities in German public life.

29. Keesings Archiv der Gegenwart, 1931/1932-. Vienna, 1931-. (Rpt. 14 vols. [July 1931-March 1945], 1962.)

A day-by-day digest of world events, useful for dating and placing visits, meetings, and conferences, arrivals and departures, speeches, etc. Focuses more on Germany than the English edition (Keesing's Contemporary Archives, London, 1931-; available also on microfiche). Cumulative name and subject indexes.

A day-by-day digest of international affairs is in The Bulletin of International News, 22 vols., London, 1925-45.

30. Overesch, Manfred, and Saal, Friedrich Wilhelm. Chronik deutscher Zeitgeschichte: Politik, Wirtschaft, Kultur. 2 vols. Düsseldorf, 1982-83.

A modern Geschichtskalendarium, a day-by-day summary of events. Suffers from lack of discrimination between what is important and what is not, and too often interlards straight reporting with editorial comment. The first volume covers the Weimar Republic; the second, divided into two parts, Nazi Germany.

31. Purlitz, Friedrich, ed. Deutscher Geschichtskalender. 49 vols. (1885-1933). Leipzig, 1886-1934.

A detailed chronicle of events, with excerpts from official documents, government and party proclamations, newspaper articles and editorials. Volumes appeared annually in two parts, one relating to Germany, the other to foreign countries.

Supplementary volumes exist on the German revolution (2 vols., 1932) and on the armistice and peace negotiations (1932).

32. Schulthess' Europäischer Geschichtskalender. Edited by Ulrich Thürauf et al. 82 vols. (1860-1942). Nördlingen, 1861-89; Munich, 1890-1965.

Similar to Purlitz, but more emphasis on developments in European countries and on international affairs.

33. Toynbee, Arnold J., et al., eds. Survey of International Affairs. 28 vols. (1920/23-1946). London, 1925-58.

An annual series describing and analyzing world events, published under the auspices of the Royal Institute of International Affairs. Important not only as a source of reference but also as an indication of how the world looked to informed observers. Of high quality, though here and there a bit out of date. The series is divided into a prewar set (1920-38) and a wartime set (1939-46). Notable are the volumes on The World in March 1939 (1952), The Eve of War (1958), The Initial Triumph of the Axis (1958), and Hitler's Europe (1954).

A companion series is J.W. Wheeler-Bennett et al., eds., Documents on International Affairs (13 vols. [1928-46]; London, 1929-54), also published annually, with state papers, speeches, exchanges of diplomatic notes, etc.

There is a Consolidated Index to the Survey of International Affairs, 1920-38, and Documents on International Affairs, 1920-38, edited by Edith M.R. Ditmas, London, 1967.

Handbooks and Directories

34. Almanach de Gotha: annuaire généalogique, diplomatique et statistique. Gotha, 1763-1944. (Available on microfiche)

This annual handbook, best known as the standard source on the genealogies of noble families, also contains information on states and governments, and it lists the diplomatic and consular officials stationed in the different countries.

The German edition appeared as Gothaischer Kalender (and slightly different titles) every year until 1942. It gave more space to German affairs.

35. Handbuch des öffentlichen Lebens. Edited by Maximilian Müller-Jabusch. Vols. 5, 6. Leipzig, 1929-31. (The first four volumes appeared as Politischer Almanach, Berlin, 1923-27).

A comprehensive directory of public life in Germany and, to a lesser extent, in foreign states and international organizations. Has information on offices and officials in the government, the diplomatic corps, the armed forces, the political parties, economic organizations and associations, etc. Has sections on Deutschtum organizations, newspapers and political journals, and vital statistics from around the world. Also provides biographical data on public figures in Germany and elsewhere.

36. Handbuch für das Deutsche Reich. Edited by Reichministerium des Innern. Vols. 41-46. Berlin, 1922-36.

A government manual, issued every other year or so. Lists the government authorities, senior officials in the ministries, foreign diplomats in Germany, military officers, etc. Has bibliography of official publications.

37. The Statesman's Year-Book, 1864-. London, 1864-.

Annual statistical and historical reference volume on the states of the world and international organizations. Current information on political institutions, the economy, social services, religious and cultural features. Good bibliographies of government publications.

Biographical Indexes

38. Das deutsche Führerlexikon, 1934-35. Berlin, 1934. (Available on microfilm)

Biographical dictionary of leading Nazi figures. Arranged in alphabetical order, with photographs. Blank spaces indicate last-minute deletions. Appendixes list government ministers and party organizations and provide statistics.

A more recent guide to Nazi party members, arranged alphabetically in who's-who style, is Erich Stockhorst, Fünftausend Köpfe: Wer War Was im Dritten Reich (Kettwig, 1967). Fairly comprehensive, but by no means complete.

39. Deutsches Biographisches Jahrbuch. Edited by Verband der Deutschen Akademien. Vols. 1-5 (1914-16, 1917-20, 1921, 1922, 1923), 10 (1928), 11 (1929). Stuttgart, 1925-32.

A necrology of important people who died during the period covered by the volume. Often written by close associates, the individual obituaries give detailed personal and career information. Vol. 5 has an index for the first five volumes; vols. 6-9, covering 1924-27, never appeared.

40. Kosch, Wilhelm, ed. Biographisches Staatshandbuch: Lexikon der Politik, Presse, und Publizistik. 2 vols. Berne, 1959-63.

A biographical dictionary of notable figures in German-speaking countries in the 19th and 20th centuries. Individual entries are brief, occasionally in error, and not always complete. Generally discreet on sensitive information (Nazi party membership and the like).

41. Schwarz, Max, ed. MdR: Biographisches Handbuch der deutschen Reichstage. Hanover, 1965.

Sketches of the political careers of the men and women who served in parliament between 1848 and 1933.

42. Wer Ist's? Edited by Hermann A.L. Degener. 8th ed. (1922), 9th ed. (1928), 10th ed. (1935). Leipzig, 1922-35.

The German Who's Who. Lists personal information, career, publications, club memberships, party affiliation, etc.

Atlases, Maps, Gazetteers

43. Gilbert, Martin, ed. Recent History Atlas, 1860-1960. 3d ed. London, 1977.

121 black-and-white maps, indicating political and military confrontations, alliances, treaties, territorial arrangements, and the like. See also Colin McEvedy, The Penguin Atlas of Recent History: Europe since 1815, New York, 1982.

44. Hilgemann, Werner. Atlas zur deutschen Zeitgeschichte,1918-1968. 3d ed. Munich, 1986.

Colored maps with detailed commentary, with the emphasis on the years 1933-45.

45. Kinder, Hermann, and Hilgemann, Werner, eds. DTV-Atlas zur Weltgeschichte: Karten und chronologischer Abriss. Vol. 2: Von der Französischen Revolution bis zur Gegenwart. 5th ed. Munich, 1970.

Detailed, colored maps on political, economic, international developments; charts on alliances, constitutions, government structure. Chronological text accompanies maps on facing pages. (Translated into English as The Anchor Atlas of World History, vol. 2, New York, 1977.)

46. Seltzer, Leon E., ed. The Columbia-Lippincott Gazetteer of the World. New York, 1962.

A gazetteer complements an atlas. Arranged in dictionary form, it provides information on locations, geographical features, historical significance.

47.   The Times Atlas of World History. Edited by Geoffrey Barraclough. Rev. ed. Maplewood, NJ, 1984.

A new historical atlas, reflecting recent changes in the conception of the scope and pattern of world history. Colored maps, illustrations, and text. Covers all periods and areas, and is therefore more general than either Gilbert or Kinder and Hilgemann.

3. Scholarly Journals

Scholarly journals contain the most current research, and they are generally the first to indicate new interpretations and new sources. They are also guides to current literature, for most of them carry book reviews or review articles, and some of them provide subject bibliographies. There are no journals devoted exclusively, or even largely, to German diplomatic history; researchers will have to rely on those that specialize in international affairs or contemporary history.

Individual journals can be located through the union lists of series cited above, p. 77.

Abstracts and Reviews

48.   Historical Abstracts: Bibliography of the World's Periodical Literature. Edited by Eric H. Boehm. Santa Barbara, CA, 1955-. Quarterly.

Summaries of articles published in historical journals, transactions, proceedings, yearbooks, Festschriften, and the like, often with information on sources. Covers all countries except United States and Canada. Since 1971, issued in two parts: A. Modern History Abstracts (1775-1914); B. Twentieth-Century Abstracts (1914-Present).

49.   Das Historisch-Politische Buch: Ein Wegweiser durch das Schrifttum. Vol. 1 (1953)-. Monthly.

Brief, signed reviews of books dealing with history and politics; emphasis on modern Europe. Sixty to seventy titles reviewed in each issue.

A similar journal is Neue Politische Literatur: Berichte über das internationale Schrifttum (1956-), originally Politische Literatur (1952-56), which appears quarterly with review articles and reviews of some 300-500 titles each year. Foreign Affairs (1922-), also a quarterly, has an annotated list of recent publications in the back of each issue.

Journals

50.   Aus Politik und Zeitgeschichte. Beilage zur Wochenzeitung Das Parlament. 1952-. Weekly.

Has frequent articles on foreign policy and diplomatic history, often individual chapters or condensed versions of forthcoming books.

51.   Central European History. 1968-. Quarterly.

Research articles and review articles, mostly on German history in the 19th and 20th centuries. Succeeds Journal of Central European Affairs (1941-64), but has not continued that journal's classified listing of articles in other periodicals.

52.   Geschichte in Wissenschaft und Unterricht. 1950-. Monthly.

Aimed mainly at teachers, it carries articles on a broad range of topics. Regular review articles, including an annual round-up of publications on Germany, 1933-45.

53.   International Affairs. London, 1922-. Quarterly.

Like Foreign Affairs (New York, 1922-), features articles on policy by high government officials and party spokesmen, and is therefore of interest for the interwar years. About half of each issue is devoted to book reviews.

54.   Jahrbuch des Instituts für deutsche Geschichte. Tel Aviv, 1952-.

A yearbook of essays on German history, especially German-Jewish history, since the 18th century. Occasional articles on foreign policy. In German, with summaries in Hebrew. (Beiheft 1 [1976] is devoted to "Germany and the Middle East, 1835-1939.")

55.   Jahrbuch für Wirtschaftsgeschichte. 1960-.

Research studies by East German historians, on occasion including something on the economic motivations and objectives of German foreign policy.

56.   Journal of Contemporary History. 1966-. Quarterly.

Research studies, mainly on Europe in the 20th century.

57.   Journal of Modern History. 1929-. Quarterly.

One of the leading historical journals, devoted to Europe and its relations with the rest of the world since the Renaissance. Historical and bibliographical articles; numerous short reviews; abstracts of articles available on request.

58. Militärgeschichtliche Mitteilungen. 1967-. Semi-annual.

Large volumes, virtually yearbooks, published under the auspices of the Militärgeschichtliches Forschungsamt. Articles, historical documents, and reviews; regular reports on research and archival resources.

See also, Wehrwissenschaftliche Rundschau (1951-70), with shorter articles, many on military operations but also on strategy and policy.

59. Revue d'histoire de la deuxième guerre mondiale. 1950-. Quarterly.

Articles on various aspects of World War II, many but by no means all on France. Regular bibliographical listing of current books and articles on the subject.

60. Vierteljahrshefte für Zeitgeschichte. 1953-. Quarterly.

Covers history since 1917, with emphasis on Germany during the Nazi era. Reports on historical conferences, archival repositories. Each issue has a classified bibliographical supplement.

61. Zeitschrift für Geschichtswissenschaft. 1953-. Originally bimonthly, now monthly.

Published in the German Democratic Republic. Frequent articles on foreign policy based on material in the Zentrales Staatsarchiv; also prints historical documents with editorial introduction and commentary.

B. SOURCES

1. Diplomatic Documents and Official Publications

Collections of diplomatic documents are best treated with caution. Many are published to plead a special cause, and both the documents themselves and the selection of documents may be suspect. Even documents compiled for scholarly purposes may be misleading, since editorial decisions or simply lack of space may distort the record. Whenever possible, the published documents should be checked against the originals in the archives.

Official publications (parliamentary proceedings, statistical yearbooks, compilations of laws) are less problematical, though it should be remembered that parliamentary proceedings that purport to be verbatim are often emended before publication. There are two guides to German government publications, somewhat dated now but still useful: Deutsche Bücherei, ed., <u>Monatliches Verzeichnis der reichsdeutschen amtlichen Druckschriften</u> (17 vols., Berlin, 1928-44), and Otto Neuberger, ed., <u>Official Publications of Present-Day Germany</u> (Washington, 1942).

Collections of documents on specific and narrow subjects are listed in the proper place among the secondary literature.

Government and Parliamentary Records

62.   <u>Akten der Reichskanzlei</u>. Edited by Karl Dietrich Erdmann, Wolfgang Mommsen, and Hans Booms. Boppard, 1968-.

A series of volumes, ultimately to number about twenty, containing cabinet minutes and supporting documentation from the files of the chancellery. Each volume is compiled by a different editor, who also contributes an introduction on the cabinet under review, on its administrative and political record. Listed in order of the period they cover:

Schulze, H. <u>Das Kabinett Scheidemann</u> (1971)
Golecki, A. <u>Das Kabinett Bauer</u> (1980)
Vogt, M. <u>Das Kabinett Müller I</u> (1971)
Wulf, P. <u>Das Kabinett Fehrenbach</u> (1972)
Schulze-Bidlingmeier, I. <u>Die Kabinette Wirth I, II</u> (1973)
Harbeck, K.H. <u>Das Kabinett Cuno</u> (1968)
Erdmann, K.D., and Vogt, M. <u>Die Kabinette Stresemann I, II</u> (1978)

Abramowski, G. Die Kabinette Marx I, II (1973)
Minuth, K.H. Die Kabinette Luther I, II (1976)
Vogt, M. Das Kabinett Müller II (1970)
Koops, T. Die Kabinette Brüning I, II (1982-)
Minuth, K.H. Das Kabinett Papen (1989)
Golecki, A. Das Kabinett Schleicher (1986)
Minuth, K.H. Die Regierung Hitler (1983-)

63. Matthias, Erich, and Morsey, Rudolf, eds. Die Regierung Max von Baden. Düsseldorf, 1962.

Matthias, Erich, and Miller, Susanne, eds. Die Regierung der Volksbeauftragten 1918/19. 2 vols. Düsseldorf, 1969.

Carefully edited collections of the minutes of the German cabinet, with supporting documents, from October 1918 to February 1919. See review essay by Klaus Epstein, Review of Politics, 26 (1964), 215-43.

64. Maurer, Ilse, and Wengst, Udo, eds. Politik und Wirtschaft in der Krise, 1930-1932: Quellen zur Ära Brüning. 2 vols. Düsseldorf, 1980.

Documents on political and economic issues, including reparations and the proposed customs union with Austria. Introduction by Gerhard Schulz reviews the literature on Brüning's economic policy.

65. Reichsgesetzblatt (RGBl). Edited by Reichsministerium des Innern. Berlin, 1871-. Weekly, or as necessary. (Available on microfiche)

Official compilation of legislation and treaties affecting Germany. Between 1939 and 1945 also included laws affecting annexed and occupied territories.

66. Statistisches Jahrbuch für das deutsche Reich. Edited by Statistisches Reichsamt. Berlin, 1880-1942. (Available on microfiche)

Annual publication listing the principal results of the official statistical surveys. A more specialized statistical source, issued monthly, is Monatliche Nachweise über den auswärtigen Handel Deutschlands (Berlin, 1892-1939).

67. Stenographische Berichte über die Verhandlungen des deutschen Reichstages. Vols. 344-460. Berlin, 1920-42. (Available on microfilm and microfiche)

Stenographic record of the parliamentary proceedings from June 1920 to April 1942, supplemented by the Anlagen zu den Stenographischen Berichten (also called Drucksachen des Reichstags). The Anlagen, which are numbered consecutively, include bills, committee reports, state papers, and the lists of members of the Reichstag and Reichsrat.

The proceedings of the Reichstag meeting as a constituent assembly, 1919-20, are in Verhandlungen der verfassunggebenden Deutschen Nationalversammlung, vols. 326-43 (Berlin, 1919-20).

68. Stenographische Berichte über die Verhandlungen des Vorläufigen Reichswirtschaftsrats. Berlin, 1920-34.

Proceedings of the provisional economic council.

Documentary Series (German)

69. Akten zur deutschen auswärtigen Politik, 1918-1945 (ADAP). Baden-Baden and Göttingen, 1950-.

Collection of German diplomatic documents edited by a commission composed of American, English, French, and German historians. It offers a chronological record of German policy on the basis of documents from the foreign ministry and, in some volumes, from the chancellery, the armed forces, and the economic ministry. The documents are printed in chronological order, but each volume has an analytical table of contents, which describes the documents briefly and lists them by subject. The volumes also contain biographical data, organizational charts, and, on occasion, reproductions of maps that were part of the documents.

There are five series:

Serie A: Nov. 1918-Nov. 1925. 6 vols. to date, covering the period to Dec. 1922.
Serie B: Dec. 1925-Jan. 1933. 21 vols., covering the entire period.
Serie C: Jan. 1933-Nov. 1937. 6 vols., covering the entire period.
Serie D: Sept. 1937-Dec. 1941. 13 vols., covering the entire period.
Serie E: Dec. 1941-May 1945. 8 vols., covering the entire period.

70. Documents on German Foreign Policy, 1918-1945 (DGFP). Washington and London, 1949-83.

Translation of no. 69, series C and D. (The French translation--Les archives secrètes de la Wilhelmstrasse [Paris, 1950-]--is a selection of the documents in the German and English editions and is not recommended.)

71. The Department of State Bulletin. Vols. 14, 15. Washington, 1946.

A series of German diplomatic documents in translation, published at the time of the war crimes trials in order to acquaint the American public with the issues.

Volume 14:

"Documents concerning Relations between the Spanish
Government and the European Axis, [1940-43]," pp. 413-27.

"German Documents on. . .
the Sumner Welles Mission, 1940," pp. 259-60, 459-66;
the Invasion of Norway, 1940," pp. 699-703;
Hitler's Plans for the Future of Norway and Denmark, 1942,"
pp. 936-40;
Hungary [1938, 1941-42]," pp. 984-86;
Relations with Japan [1939-41]," pp. 1038-41, 1050.

"German Documents: Conference with Axis Leaders [1941]," pp.
1103-07, 1124.

Volume 15:
"German Documents: . . .
Conference with Axis Leaders [1942]," pp. 57-63;
Conference with Axis Leaders (1943)," pp. 197-201, 236;
Conference with Japanese Representatives [1943]," pp. 399-
403, 427, 480-86, 564-69;
Conference with Axis Leaders [1943]," pp. 607-14, 639;
Conference with Axis Leaders, 1944," pp. 695-99;
Conference with Axis Leaders, 1944," pp. 1040-47, 1061.

72. Documents and Materials Relating to the Eve of the Second World
War. Edited by the Ministry of Foreign Affairs of the USSR. 2
vols. Moscow, 1948-49.

Mostly German diplomatic documents in English translation. The first
volume is about Munich and its origins (1937-38), the second about
the events leading up to the outbreak of war (1938-39). Many of the
documents, especially in vol. 2, are drawn from the Dirksen papers,
which were captured by the Soviets. Copies of most of the
documents are in the ADAP volumes or in the archives. (The two
volumes are also available in the original German.)

The Ministry of Foreign Affairs also published another collection of
captured German documents, this one intended to prove that certain
European states had collaborated closely with Nazi Germany:
Documents secrets du Ministère des affaires étrangères d'Allemagne
(3 vols., Paris, 1946-47). The first volume deals with Turkey (1941-
43), the second with Hungary (1937-42), and the third with Spain
(1936-43). The first also appeared in English.

73. Nazi-Soviet Relations, 1939-1941: Documents from the Archives of
the German Foreign Office. Edited by Raymond J. Sontag and
James Stuart Beddie. Washington, 1948.

The most significant documents bearing on German-Soviet relations
between April 1939 and June 1941. Superseded now by the relevant
volumes of ADAP.

The German edition--<u>Das nationalsozialistische Deutschland und die Sowjetunion, 1939-1941</u> (Berlin, 1948)--was edited by E.M. Carroll and F.T. Epstein.

A variant of this collection, containing some documents not in the Sontag/Beddie volume, is Alfred Seidl, <u>Die Beziehungen zwischen Deutschland und der Sowjetunion, 1939 bis 1941</u> (Tübingen, 1949). Seidl was a defense attorney at Nuremberg and used documents made available to him there.

74. <u>Staatsmänner und Diplomaten bei Hitler: Vertrauliche Aufzeichnungen über Unterredungen mit Vertretern des Auslandes</u>. Edited by Andreas Hillgruber. 2 vols. Frankfurt/M., 1967-70.

German records of Hitler's interviews with foreign statesmen and diplomats, 1939-44. Many of the documents are also in Department of State <u>Bulletin</u> (no. 71).

75. <u>Gustav Stresemann; Vermächtnis</u>. Edited by Henry Bernhard. 3 vols. Berlin, 1932-33.

Personal and official papers from Stresemann's <u>Nachlass</u>, selected and edited by his confidential secretary. On the selection and editing, see Hans Gatzke, "The Stresemann Papers," <u>Journal of Modern History</u>, 26 (1954), pp. 49-59.

For a further selection, including documents not in <u>Vermächtnis</u>, see <u>Gustav Stresemann: Schriften</u>, edited by Arnold Harttung (Berlin, 1976).

The full <u>Nachlass</u> is available in the Politisches Archiv, Bonn, and on microfilm.

76. <u>Die Weizsäcker-Papiere, 1900-1932</u>. Edited by Leonidas E. Hill. Berlin, 1982.

<u>Die Weizsäcker-Papiere, 1933-1950</u>. Edited by Leonidas E. Hill. Berlin, 1974.

Collection of diary entries, family letters, notes, and official documents drawn from the Weizsäcker <u>Nachlass</u> (in family hands). Coverage most extensive for the middle years (1937-43), when Weizsäcker was chief of the political department and then state secretary. Annotations, bibliography, and a somewhat uncritical introduction.

White Books

These are collections of diplomatic documents published by the German government to justify its course of action and generally issued soon after the events to which they refer. For discussion, see Toscano (no. 13), pp. 88-103, 316-22, and Günter Kahle, "Die Publikation des Deutschen Weissbuches Nr. 6:

Zur Reaktion in London, Moskau, Ankara und Teheran," in Helmut Berding et al., eds., Vom Staat des Ancien Regime zum Modernen Parteienstaat (Munich, 1978), pp. 451-66.

77.   German White Books, edited by the Auswärtiges Amt:

Urkunden zur letzten Phase der deutsch-polnischen Krise (Weissbuch 1939, Nr. 1). Berlin, 1939.

Dokumente zur Vorgeschichte des Krieges (Weissbuch 1939, Nr. 2). Berlin, 1939.

Polnische Dokumente zur Vorgeschichte des Krieges (Weissbuch 1940, Nr. 3). Berlin, 1940.

Dokumente zur englisch-französischen Politik der Kriegsausweitung (Weissbuch 1940, Nr. 4). Berlin, 1940.

Weitere Dokumente zur Kriegsausweitungspolitik der Westmächte (Weissbuch 1940, Nr. 5). Berlin, 1940.

Die Geheimakten des französischen Generalstabes (Weissbuch 1941, Nr. 6). Berlin, 1941.

Dokumente zum Konflikt mit Jugoslawien und Griechenland (Weissbuch 1941, Nr. 7). Berlin, 1941.

These books contain documents from German archives and from enemy archives captured in the course of military operations. They were also published in translation (English and French, and in some cases in other languages as well).

A concordance of the documents printed in Weissbuch 1939, Nr. 2 and the originals is in ADAP, Serie C, Vol. 2, pp. 905-6, and in ADAP, Serie D, Vol. 7, pp. 557-63.

78.   Colored books by other European governments:

Belgium, Ministry of Foreign Affairs. The Official Account of What Happened, 1939-1940. New York, 1940.

France, Ministry of Foreign Affairs. The French Yellow Book: Diplomatic Documents concerning the Events and Negotiations which preceded the Opening of Hostilities. . . . London, 1940.

Great Britain, Foreign Office. British War Blue Book: Documents concerning German-Polish Relations and the Outbreak of Hostilities. . . . London, 1939.

Netherlands, Ministry of Foreign Affairs. Netherlands Orange Book: Summary of the Principal Matters dealt with. . .in Connection with the State of War. . . . Leyden, 1940.

Poland, Ministry of Foreign Affairs. The Polish White Book: Official Documents Concerning Polish-German and Polish-Soviet Relations (1933-1939). London, 1940.

Documentary Series (Non-German)

The list that follows is no more than a selection. Information on these collections will be found in other volumes of this series of handbooks.

79. Der Notenwechsel zwischen dem Heiligen Stuhl und der Deutschen Reichsregierung. Edited by Dieter Albrecht. 3 vols. Mainz, 1965-80.

Actes et documents du Saint Siège relatifs à la seconde guerre mondiale. Edited by Pierre Blet et al. Vatican City, 1965-.

80. Documents diplomatiques belges, 1920-1940. Edited by Charles de Visscher and Fernand Vanlangenhove. 5 vols. Brussels, 1964-66.

81. Documents diplomatiques français, 1932-1939. Edited by Ministère des Affaires Étrangères. Paris, 1963-.

Les événements survenus en France de 1933 à 1945. Témoignages et documents recueillis par la commission d'enquête parlementaire. 11 vols. Paris, 1947.

La délégation française auprès de la commission allemande d'armistice: recueil de documents publiés par le gouvernement français. 5 vols. Paris, 1947-59.

Le procès Flandin devant la Haute Cour de Justice, 23-26 juillet 1946. Paris, 1946.

Le procès Benoist-Méchin (29 mai-6 juin 1947). Paris, 1948.

Le procès de la collaboration: Fernand de Brinon, Joseph Darnand, Jean Luchaire. Paris, 1948.

82. Documents on British Foreign Policy, 1919-1939. Edited by E.L. Woodward et al. London, 1946-.

The British regularly published foreign office documents, including correspondence with Germany, as Command Papers. They are listed in Robert Vogel, A Breviate of British Diplomatic Blue Books, 1919-1939 (Montreal, 1963).

83. Foreign Relations of the United States: Diplomatic Papers. Edited by Department of State. Washington, 1943-.

84. I documenti diplomatici italiani, 1861-1943. Edited by Ministerio degli Affari Esteri. Rome, 1952-.

85.   League of Nations. Official Journal, 1920-1946, and Official Journal, Special Supplements, 1920-1946. Geneva, 1920-46.

86.   Soviet Documents on Foreign Policy, 1917-1941. Edited by Jane Degras. 3 vols. London, 1951-53.

Treaty Collections

87.   Bruns, Victor, ed. Politische Verträge: Eine Sammlung von Urkunden. 5 vols. Berlin, 1936-42.

Compilation of treaties concluded between 1920 and 1940 (treaties of guarantee, alliance, and political cooperation; non-aggression pacts; declarations of neutrality). In the original languages.

88.   Kraus, Herbert, ed. Internationale Schiedssprechung: Eine Sammlung der für das Deutsche Reich verbindlichen Verträge und Vertragsbestimmungen, die sich auf internationale Gerichtsbarkeit, Schiedsgerichtsbarkeit sowie Vergleichsverfahren beziehen, nebst den dazugehörigen deutschen Regierungsdenkschriften. Berlin, 1929.

Collection of treaties and agreements on international arbitration and mediation together with relevant German documentation.

89.   League of Nations. Treaty Series. 205 vols. Geneva, 1920-46.

Full texts of treaties registered with the secretariat of the League between 1920 and 1946. In the original language as well as French and English. Organized by date of registration, not signature or ratification.

The treaties are indexed in Peter H. Rohn, ed., World Treaty Index (Santa Barbara, CA, 1974).

90.   Rönnefarth, Helmut K.G., and Euler, Heinrich, eds. Konferenzen und Verträge: Ein Handbuch geschichtlich bedeutsamer Zusammenkünfte und Vereinbarungen. Vol. 4 (1914-59). Würzburg, 1959.

Information on international conferences and agreements--participants, partners, and signatories, aims and purposes, content, language, date of meeting and ratification. In chronological order.

91.   Triepel, Heinrich, et al., eds. G.F. de Martens: Nouveau recueil général de traités et autres actes relatifs aux rapports de droit international. 3d series. 41 vols. Leipzig, 1909-44.

A general collection of treaties through 1942. In the original languages and in French.

2. Diplomatic Handbooks

Handbooks available and used by diplomats offer some insight into the procedures and protocol used in official transactions, and they are ready tools for researchers who need to know the terms and forms by which diplomats carried out their duties. They will also serve as a context for assessing the sorts of information available to members of the foreign service, and, further, as an indication of the kind of information that was authorized for distribution.

92.   Deutsches Institut für Aussenpolitische Forschung. Materialien zur Neuordnung. 7 vols. Berlin, 1942-43.

Each volume provides statistics, dates, and other data on a particular country or territorial issue. Prepared by the institute in close collaboration with the foreign ministry, which had requested the volumes for internal use; plans existed for more than 100 volumes to cover the entire world.

93.   Huber, Ernst Rudolf. Verfassungsrecht des grossdeutschen Reiches. Hamburg, 1939.

A semi-official interpretation and commentary on German constitutional law.

94.   Jahrbuch der Auslands-Organisation der NSDAP. 4 vols. Berlin, 1938-42.

The annual publication of the AO, with information on the AO's attempts to organize and indoctrinate German nationals abroad. Illustrations, diagrams, tables.

95.   Jahrbuch der Hochschule für Politik. Berlin, 1938-41. (Continued as Jahrbuch für Politik und Auslandskunde [1942] and then as Jahrbuch der Weltpolitik [1942-44].)

Descriptive pieces on Germany, foreign states, and on the annexed and occupied territories (Government General in Poland; Reichskommissariat Ostland).

96.   Jahrbuch für Auswärtige Politik, Internationale Wirtschaft und Kultur, Weltverkehr und Völkerrecht. 9 vols. Berlin, 1929-44 (suspended publication 1932-37).

An annual reference manual, conceived as a counterpart to The Statesman's Year-Book (above, no. 37), edited first by Hartmann von Richthofen, then by Fritz (after 1942, Friedrich) Berber. Each volume surveyed the year with a chronicle of events, articles on foreign policy and international developments, diplomatic documents, and a classified list of new books on foreign affairs. Also contained lists of German ministries and agencies (and their personnel) and of the diplomatic corps in Berlin, and information on the governments in foreign countries and the administrations in the occupied territories.

97.   Kraske, Erich, ed. <u>Handbuch des auswärtigen Dienstes</u>. Halle, 1939.

Kraske's book was put together at the request of the Foreign Ministry. Together with Herbert Kraus, <u>Der Auswärtige Dienst des Deutschen Reiches</u>, Berlin, 1932, it is a useful source of information on organization, procedures, internal policies, etc.

98.   Pohl, Heinrich. <u>Völkerrecht und Aussenpolitik in der Reichsverfassung</u>. Berlin, 1929.

On the legal aspects of foreign policy, as defined by the Weimar constitutions.

99.   Schifferdecker, Otto. <u>Die Organisation des Auswärtigen Dienstes im alten und neuen Reich</u>. Heidelberg, 1932.

100.   Stuckart, Wilhelm. <u>Neues Staatsrecht</u>. Leipzig, 1943.

Handbook on occupation and annexation policies, by the state secretary in the ministry of interior.

101.   Wahl, Kurt H. <u>Die deutschen Länder in der Aussenpolitik</u>. Stuttgart, 1930.

Information on the role and function of the German states in the making of foreign policy.

3. Memoirs and Diaries

The memoir literature is prone to all sorts of distortions. Personal biases and lapses of memory lead to omissions and errors; attempts to justify past actions and minimize past responsibilities skew the record. Yet memoirs cannot be dismissed, for they are often the only sources on matters that did not get on the record--telephone conversations, private conferences, negotiations conducted outside official channels. The extent to which we can rely on memoirs depends on our impression of their verisimilitude and on what we find when chance permits us to compare them with the documents.

None of the German foreign ministers left genuine memoirs, nor did any of the leading Nazi emissaries. German diplomats were less reticent, and their memoirs, together with those written by foreign diplomats stationed in Berlin, make up the bulk of those listed below. Also included are the memoirs of government officials, civil servants, and publicists who were directly involved in foreign affairs. (Memoirs limited to narrow periods or topics are mentioned below among the secondary literature.)

Many of the German diplomatic memoirs were written under the impact of the lost war and the war crimes trials. An assessment of their value and accuracy is in Lewis Namier, <u>Diplomatic Prelude, 1938-1939</u> (London, 1948), <u>Europe in Decay</u> (London, 1950), and <u>In the Nazi Era</u> (London, 1952). More

100

sympathetic is Walther Hubatsch, <u>Deutsche Memoiren, 1945-1955</u> (Laupheim, Württ., 1956).

German

102.   Abetz, Otto. <u>Das offene Problem: Ein Rückblick auf zwei Jahrzehnte deutscher Frankreichpolitik</u>. Cologne, 1951.

Ribbentrop's expert on France and ambassador in Paris, 1940-44. On Abetz's life and career, see John E. Wallace, "Otto Abetz and the Question of a Franco-German Reconciliation, 1919-1939," <u>Southern Quarterly</u>, 13 (1975), 189-206.

103.   Bargatzky, Walter. <u>Hotel Majestic: Ein Deutscher im besetzten Frankreich</u>. Freiburg i.B., 1987.

A member of the military administration in occupied France, 1940-44.

104.   Bernstorff, Johann Heinrich von. <u>Erinnerungen und Briefe</u>. Zurich, 1936.

DDP deputy in the Reichstag and president of the Deutsche Liga für Völkerbund. Frequent delegate to the League; representative on the preparatory commission for the disarmament conference, 1926-30.

105.   Blücher, Wipert von. <u>Deutschlands Weg nach Rapallo: Erinnerungen eines Mannes aus dem zweiten Gliede</u>. Wiesbaden, 1951.

————. <u>Am Rande der Weltgeschichte: Marokko, Schweden, Argentinien</u>. Wiesbaden, 1958.

————. <u>Zeitenwende in Iran: Erlebnisse und Beobachtungen</u>. Biberach, 1949.

————. <u>Gesandter zwischen Diktatur und Demokratie: Erinnerungen aus den Jahren 1935-1944</u>. Wiesbaden, 1951.

Listed here in accordance with the chronology of the author's career, these volumes deal with Germany's relations with Russia (1918-22), Sweden (1922-26), Argentina (1926-29), Iran (1931-35), and Finland (1935-44).

106.   Bonn, Moritz J. <u>So macht man Geschichte: Bilanz eines Lebens</u>. Munich, 1953.

Economic expert, consultant to the government; at Versailles and subsequent reparations conferences. <u>Nachlass</u>, Bundesarchiv, Koblenz.

107.   Bräutigam, Otto. <u>So hat es sich zugetragen: Ein Leben als Soldat und Diplomat</u>. Würzburg, 1968.

The deputy chief of the political division of the Ministry of Occupied Eastern Territories, 1941-45, involved in framing and executing Nazi policies in Eastern Europe. Diary, Library of Congress.

108. Brüning, Heinrich. Memoiren, 1918-1934. Stuttgart, 1970.

Written in exile in the 1930s, informative on Brüning's conservative outlook and his foreign policy as chancellor, 1930-32. See Rudolf Morsey, Zur Entstehung, Authentizität und Kritik von Brünings "Memoiren, 1918-1934" (Opladen, 1975); and the reviews by Karl Dietrich Bracher (Vierteljahrshefte für Zeitgeschichte 19 [1971], pp. 113-23) and Arnold Brecht (Politische Vierteljahresschrift 12 [1971], pp. 607-40).

109. Cahén, Fritz Max. Der Weg nach Versailles: Erinnerungen, 1912-1919. Boppard, 1963.

Memoirs of a journalist who served as Brockdorff-Rantzau's spokesman, 1918-19.

110. Curtius, Julius. Sechs Jahre Minister der deutschen Republik. Heidelberg, 1948.

Thin and somewhat apologetic account of his career as minister of economics (1926-29) and foreign minister (1929-31). On his controversial policies, see Bemühungen um Österreich: Das Scheitern des Zollunionsplans von 1931 (Heidelberg, 1947), and Der Young-Plan: Entstellung und Wahrheit. (Stuttgart, 1950).

111. Dennler, Wilhelm. Die Böhmische Passion: Prager Tagebuch, 1939-1947. Freiburg i.B., 1953.

Diary of an official in the office of the Reichsprotektor.

112. Dirksen, Herbert von. Moskau, Tokio, London: Erinnerungen und Betrachtungen zu 20 Jahren deutscher Aussenpolitik, 1919-1939. Stuttgart, 1949.

Assigned to East European affairs (1920-28); ambassador at three major posts (1928-39). The English version (Moscow, Tokyo, London [Norman, OK, 1952]) is abridged. See also Documents (no. 72).

113. Dollmann, Eugen. Roma nazista. Milan, 1949. (Trl. as Dolmetscher der Diktatoren [Bayreuth, 1963] and as The Interpreter: Memoirs [London, 1967].)

On the relations between the Axis powers and on the German role in Italian affairs, by the official interpreter attached to the German forces in Italy.

114. Faber du Faur, Moriz von. Macht und Ohnmacht: Erinnerungen eines alten Offiziers. Stuttgart, 1953.

   Served as military attaché in Belgrade, 1935-40.

115. Lowenthal-Hensel, Cécile, and Paucker, Arnold, eds. Ernst Feder: heute sprach ich mit. . . Tagebücher eines Berliner Publizisten, 1926-1932. Stuttgart, 1971.

   Extracts from the diaries of the political editor of the Berliner Tageblatt (1919-31). Had access to foreign ministers and diplomats; accompanied German delegations to Geneva.

116. Frank, Hans. Im Angesicht des Galgens: Deutung Hitlers und seiner Zeit. Munich, 1953.

   Musings on Hitler, Nazism, and Germany, with a few autobiographical allusions. Little on his service as governor general in occupied Poland. Nachlass, Politisches Archiv, Bonn.

117. Fromm, Bella. Blood and Banquets: A Berlin Social Diary. New York, 1942.

   Diplomatic columnist of the Vossische Zeitung, concerned mainly with diplomatic dinners and receptions, but with occasional snippets of interest.

118. Gärtner, Margarete. Botschafterin des guten Willens: Aussenpolitische Arbeit. 1914-1950. Bonn, 1955.

   Detailed account of revisionist propaganda activities, by the head of the Wirtschaftspolitische Gesellschaft, an organization subsidized by the government and by industry. Nachlass, Geheimes Staatsarchiv, Berlin.

119. Die Tagebücher von Joseph Goebbels: Sämtliche Fragmente. 4 vols. Edited by Elke Fröhlich. Munich, 1987.

   Goebbels Tagebücher aus den Jahren 1942-1943. Edited by Louis P. Lochner. Zurich, 1948.

   Tagebücher 1945: die letzten Aufzeichnungen. Edited by Peter Stadelmayer. Hamburg, 1977.

   Diary entries, left unedited by the diarist, with comments on German policies and international developments. An English translation of part of these diaries--The Goebbels Diaries, 1939-1941 (London, 1982)--is incomplete and error-ridden. For a biography, see Helmut Heiber, Joseph Goebbels (Berlin, 1962).

120. Grimm, Friedrich. Frankreich-Berichte 1934 bis 1944. Bodman, 1972.

Vice president of the Deutsch-Französische Gesellschaft (the German counterpart of the Comité France-Allemagne), a group interested in pressing the German case in France. His reports on France were passed on to members of the Nazi government.

121.   Grobba, Fritz. Männer und Mächte im Orient: 25 Jahre diplomatischer Tätigkeit im Orient. Göttingen, 1967.

Stationed at Kabul, Jidda, Baghdad in the 1930s; negotiated with the Grand Mufti of Jerusalem during the war.

122.   Groscurth, Helmut. Tagebücher eines Abwehroffiziers, 1938-1940. Edited by Helmut Krausnick and Harold C. Deutsch. Stuttgart, 1970.

As a member of the Abwehr, Groscurth was privy to a great deal of information about foreign policy.

123.   Halder, Franz. Kriegstagebuch: Tägliche Aufzeichnungen des Chefs des Generalstabes des Heeres, 1939-1942. Edited by Hans-Adolf Jacobsen. 3 vols. Stuttgart, 1962-64. (For a mimeographed translation, see The Halder Diaries [7 vols., Washington, 1950].)

A private diary, kept from August 1939 to September 1942 by the chief of the general staff. Especially valuable because the official war diary of the general staff is lost. See the editor's "Das 'Halder-Tagebuch' als historische Quelle," in Festschrift Percy Ernst Schramm (Wiesbaden, 1964), pp. 251-68.

124.   [Hassell, Ulrich von]. Ulrich von Hassell: Die Hassell-Tagebücher 1938-1944: Aufzeichnungen vom anderen Deutschland. Edited by Friedrich Freiherr Hiller von Gaertringen. Berlin, 1988.

Diaries from the years after he had left active service; recounts conversations with former colleagues, but mainly on the activities of the anti-Hitler resistance. This edition, extensively and carefully annotated, represents almost the entire diary, omitting only personal items, and is about two-thirds larger than the previous edition (Vom anderen Deutschland: Aus den nachgelassenen Tagebüchern des ehemaligen Botschafters von Hassell, 1938-1944, Zurich, 1946).

125.   Heller, Gerhard. Un Allemand à Paris, 1940-1944. Paris, 1981. (Trl. as "In einem besetzten Land" -- NS-Kulturpolitik in Frankreich: Erinnerungen 1940-1944 [Cologne, 1982].)

Was a member of the German occupation authorities charged with implementing and encouraging National Socialist cultural policy.

126.   Hencke, Andor. Augenzeuge einer Tragödie: Diplomatenjahre in Prag, 1936-1939. Munich, 1977.

Served in Prague as counselor of legation and deputy to minister Eisenlohr. Subsequently was under state secretary in the foreign ministry.

127. Henle, Günter. Weggenosse des Jahrhunderts. Stuttgart, 1968.

Member of the diplomatic service in the 1920s and 1930s; served at The Hague, Buenos Aires, and, between 1931 and 1936, in London.

128. Hentig, Werner Otto von. Mein Leben eine Dienstreise. 2d ed. Göttingen, 1963.

On assignments in the United States and South America in the late 1920s and early 1930s, and as special plenipotentiary in Cairo, 1939. Nachlass, Politisches Archiv, Bonn.

129. Herwarth, Hans von. Zwischen Hitler und Stalin: Erlebte Zeitgeschichte, 1931-1945. Frankfurt/M., 1982. (Trl. as Against Two Evils [New York, 1981].)

Served under ambassadors Dirksen, Nadolny, and Schulenburg in the embassy in Moscow, 1931-39.

130. Hesse, Fritz. Das Spiel um Deutschland. Munich, 1953.

Correspondent for DNB in London (1933-39) and a specialist on British affairs in Ribbentrop's entourage. His memoirs have been sharply criticized by Helmut Krausnick in "Legenden um Hitlers Aussenpolitik," Vierteljahrshefte für Zeitgeschichte, 2 (1954), 217-39.

131. Hilger, Gustav. Wir und der Kreml: Deutsch–sowjetische Beziehungen, 1918-1941. 2d ed. Frankfurt/M., 1956.

Spent virtually his entire professional life at the embassy in Moscow (1922-41). Interpreter at many important conferences.

132. Hossbach, Friedrich. Zwischen Wehrmacht und Hitler, 1934-1938. Rev. ed. Göttingen, 1965.

Hitler's military adjutant, 1934-38. His famous memorandum is reprinted in an appendix.

133. Jäckh, Ernst. Der goldene Pflug. Stuttgart, 1954.

————. Weltsaat: Erlebtes und Erstrebtes. Stuttgart, 1960.

Founder of the Deutsche Liga für Völkerbund; advocate of German membership in the League.

134. [Keitel, Wilhelm]. Generalfeldmarschall Keitel: Verbrecher oder Offizier? Edited by Walter Görlitz. Göttingen, 1961.

An ex parte account by the chief of the armed forces high command (1938-45), written in a Nuremberg cell. The English version (The Memoirs of Field-Marshal Keitel [London, 1965]) omits the chapters on 1933-37 but adds documents not in the German edition.

135.　　Kessler, Harry. Tagebücher, 1918-1937. Frankfurt/M., 1961. (Rpt. in paperback, 1982)

On diplomatic missions to Warsaw (1918), Genoa (1922), London (1923), and Geneva (1924). Close to Rathenau and to senior officials in the foreign ministry.

136.　　Kleist, Peter. Zwischen Hitler und Stalin, 1939-1945: Aufzeichnungen. Bonn, 1950.

The German-Soviet rapprochement, 1939-41, and the administration of German-occupied Soviet territory, by a member of Dienststelle Ribbentrop (1936-43) and the Ministry of Occupied Eastern Territories. Unreliable.

137.　　[Köstring, Ernst]. General Ernst Köstring: Der militärische Mittler zwischen dem Deutschen Reich und der Sowjetunion, 1921-1941. Edited by Hermann Teske. Frankfurt/M., 1966.

Autobiographical sketch by the military attaché in Moscow (1931-33, 1935-41), with copies of many of his letters and reports.

138.　　Kordt, Erich. Nicht aus den Akten. . . : Die Wilhelmstrasse in Frieden und Krieg. Stuttgart, 1950.

————. Wahn und Wirklichkeit: Die Aussenpolitik des dritten Reiches. Stuttgart, 1948.

Liaison to Dienststelle Ribbentrop and then head of Büro RAM; well informed on Ribbentrop and his policies. Akten is autobiographical; Wahn is a history, with some personal glimpses, now largely superseded by the documents.

139.　　Krogmann, Carl Vincent. Es ging um Deutschlands Zukunft, 1932-1939. Leoni, 1976.

Memoirs of a Nazi mayor of Hamburg, with extracts from his diary. Close to Hitler.

140.　　Kroll, Hans. Lebenserinnerungen eines Botschafters. Cologne, 1967.

Ritter's assistant in the ministry (1929-36), then counselor of embassy in Ankara till 1945.

141. Luther, Hans. <u>Vor dem Abgrund, 1930-1933: Reichsbankpräsident in Krisenzeiten</u>. Berlin, 1964.

Worked with Brüning on economic and reparations policies. His memoirs of the years as chancellor (<u>Politiker ohne Partei: Erinnerungen</u> [Stuttgart, 1960]) are superficial.

142. Meissner, Otto. <u>Staatssekretär unter Ebert, Hindenburg, Hitler</u>. Hamburg, 1950.

State secretary in the president's office, 1920-45. Reticent, sometimes inaccurate.

143. Möllhausen, Eitel Friedrich von. <u>Il giucco è fatto!</u> Florence, 1951; <u>La carta perdente: Memorie diplomatiche</u>. Rome, 1948.

Rahn's deputy and collaborator in Paris and in Rome (1940-45), often entrusted with special missions. The second volume was translated into German as <u>Die gebrochene Achse</u> (Alfeld, 1949).

144. Nadolny, Rudolf. <u>Mein Beitrag</u>. Wiesbaden, 1955. (An enlarged, annotated version, edited by Günter Wollstein, was published as <u>Mein Beitrag: Erinnerungen eines Botschafters des Deutschen Reiches</u> [Cologne, 1985].)

One of the more outspoken diplomats--minister in Sweden, ambassador in Turkey and Soviet Russia, head of the German disarmament delegation (1932-33). See also, Günter Wollstein, "Rudolf Nadolny--Aussenminister ohne Verwendung," <u>Vierteljahrshefte für Zeitgeschichte</u>, 28 (1980), 47-93.

145. Neubacher, Hermann. <u>Sonderauftrag Südost, 1940-1945: Bericht eines fliegenden Diplomaten</u>. Göttingen, 1956. (3d ed., Seeheim, 1966)

One of the most active and influential German agents in the Balkans.

146. Papen, Franz von. <u>Der Wahrheit eine Gasse</u>. Munich, 1952. (Trl. as <u>Memoirs</u> [London, 1952].)

Information on his service as chancellor (1932), negotiator at the Vatican (1933), and envoy to Austria and Turkey (1934-44). Attempts to rehabilitate his reputation by doctoring the record. See reviews by Werner Conze (<u>Historische Zeitschrift</u> [1953], pp. 307-17] and by Rudolf Pechel (<u>Deutsche Rundschau</u> [1952], pp. 1231-34).

Papen's <u>Vom Scheitern einer Demokratie, 1930-1933</u> (Mainz, 1968) is an expansion of the second section of the memoirs, as self-righteous and purblind as they are.

147. Prittwitz und Gaffron, Friedrich von. Zwischen Petersburg und Washington: Ein Diplomatenleben. Munich, 1952.

Counselor of embassy in Rome, then ambassador in Washington (1927-33). The only German ambassador to resign in 1933.

148. [Prüfer, Curt]. Rewriting History: The Original and Revised World War II Diaries of Curt Prüfer, Nazi Diplomat. Edited by Donald M. McKale. Kent, OH, 1988.

Diaries of the years 1942-43, while attached to the foreign ministry after his return from Brazil, where he was ambassador 1939-42. There are two versions: the contemporary version and another, embroidered and sanitized, dating from after the war. For a biography, see Donald M. McKale, Curt Prüfer: German Diplomat from the Kaiser to Hitler (Kent, OH, 1987).

149. Pünder, Hermann. Politik in der Reichskanzlei: Aufzeichnungen aus den Jahren 1929-1932. Stuttgart, 1961.

State secretary in the chancellery, 1926-32, and, as such, adviser on policy. Regular member of the German delegation to Geneva. See also his memoirs (Von Preussen nach Europa [Stuttgart, 1968]), with a long section on the Weimar years. Nachlass, Bundesarchiv, Koblenz.

150. Putlitz, Wolfgang Gans Edler Herr zu. Unterwegs nach Deutschland: Erinnerungen eines ehemaligen Diplomaten. Berlin, 1956.

Scornful and disparaging comments by a minor diplomat between the wars (Washington, London), who after the war settled in the German Democratic Republic. The English version (The Putlitz Dossier [London, 1957]) is abridged.

151. Rahn, Rudolf. Ruheloses Leben: Aufzeichnungen und Erinnerungen. Düsseldorf, 1949.

Interesting for the war years, when he was counselor of embassy at Paris (1940-43) and ambassador to Mussolini's Italy (1943-45). One of Ribbentrop's special envoys and troubleshooters.

152. Rathenau, Walther. Tagebuch, 1907-1922. Edited by Hartmut Pogge von Strandmann. Düsseldorf, 1967.

Some notes on the reparations conference at Spa (1921) and on conversations with foreign diplomats.

153. Rheinbaben, Werner von. Viermal Deutschland: Aus dem Erleben eines Seemanns, Diplomaten, Politikers, 1895-1954. Berlin, 1954.

State secretary in Stresemann's chancellery (1923), delegate to the League and to the disarmament conference (1926-33), proponent of an aggressive revisionist policy. His <u>Kaiser, Kanzler, Präsidenten</u> (Mainz, 1968) has portraits of leading Weimar personalities, drawn from memory but obviously modified by reading.

154. Ribbentrop, Joachim von. <u>Zwischen London und Moskau:</u> <u>Erinnerungen und letzte Aufzeichnungen</u>. Leoni, 1953.

Autobiographical notes, written at Nuremberg, on his career as ambassador and foreign minister, predictably tendentious and apologetic. Further attempts to rehabilitate Ribbentrop are in the volumes edited by his wife, Annelies von Ribbentrop:

<u>Deutsch-englische Geheimverbindungen</u> (Tübingen, 1967);

<u>Die Kriegsschuld des Widerstandes: Aus britischen</u> <u>Geheimdokumenten 1938/39</u> (2d ed., Leoni, 1975);

<u>Verschwörung gegen den Frieden</u> (Leoni, 1962).

155. Riesser, Hans Eduard. <u>Von Versailles zur UNO: Aus den</u> <u>Erinnerungen eines Diplomaten</u>. Bonn, 1962.

Assigned to diplomatic posts in the United States and Western Europe, 1918-33. Interesting chiefly for his comments on fellow diplomats. For more such comments, see his <u>Haben die deutschen</u> <u>Diplomaten versagt?</u> (Bonn, 1959).

156. Rintelen, Enno von. <u>Mussolini als Bundesgenosse: Erinnerungen des</u> <u>deutschen Militärattachés in Rome, 1936-1943</u>. Tübingen, 1951.

The long-term military attaché in Rome, closely involved in German-Italian affairs.

157. Rosen, Friedrich. <u>Aus einem diplomatischen Wanderleben</u>. Vols. 3, 4. Wiesbaden, 1959.

Reflections on the foreign ministry and foreign policy in the early twenties, by a professional diplomat who served briefly as foreign minister (1921). There is a short biography by Herbert Müller-Werth, <u>Friedrich Rosen: Ein staatsmännisch denkender Diplomat</u> (Wiesbaden, 1969).

158. Rosenberg, Alfred. <u>Das politische Tagebuch Alfred Rosenbergs aus</u> <u>den Jahren 1934/35 und 1939/40</u>. Edited by Hans-Günther Seraphim. Göttingen, 1956.

Diary entries on contacts with Britain (1934-35) and on conversations with Hitler (1939-40), with an appendix of pertinent documents drawn from the Nuremberg trials.

His <u>Portrait eines Menschheitsverbrechers: Nach den hinterlassenen</u> <u>Memoiren des ehemaligen Reichsministers</u> (Edited by Serge Lang and

Ernst von Schenk [St. Gallen, 1947]) consists of autobiographical snippets arranged by the editors, who also supply extensive commentary. Mainly on his personal life; vague and distorted.

Robert Cecil's The Myth of the Master Race (New York, 1972) deals with Rosenberg's ventures into foreign affairs and has a complete bibliography of his writings.

159. Roskothen, Ernst. Gross-Paris, Place de la Concorde, 1941-1944: Ein Wehrmachtsrichter erinnert sich.... Bad Dürrheim, 1977.

A member of the German military administration in Paris, attached to the judicial branch.

160. Sahm, Heinrich. Erinnerungen aus meinen Danziger Jahren, 1919-1930. Marburg, 1958 (mimeograph).

Expanded version of his diary as president of the Danzig Senate, 1920-30. An unpublished diary for the years 1934-39, when he was German minister in Oslo, is in family hands. See also the very thorough biography by Heinrich Sprenger, Heinrich Sahm: Kommunalpolitiker und Staatsmann (Spich b. Köln, 1968).

161. Schacht, Hjalmar. Abrechnung mit Hitler. Hamburg, 1948.

————. 76 Jahre meines Lebens. Bad Wörishofen, 1953.

His life as president of the Reichsbank and minister of economics, 1923-39. The second version has additional material on the 1920s.

The best biography is by Edward N. Peterson (Hjalmar Schacht: For and Against Hitler [Boston, 1954]), but see also Helmut Müller, Die Zentralbank--eine Nebenregierung: Reichsbankpräsident Schacht als Politiker der Weimarer Republik (Opladen, 1973).

162. Schellenberg, Walter. Memoiren. Cologne, 1959.

Somewhat fanciful memoirs of one of Himmler's leading agents, involved in clandestine peace negotiations during the war.

163. Schlesinger, Moritz. Erinnerungen eines Aussenseiters im diplomatischen Dienst. Cologne, 1977.

German-Russian relations, 1918-22, by one of the major figures involved. Takes issue with Blücher's account (no. 105); and includes a selection of letters.

164. Schmidt, Paul. Statist auf diplomatischer Bühne, 1923-45. Bonn, 1950. (14th ed., Wiesbaden, 1986.)

Foreign ministry interpreter from 1923 to 1945. Witnessed many important meetings, especially in the Nazi era, and recorded the proceedings.

165. Schwerin von Krosigk, Lutz. Es geschah in Deutschland. Tübingen, 1951.

———. Memoiren. Stuttgart, 1977.

———. Staatsbankrott: Die Geschichte der Finanzpolitik des Deutschen Reiches von 1920 bis 1945. Göttingen, 1974.

Finance minister from 1932 to 1945; foreign minister at the time of capitulation. The first of these works consists of interpretive sketches of government and party leaders; the third is more a history of government finance with some autobiographical references.

166. Sonnenhol, Gustav Adolf. Untergang oder Übergang. Stuttgart, 1984.

Joined the foreign service in 1939; served as consul in North Africa in 1942-44 and in Geneva 1944-45.

167. Stern-Rubarth, Edgar. . . .Aus zuverlässiger Quelle verlautet. . . . Stuttgart, 1964.

Government spokesman in the 1920s; member of the delegations at Locarno and Geneva.

168. Vogel, Georg. Diplomat unter Hitler und Adenauer. Düsseldorf, 1969.

At diplomatic posts in Prague, London, and Athens (1936-40), liaison with Dienststelle Altenburg in occupied Greece, frequently at Ribbentrop's mobile headquarters (1943-44).

169. Warburg, Max M. Aus meinen Aufzeichnungen. New York, 1952.

Prominent Hamburg banker, member of the peace delegation at Versailles, consultant to the government on reparations.

170. Warlimont, Walter. Im Hauptquartier der deutschen Wehrmacht, 1939-1945. Frankfurt/M., 1962.

Jodl's deputy in Hitler's headquarters, and as such a good source on Hitler's views and strategies.

171. Weizsäcker, Ernst von. Erinnerungen. Munich, 1950.

A diplomat of the old school, he was Ribbentrop's state secretary, 1938-43. He took a position midway between loyalty and disloyalty, and the ambiguities of this position permeate his memoirs. For a close examination, see Leonidas E. Hill, "The Genesis and Interpretation of the Memoirs of Ernst von Weizsäcker," German Studies Review, 10 (1987), pp. 443-80. See also Papiere (no. 76).

172. Wiedenfeld, Kurt. Zwischen Wirtschaft und Staat. Edited by Friedrich Bülow. Berlin, 1960.

In the foreign ministry's foreign trade department (1918-21), then liaison agent in Moscow (1921-22). Includes letters.

173. Winnig, August. Am Ausgang der deutschen Ostpolitik: Persönliche Erlebnisse und Erinnerungen. Berlin, 1921.

————. 400 Tage Ostpreussen. Dresden, 1927.

Plenipotentiary in the Baltic states (1918-19), then Reichskommissar in East Prussia (1919-20). Nachlass, Bundesarchiv, Koblenz.

174. Zechlin, Walter. Pressechef bei Ebert, Hindenburg und Kopf. Hanover, 1956.

Member, then director, of the Presseabteilung for most of the Weimar period.

175. Ziehm, Ernst. Aus meiner politischen Arbeit in Danzig, 1914-1939. Marburg, 1960 (mimeograph).

President of the Danzig Senate, 1930-33. On the growing Nazi movement in the free city, meetings with Hitler, negotiations at Geneva.

Non-German

176. Alfieri, Dino. Due dittatori di fronte: Roma-Berlino, 1939-1943. Milan, 1948. (Trl. as Dictators Face to Face [New York, 1954].)

Italian ambassador in Berlin, 1940-43, present at high-level German-Italian conferences.

177. Anfuso, Filippo. Du palais de Venise au lac du Garde. Paris, 1949. (Trl. as Rom-Berlin im diplomatischen Spiegel [Essen, 1951].)

Italian career diplomat, Ciano's chef de cabinet (1938-41), ambassador to Berlin (1943-45).

178. Berezhkov, Valentin Mikhailovich. In diplomatischer Mission bei Hitler in Berlin, 1940-1941. Frankfurt/M., 1967.

First Secretary at the Soviet embassy in Berlin, 1940-41.

179. Beus, Jacobus Gijsbertus de. Morgen bei Tagesanbruch: Dramatische Stunden im Leben eines Diplomaten. Berlin, 1982.

Member of the Dutch foreign service, who began his career as secretary of legation in the Dutch legation in Berlin in the late 1930s.

180.   Brinon, Fernand de. Mémoires. Paris, 1949.

A member of Abetz's Comité Franco-Allemagne before the war; collaborator and Vichy representative at Paris during the war. See also, Procès (no. 81).

181.   Burckhardt, Carl Jacob. Meine Danziger Mission, 1937-1939. Munich, 1960.

The last League high commissioner in Danzig, in contact with the German foreign ministry, with Hitler, and, on the spot, with Forster and Greiser.

182.   Ciano, Galeazzo. Diario, 1937-38. Bologna, 1948; Diario, 1939-43. 2 vols. Milan, 1946.

Daily entries by Mussolini's son-in-law and foreign minister (1936-43). Also exist in English, French, and German editions; the French is considered the most complete on 1939-43.

L'Europa verso la catastrofe (Milan, 1948), which was translated as Ciano's Diplomatic Papers (London, 1948), is a record of Ciano's conversations with foreign diplomats between 1936 and 1942. Supplements the diaries. Both diaries and documents are to be used with caution.

183.   Coulondre, Robert. De Staline à Hitler: souvenirs de deux ambassades, 1936-1939. Paris, 1950.

French ambassador in Berlin, Nov. 1936 to Oct. 1938; well informed and valuable memoirs. Also in German translation.

184.   D'Abernon, Edgar Vincent, Viscount. The Diary of an Ambassador. 3 vols. New York, 1929-31.

Justly famous diary of the British ambassador in Berlin, 1920-26.

185.   Davignon, Jacques. Berlin, 1936-1940: souvenirs d'une mission. Paris, 1951.

Belgium's minister, then ambassador, in Berlin, 1936-40. Especially interesting on 1939-40.

186.   Dodd, William E. Ambassador Dodd's Diary, 1933-1938. New York, 1941.

American ambassador in Berlin, 1933-37, whose revulsion of Nazism caused him to shun contact and to limit his sources of information.

187. François-Poncet, André. Souvenirs d'une ambassade à Berlin, Septembre 1931-Octobre 1938. Paris, 1946.

Based largely on his official correspondence with Paris, which is now available in the French documentary series (no. 81). Also available in German and, abridged, in English.

188. Gheorghe, Ion. Rumäniens Weg zum Satellitenstaat. Heidelberg, 1952.

Rumanian military attaché and later ambassador in Berlin (1943-45). Iron Guard sympathies.

189. Hägglöf, Gunnar. Diplomat: Memoirs of a Swedish Envoy. London, 1972.

Senior Swedish diplomat, responsible for German affairs, 1934-44; member of the Dahlerus mission (1939) and in Berlin off and on throughout the war.

190. Hedin, Sven. Ohne Auftrag in Berlin. Tübingen, 1950.

Swedish explorer; frequent visitor to Nazi Germany. Informal intermediary between Germany and the Allies during the war. Inaccuracies.

191. Henderson, Nevile. Failure of a Mission: Berlin, 1937-1939. London, 1940.

British ambassador, 1937-39, determined to promote Anglo-German understanding. Informative on Anschluss, Munich, and the crisis over Danzig, though in part superseded by the documents.

See also, Rudi Strauch, Sir Nevile Henderson: Britischer Botschafter in Berlin von 1937 bis 1939 (Bonn, 1959).

192. Kirkpatrick, Ivone. The Inner Circle: Memoirs. London, 1959.

First Secretary at the British embassy in Berlin, 1933-38; Chamberlain's interpreter in Sept. 1938.

193. Labougle, Eduardo. Misión en Berlín. Buenos Aires, 1946.

Argentine ambassador in Berlin, 1932-39.

194. La Tournelle, Guy de. "A Dantzig de Décembre 1934 à Septembre 1939." Revue d'Histoire Diplomatique, 92 (1978), 321-47.

French consul stationed in Danzig, 1934-39.

195. [Lipski, Józef]. Diplomat in Berlin, 1933-1939. Edited by Waclaw Jedrzejewicz. New York, 1968.

Polish ambassador in Berlin, 1933-39. Correspondence with Warsaw, including reports on conversations with German diplomats and Nazi leaders.

196. Magistrati, Massimo. Il prologo del dramma: Berlino, 1934-37. Milan, 1971.

———. L'Italia a Berlino, 1937-1939. Milan, 1956.

Minister-counsellor at the Italian embassy in Berlin (1934-40), and closely associated with ambassador Attolico. Much of this material has appeared also in Rivista di Studi Politici Internazionali (1948-53).

197. Navarro, Francisco. Alemania por Deutro, 1941-1942. Mexico City, 1943.

Senior official at the Mexican legation in Berlin in the early years of the war.

198. Petresco-Comnène, Nicolas. I responsabili. Milan, 1949; Preludi del grande dramma. Rome, 1947.

Rumanian minister to Germany (1932-38). These memoirs are more historical reconstruction than personal recollections.

199. Simoni, Leonardo [pseud. of Michele Lanza]. Berlino: ambasciata d'Italia, 1939-1943. Rome, 1946.

First Secretary at the Italian embassy in Berlin (1939-43). Ostensibly diary entries but in fact excerpted from official documents.

200. [Smith, Truman]. Berlin Alert: The Memoirs and Reports of Truman Smith. Edited by Robert Hessen. Stanford, 1984.

Military attaché at the American embassy in Berlin, 1935-39.

201. Stehlin, Paul. Témoignage pour l'histoire. Paris, 1964.

Air attaché at the French embassy in Berlin, 1935-39.

202. Tabouis, Geneviève. They Called Me Cassandra. New York, 1942; Vingt ans de "suspense" diplomatique. Paris, 1958.

One of the best informed diplomatic correspondents between the wars. Mostly on France, but useful also for the politics at Geneva.

203. Vauhnik, Vladimir. Memoiren eines Militärattachés: Ein Kampf gegen das Fingerspitzengefühl Hitlers. Klagenfurt, 1967.

Military attaché at the Yugoslav legation in Berlin, 1938-41.

204.   [Wilson, Hugh R.]. A Career Diplomat. The Third Chapter: The Third Reich. Edited by Hugh R. Wilson, Jr. New York, 1961.

Selections from the diary and correspondence of the American ambassador in Berlin, 1938-40.

4. Contemporary Commentaries

Contemporary works on foreign policy are by and large polemical, even though they appear in the guise of scholarship. Most of them, whether attacking or defending government policy, were written in order to influence internal, not external, affairs. Those that were subsidized by the foreign ministry and disseminated abroad, adhered to the official line, whatever it might be at the time. These works enable us to gauge opinion, to locate sources of pressure, and in general to determine the focus and terms of debate.

The number of such works published in Germany between 1918 and 1945 runs into the thousands. The Institut für Auswärtige Politik in Hamburg, the Deutsches Auslandswissenschaftliches Institut and the Deutsches Institut für Aussenpolitische Forschung, both in Berlin, were prolific in sponsoring monograph series, document collections, journals, yearbooks, and the like. Listed below is only a representative sampling.

Contemporary Bibliographies

205.   Deutsches Auslandswissenschaftliches Institut. Europa-Bibliographie. 8 parts. Edited by Fritz Prinzhorn. Leipzig, 1941-44.

206.   Gunzenhäuser, Max, ed. Bibliographie zur Geschichte der deutsch-polnischen Beziehungen und Grenzlandfragen, 1919-1939. Stuttgart, 1942.

207.   Juntke, F., and Sveistrup, H., eds. Das deutsche Schrifttum über den Völkerbund, 1917-1925. Berlin, 1927.

208.   Kleinwaechter, Friedrich, and Paller, Heinz von, eds. Die Anschlussfrage in ihrer kulturellen, politischen, und wirtschaftlichen Bedeutung. Vienna, 1930.

209.   Koch, W. Verzeichnis des Schrifttums über das Saargebiet seit 1929. Berlin, 1934.

210.   Mai, Richard, and Scherer, E.C., eds. Auslandsdeutsche Quellenkunde, 1924-1933. Berlin, 1936.

See also, Deutsches Auslands-Institut, ed., Bibliographisches Handbuch des Auslandsdeutschtums (5 vols., Stuttgart, 1932-36), and the annual Bibliographie des Deutschtums im Ausland (Stuttgart, 1937-44), edited by the same institute.

211. Meyer, H.M., and Pflaume, H., eds. Wartheland-Bibliographie (1939-42). Posen, 1943.

212. Prinzhorn, Fritz, ed. Danzig-Polen-Korridor und Grenzgebiete: Eine Bibliographie. 9 vols. Danzig and Leipzig, 1932-42.

    By the same editor: Memelgebiet und Baltische Staaten: Eine Bibliographie (3 vols., Danzig, 1937-39), and Reichsgau Sudetenland, Reichsprotektorat Böhmen-Mähren (2 vols., Leipzig, 1940-41).

213. Reismüller, Georg, and Hofmann, Josef, eds. Zehn Jahre Rheinlandbesetzung: Beschreibendes Verzeichnis des Schrifttums. Breslau, 1929.

214. Schwab, Georg, ed. Versailles und Kriegsschuld: Literaturverzeichnis. 3 vols. Leipzig, 1929.

    See also H. Sveistrup, ed., Die Schuldenlast des Weltkrieges (2 vols., Berlin, 1929-31).

Documentary Collections

215. Berber, Fritz, ed. Deutschland-England, 1933-1939: Die Dokumente des deutschen Friedenswillens. 3d ed., Essen, 1942.

    ———. Deutschland-Frankreich, 1933-1939. Essen, 1942.

    The foreign ministry blocked the publication of this volume; galley proofs are in the library of the Institut für Internationale Angelegenheiten der Universität Hamburg.

    ———. Locarno: Eine Dokumentensammlung. Berlin, 1936.

    A defense of Nazi policy--to show how France destroyed Locarno and how Britain rejected all German overtures for harmonious relations.

216. ———. Das Diktat von Versailles: Entstehung, Inhalt, Zerfall. 2 vols. Essen, 1939.

    Text and documents to illustrate both the creation and the revision of each clause of the peace treaty. Extensive bibliography.

217. Freund, Michael, and Frauendienst, Werner, eds. Weltgeschichte der Gegenwart in Dokumenten. 5 vols. Essen, 1936-40.

    Freund, Michael, ed. Weltgeschichte der Gegenwart: Geschichte des Zweiten Weltkrieges in Dokumenten. 3 vols. Freiburg i.B., 1953-56.

The first set of volumes deals with 1934-38, the second with 1938-39. Emphasis on international affairs (notes, agreements, declarations) with connective text.

218. Meier-Benneckenstein, Paul, ed. Dokumente der deutschen Politik. 9 vols. Berlin, 1935-44.

An annual publication, brought out under the auspices of the Hochschule für Politik, covering the period 1933-44. Of particular interest are vols. 3 (Saar, rearmament 1935), 4 (Rhineland, peace plan of 1936), and 5 (foreign policy, 1937).

Plans to publish a series on World War I and on the Weimar Republic did not materialize. The only volume to appear was Hans Volz, ed., Novembersturz und Versailles (Berlin, 1942), which has biased evidence for the alleged partisanship within the German government and its neglect of German national interests.

Meier-Benneckenstein also edited a four-volume series entitled Das Dritte Reich im Aufbau (Berlin, 1939), a documentary history of government organization after 1933. Vol. 2 has an article on the AO, vol. 5 has articles on the ministries of finance and of propaganda.

Journals and Yearbooks

A list of German journals, with information on the editorial staff, place of publication, circulation, party affiliation, and the like, is in Sperlings Zeitschriften- und Zeitungs-Adressbuch: Handbuch der deutschen Presse (vols. 50-61, Leipzig, 1923-39).

219. Berliner Monatshefte. 19 vols. Berlin, 1923-44.

The journal, which appeared monthly, carried articles mainly on Versailles, and especially on war guilt, in order to substantiate Germany's position. The first five volumes were entitled Die Kriegsschuldfrage: Monatsschrift für internationale Aufklärung. Indirectly subsidized by the foreign ministry.

220. Deutsches Grenzland: Jahrbuch des Instituts für Grenz- und Auslandsstudien. 5 vols. Edited by Max Hildebert Boehm and Karl C. von Loesch. Berlin, 1936-40.

The annual publication of the Institut für Grenz- und Auslandsstudien in Berlin. See below, no. 233.

221. Europa: Handbuch der politischen, wirtschaftlichen und kulturellen Entwicklung des neuen Europa. Edited by Deutsches Institut für Aussenpolitische Forschung; Preface by Joachim von Ribbentrop. Leipzig, 1942.

26 articles on Hitler's Europe, some written by authors from Germany's wartime allies, accounting for the changes that have taken

place and showing what they mean for the future. The purpose was to glorify and reinvigorate the war effort.

222. Europäische Gespräche. 11 vols. Vols. 1-4, Stuttgart, 1923-26; vols. 5-11, Berlin, 1927-33.

A semi-official journal on foreign policy, with frequent contributions by politicians and diplomats. Edited by A. Mendelssohn-Bartholdy of the Institut für Auswärtige Politik, Hamburg.

Superseded by Hamburger Monatshefte für Auswärtige Politik (3 vols., Hamburg, 1934-36), by Monatshefte für Auswärtige Politik (5 vols., Essen, 1937-41), and by Auswärtige Politik (3 vols., Berlin, 1942-44).

223. Europäische Revue. 19 vols. Berlin, 1925-44.

German views on European unity--political, cultural, and economic. In 1939, absorbed Völkerbund und Völkerrecht (edited by the Deutsche Gesellschaft für Völkerrecht; 1934-38), which carried articles, documents, and reviews on the League of Nations and League affairs.

224. Nation und Staat: Deutsche Zeitschrift für das europäische Minoritätenproblem. 17 vols. Vienna, 1927-44.

Analyses of political and legal issues affecting minorities; pleads the German case. Subsidized and supplied with material by the foreign ministry.

225. Völkerbund-Fragen. Edited by Deutsche Gesellschaft für Völkerbundfragen. 4 vols. Berlin, 1924-27. (Superseded by Völkerbund: Chronik, Materialien, Kritik, edited by the Deutsche Liga für Völkerbund [1928-31].)

German views on the League of Nations and on Germany's membership in the League, expressed by academics and lawyers and sometimes by members of the government. The foreign ministry subsidized both the Deutsche Gesellschaft and the Deutsche Liga.

226. Der Weg zur Freiheit: Monatsschrift des Arbeitsausschusses deutscher Verbände. 17 vols. Berlin, 1920-37.

A monthly newsletter of the confederation of revisionist lobbies, reporting on the activities of its corporate members.

227. Zeitschrift für ausländisches öffentliches Recht und Völkerrecht. 12 vols. Leipzig, 1929-44.

Interpretations of international law (both doctrine and practice) from the German point of view. Documents on international affairs reproduced in the original. Bibliography of articles, often with abstracts, from around 500 journals.

228. Zeitschrift für Geopolitik. Edited by Karl Haushofer. 21 vols. Berlin, 1924-44.

Review of current events. Articles often with strong theoretical bias; review essays.

Monographs

229. Anon. Der Kampf um die deutsche Aussenpolitik. Leipzig, 1931.

Explores the pros and cons of the various issues confronting Germany in foreign affairs. Said to have been written by a senior member of the foreign ministry.

230. Beer, Max. Die auswärtige Politik des Dritten Reiches. Zurich, 1934.

Author was a German journalist in Geneva and an official of the League secretariat in the 1920s. Contrasts Nazi policies and its characteristics with Weimar policy and its accomplishments.

231. Berber, Fritz. Die völkerrechtspolitische Lage Deutschlands. Berlin, 1936.

Legal analysis and defense of Germany's international position, by the then director of studies of the Institut für Auswärtige Politik, Hamburg.

232. Bitter, F.W., and Zelle, Arnold. Die Krankheit Europas: Handbuch für die deutsche Freiheitspolitik. Freiburg i.B., 1932.

Argues that the peace treaty must be revised before Europe can recover politically and spiritually.

233. Boehm, Max Hildebert. Die deutschen Grenzlande. Berlin, 1925.

A sequel to his Europa Irredenta (1924), both a history of Germany's borderlands and a drawn-out defense of her rights and claims to these lands. Boehm was director of the Institut für Grenz- und Auslandsstudien in Berlin.

234. Bülow, Bernhard W. von. Der Versailler Völkerbund: Eine vorläufige Bilanz. Stuttgart, 1923.

A critical analysis of the League of Nations, with recommendations for German policy, by the head of the foreign ministry's Völkerbundsreferat and later state secretary.

235. Deutsche Liga für Völkerbund, ed. Deutschland und der Völkerbund. Berlin, 1926.

A semi-official tract, by the German League-of-Nations Union, advocating membership in the League. See also Die Politik Deutschlands im Völkerbund (Geneva, 1932), by Ernst Jäckh and Wolfgang Schwarz, both of whom were associated with the Deutsche Liga.

236. Dewall, Wolf von. Der Kampf um den Frieden: Deutschland-Frankreich in der europäischen Politik. Frankfurt/M., 1929.

A history of Germany's attempt to achieve reconciliation with France, by a journalist of the Frankfurter Zeitung. Indicative of its tenor is the dedication to Stresemann, Schubert, and Gaus.

237. Dieckhoff, Hans Heinrich. Zur Vorgeschichte des Roosevelt-Krieges. Berlin, 1943.

By the former German ambassador to the United States (1937-41), the first volume of a series entitled Die Entstehung des Krieges von 1939, published under the auspices of the Deutsches Institut für Aussenpolitische Forschung.

238. Draeger, Hans. Die deutsche Revisionsbewegung: Ihre bisherige Entwicklung und künftige Ziele. Berlin, 1927.

A brief description of Germany's "revisionist movement," by the head of the Arbeitsausschuss deutscher Verbände.

239. Freytagh-Loringhoven, Axel von. Deutschlands Aussenpolitik, 1933-1941. 11th ed. Berlin, 1943.

Author was professor of law at Breslau and a member of the Reichstag, where he belonged to the right wing of the DNVP, from 1924 to 1933. This account, a quasi-scholarly defense of Nazi policy, was updated regularly.

240. ———. Kriegsausbruch und Kriegsschuld, 1939. Essen, 1940.

A critique of the various "colored books" on the origins and outbreak of war.

241. Funk, Walther. Grundsätze der deutschen Aussenpolitik und das Problem der internationalen Verschuldung. Berlin, 1938.

Treatise on the essential elements of Nazi foreign policy as related to the international debt problem, by the Minister of Economics (1933-45).

242. Heiss, Friedrich, and Ziegfeld, A. Hillen, eds. Deutschland und der Korridor. Berlin, 1933 (republished in 1939 by Friedrich Heiss et al.).

Colorful descriptions of the "bleeding" borders in the East. See also Fritz Rathenau, Deutschlands Ostnot (3d ed., Berlin, 1931); author was an official in the Prussian ministry of interior.

243. Hoetzsch, Otto, and Freytagh-Loringhoven, Axel von. Deutsche Aussenpolitik und Nationale Opposition. Berlin, 1926.

Harsh critique of Stresemann's policy by members of the DNVP Fraktion in the Reichstag. Similarly, Karl Mehrmann, Locarno-Thoiry-Genf in Wirklichkeit (Berlin, 1928).

244. Koch-Weser, Erich. Deutschlands Aussenpolitik in der Nachkriegszeit, 1919-1929. 3d ed. Berlin, 1930.

Review of policy, with some recommendations, by the chairman of the DDP.

245. Kriegk, Otto. Das Ende von Versailles: Die Aussenpolitik des Deutschen Reiches. Oldenburg, 1934.

Representative of the conservative interpretation of the focus and direction of German foreign policy.

246. Rheinbaben, Werner von. Von Versailles zur Freiheit: Weg und Ziel der deutschen Aussenpolitik. Hamburg, 1927.

A clear statement of Germany's revisionist case in the 1920s, by a member of Stresemann's party in the Reichstag and for a while Stresemann's state secretary in the chancellery. His views a dozen years later are in Um ein neues Europa (Berlin, 1939).

247. Rogge, Heinrich. Hitlers Friedenspolitik und das Völkerrecht. Berlin, 1935.

―――. Kollektivsicherheit, Bündnispolitik, Völkerbund. Berlin, 1937.

―――. Hitlers Versuche zur Verständigung mit England. Berlin, 1940.

On Hitler's efforts to work toward a peaceful Europe within the framework of international law, defeated by self-centered and hostile powers. The last of the three is part of a series--Das Britische Reich in der Weltpolitik--published by the Deutsches Institut für Aussenpolitische Forschung.

248. Schacht, Hjalmar. Das Ende der Reparationen. Berlin, 1931.

Author was president of the Reichsbank and involved in the reparations negotiations of 1929. He attacks the government for alleged flaws in the settlement. For a government rejoinder, see below, no. 437.

249. Schmidt, Richard, and Grabowsky, Adolf, eds. <u>Deutschlands Kampf um Gleichberechtigung</u>. Berlin, 1934. (Trl. as <u>Disarmament and Equal Rights</u> [Berlin, 1934].)

A collection of documents and of essays by members of Germany's disarmament delegation, all offered in evidence for the futility of the disarmament negotiations of 1933-34.

250. Schnee, Heinrich, and Draeger, Hans, eds. <u>Zehn Jahre Versailles</u>. 3 vols. Berlin, 1929-30.

The first two volumes deal with Germany's legal right to the revision of the treaty and with the economic and political implications of its terms. The third, edited by K.C. von Loesch and M.H. Boehm, focuses on the territorial and demographic consequences of the treaty.

251. Schwendemann, Karl. <u>Versailles nach 15 Jahren</u>. Berlin, 1935.

A review of the treaty after fifteen years: each individual clause is examined for what it is, what it did, and what became of it.

252. Schwendemann, Karl, ed. <u>Abrüstung und Sicherheit</u>. 2d ed. 2 vols. Leipzig, 1933-34.

————. <u>Gleiches Recht und gleiche Sicherheit</u>. Berlin, 1934.

On the disarmament conference and its failure to provide Germany with equal rights. The first title is an account of the negotiations through 1934, with an appendix of numerous documents, especially German documents. The second is a statement of official grievances. Author was an official in the foreign ministry.

253. Troeltsch, Ernst. <u>Spektator-Briefe: Aufsätze über die deutsche Revolution und die Weltpolitik, 1918-1922</u>. Tübingen, 1924.

Essays on political and diplomatic developments, often based on inside information.

254. Truckenbrodt, Walter. <u>Deutschland und der Völkerbund: Die Behandlung reichsdeutscher Angelegenheiten im Völkerbundsrat, 1920-1939</u>. Essen, 1941.

Criticizes League action (or inaction) on issues of interest to Germany. Herbert Michaelis's <u>Der Völkerbund im Dienste von Versailles</u> (Berlin, 1941) sticks closely to Truckenbrodt's documentation.

255. Truhart, Herbert von. <u>Völkerbund und Minderheitenpetitionen</u>. Vienna, 1931.

Analysis of the League's response to minority petitions, especially from German minorities, by a member of the Ausschuss für Minderheitenrecht.

A collection of essays indicating the kinds of redress Germans expected the minorities to get is Fritz Wertheimer, <u>Deutschland, die Minderheiten und der Völkerbund</u> (Berlin, 1926).

256.   Wentzcke, Paul. <u>Ruhrkampf: Einbruch und Abwehr im rheinisch-westfälischen Industriegebiet</u>. 2 vols. Berlin, 1930-32.

A detailed, heavily documented history of the occupation of the Ruhr, as seen through German eyes.

257.   Ziegler, Wilhelm. <u>Versailles: Die Geschichte eines missglückten Friedens</u>. 3d ed. Hamburg, 1933.

Typical of the nationalist view of what happened at Versailles and why it happened. Uses extensive documentation (virtually all that was available at the time), but only to prove his case.

C. HISTORIES

1. General Histories of Germany, 1918-45

This is not a historiographical survey, but a selection of recent works on German history and especially on German diplomatic history. It provides insight into the current state of research and trends of interpretation. Works addressing themselves primarily to questions of interpretation are listed below under Interpretations and Perspectives (pp. 129-30).

General histories of international affairs between the wars necessarily deal extensively with Germany. The most thorough and informative among these are Maurice Baumont's La faillite de la paix (5th ed., Paris, 1967-68), Jean-Baptiste Duroselle's Histoire diplomatique de 1919 à nos jours (7th ed., Paris, 1978), and Pierre Renouvin's Les crises du 20e siècle (5th ed., Paris, 1970). Gordon A. Craig and Felix Gilbert, eds., The Diplomats, 1919-1939 (Princeton, 1953), reconstructs the diplomatic history of those years through the careers of leading diplomats.

An extensive, annotated bibliography on the Weimar Republic is Peter D. Stachura, The Weimar Era and Hitler, 1918-1933 (Oxford, 1977). There is nothing like it for the Nazi regime, though Peter Hüttenberger's Bibliographie zum Nationalsozialismus (Göttingen, 1980) and the list of books in Bracher and in Hildebrand (below, no. 259) are some compensation.

Documentary Collection

258.   Michaelis, Herbert, et al., eds. Ursachen und Folgen: Vom deutschen Zusammenbruch 1918 und 1945 bis zur staatlichen Neuordnung Deutschlands in der Gegenwart. Berlin, 1958-.

   Designed for general audiences, it is one of the most useful series of its kind. Diplomatic documents, government declarations, party programs, speeches and letters, all arranged chronologically by subject. The first volume of a two-volume biographical index, a virtual who's who on 1919-45, appeared in 1979.

General Histories

259.   Bracher, Karl Dietrich. Die deutsche Diktatur. Cologne, 1969. (Trl. as The German Dictatorship [New York, 1970].)

The best introduction to the subject--well informed, judicious. Good bibliography.

A briefer synthesis, reflecting the scholarship of the intervening years, is Klaus Hildebrand, Das Dritte Reich (3d ed., Munich, 1987). Includes a survey of past and present research, and a classified bibliography of published sources and secondary literature.

260. Bracher, Karl Dietrich, Funke, Manfred, and Jacobsen, Hans-Adolf, eds. Nationalsozialistische Diktatur, 1933-1945: Eine Bilanz. Düsseldorf, 1983.

A collection of essays previously published, primarily by German authors.

261. ———. Die Weimarer Republik, 1918-1933: Politik, Wirtschaft, Gesellschaft. Düsseldorf, 1987.

Similar to the anthology above (no. 260), a useful compendium of current scholarship, with a good bibliography.

See also, Karl-Dietrich Erdmann and Hagen Schulze, eds., Weimar: Selbstpreisgabe einer Demokratie (Düsseldorf, 1980), another such collection.

262. Bruno Gebhardt: Handbuch der deutschen Geschichte. Edited by Herbert Grundmann. Vol. 4. 9th ed. Stuttgart, 1973-76.

Handbuch der deutschen Geschichte. Edited by Leo Just et al. Vol. 4. Konstanz, 1968-71.

Two standard handbooks on German history, useful for reference. Different chapters are written by different historians: the chapters on Germany between 1918 and 1945 were done by Erdmann (in Gebhardt) and by Schwarz, Hofer, and Michaelis (in Just). Compendious; good bibliographies.

263. Craig, Gordon A. Germany, 1866-1945. New York, 1978.

Strong on political and diplomatic developments, likely to remain a standard reference work for some time to come.

See also, Hajo Holborn, A History of Modern Germany, 1840-1945 (New York, 1969), and A.J. Ryder, Twentieth-Century Germany (New York, 1973), a good introduction.

264. Heiber, Helmut, et al. Deutsche Geschichte seit dem ersten Weltkrieg. 3 vols. Stuttgart, 1971-73.

Written by members of the Institut für Zeitgeschichte in Munich. The first two volumes contain carefully coordinated book-length studies of the Weimar Republic (Heiber), Nazi Germany (Broszat), Germany's interwar economy (Petzina), international affairs between the wars (Graml), and World War II (Gruchmann). These are also available separately in paperback. The third volume, an archival guide and bibliography, is listed above (no. 7).

265. Schulz, Gerhard. <u>Deutschland seit dem Ersten Weltkrieg, 1918-1945</u>. 2d ed. Göttingen, 1982.

Brief survey, with special interest in tracing the connections between politics and economics and between internal and external affairs, and in placing German affairs into their international setting. Bibliographical essay.

See also, Jacques Bariéty and Jacques Droz, <u>République de Weimar et régime hitlérien, 1918-1945</u> (Paris, 1973).

266. Schulze, Hagen. <u>Weimar: Deutschland 1917-1933</u>. Berlin, 1982.

A sophisticated, comprehensive text.

For an introductory summary of the history of Weimar, a survey of the literature and current research, and an extensive bibliography, see Eberhard Kolb, <u>Die Weimarer Republik</u> (2d ed., Munich, 1988), trl. as <u>The Weimar Republic</u> (London, 1988).

267. Thamer, Hans-Ulrich. <u>Verführung und Gewalt: Deutschland 1933-1945</u>. Berlin, 1986.

In the same series as Schulze (no. 266); comprehensive and up to date.

2. Diplomatic Histories of Germany, 1918-45

268. Hiden, John W. <u>Germany and Europe, 1919-1939</u>. London, 1977.

Introductory survey of German foreign relations, with equal attention to the Weimar and the Nazi phases. Stresses the importance of economic factors and domestic context, and argues for the unique and strongly ideological quality of Hitler's policy.

269. Hillgruber, Andreas. <u>Die Zerstörung Europas: Beiträge zur Weltkriegsepoche 1914 bis 1945</u>. Berlin, 1988.

A collection of essays by the author, including essays on German foreign policy in Southeastern Europe, on the relations between Germany and Poland, 1933-45, and on Hitler's policy toward the USSR and toward his allies.

270. Kochan, Lionel. <u>The Struggle for Germany, 1914-1945</u>. Chicago, 1963.

A deliberately provocative essay on the diplomatic contest between Russia and the West for Germany's allegiance.

271. Krüger, Peter. Die Aussenpolitik der Republik von Weimar. Darmstadt, 1985.

The first modern history of the subject, based on thorough archival research. Ranges broadly over the entire subject, from 1918 to 1930, with the central argument that Weimar foreign policy must be seen as more complex and ramified than mere revisionism, especially under Stresemann, when it became a policy of conciliation with the objective of returning Germany to the rank of great powers, and more than merely a phase in the continuity of policy from the Empire to the Third Reich.

272. ———. Versailles: Deutsche Aussenpolitik zwischen Revisionismus und Friedenssicherung. Munich, 1986.

Not just a summary or recapitulation of his larger work (no. 271), this book focuses on the problems of a foreign policy seeking to adjust and relate to the policies of the western democracies, the requirements of a highly developed industrial power, and the dilemma of traditional nationalism and international linkages.

273. Rössler, Hellmuth, ed. Ideologie und Machtpolitik, 1919. Göttingen, 1966.

———. Die Folgen von Versailles, 1919-1924. Göttingen, 1969.

———. Locarno und die Weltpolitik, 1924-1932. Göttingen, 1969.

Hauser, Oswald, ed. Weltpolitik, 1933-1939. Göttingen, 1973.

———. Weltpolitik, 1939-1945. Göttingen, 1975.

Papers and proceedings from a series of conferences on world politics between 1919 and 1945. Some of the essays stand out: that by Deist on disarmament (v. 3), those by Jacobsen and Hillgruber on 1938-39 (v. 4), and those by Hillgruber and Hildebrand on World War II (v. 5).

274. Weinberg, Gerhard L. The Foreign Policy of Hitler's Germany: Diplomatic Revolution in Europe, 1933-1936. Chicago, 1970.

———. The Foreign Policy of Hitler's Germany: Starting World War II, 1937-1939. Chicago, 1980.

Based on an unrivaled knowledge of the sources, this is the foremost history of Hitler's policy and diplomacy in the 1930s.

275. Wendt, Bernd-Jürgen. Grossdeutschland: Aussenpolitik und Kriegsvorbereitung des Hitler-Regimes. Munich, 1987.

Examines the Nazi preparation of war with a broad look at Germany's economic policy, rearmament and strategy, ideology and the mobilization of masses. Considers government decision-making, the role of personality, and pressures independent of personality. Interprets Nazi foreign policy in line of continuity since 1870.

276. Zimmermann, Ludwig. Deutsche Aussenpolitik in der Ära der Weimarer Republik. Göttingen, 1958.

An early work, based on limited sources, and written from the perspective of the interwar period. Now largely superseded by specialized studies.

An introduction, reflecting research since Zimmermann, is Marshall Lee and Wolfgang Michalka, Deutsche Aussenpolitik, 1917-1933: Kontinuität oder Bruch? (Stuttgart, 1980), trl. as German Foreign Policy, 1917-1933: Continuity or Break? (New York, 1987). It provides a useful survey of recent literature and deals with the major historiographical debates.

3. Interpretations and Perspectives

277. Calleo, David. The German Problem Reconsidered: Germany and the World Order, 1870 to the Present. New York, 1978.

A fresh look at Germany and her international position over the last hundred years. Considers previous interpretations centered too narrowly on Germany and therefore unable to answer "the big questions."

278. Dehio, Ludwig. Deutschland und die Weltpolitik im 20. Jahrhundert. Munich, 1955.

Essays on Germany's role in world affairs in the first half of this century and on the opinions of what that role should be.

279. Fischer, Fritz. Der Erste Weltkrieg und das deutsche Geschichtsbild. Düsseldorf, 1977.

————. Bündnis der Eliten: Zur Kontinuität der Machtstrukturen in Deutschland 1871-1914. Düsseldorf, 1979. (Trl. as From Kaiserreich to Third Reich, London, 1986.)

Jacobsen, Hans-Adolf. "Zur Kontinuität und Diskontinuität in der deutschen Aussenpolitik im 20. Jahrhundert." In Von der Strategie der Gewalt zur Politik der Friedenssicherung (Düsseldorf, 1977), pp. 9-32.

Jarausch, Konrad H. "From Second to Third Reich: The Problem of Continuity in German Foreign Policy." Central European History, 12 (1979), 68-82.

Stürmer, Michael. "Jenseits des Nationalstaats: Bemerkungen zum deutschen Kontinuitätsproblem." Politik und Kultur (1975), 119-38.

Turner, Henry A., Jr. "Continuity in German Foreign Policy? The Case of Stresemann." The International History Review, 1 (1979), 509-21. ("Stresemann und das Problem der Kontinuität in der deutschen Aussenpolitik," in Grundfragen der deutschen Aussenpolitik seit 1871, edited by Gilbert Ziebura [Darmstadt, 1975], pp. 284-304.)

Wereszycki, Henryk. "From Bismarck to Hitler: The Problems of Continuity from the Second to the Third Reich." Polish Western Affairs, 14 (1973), 19-32.

Contributions to the historiographical debate on continuity in German foreign policy.

280.   Hillgruber, Andreas. Deutsche Grossmacht- und Weltpolitik im 19. und 20. Jahrhundert. Düsseldorf, 1977.

———. Deutschlands Rolle in der Vorgeschichte der beiden Weltkriege. Göttingen, 1967. (Trl. as Germany and the Two World Wars [Cambridge, MA, 1981].)

———. Die gescheiterte Grossmacht: Eine Skizze des Deutschen Reiches, 1871-1945. 3rd ed., Düsseldorf, 1982.

———. Grossmachtpolitik und Militarismus im 20. Jahrhundert. Düsseldorf, 1974.

———. Kontinuität und Diskontinuität in der deutschen Aussenpolitik von Bismarck bis Hitler. Düsseldorf, 1969.

———. Die Last der Nation: Fünf Beiträge über Deutschland und die Deutschen. Düsseldorf, 1984.

Essays illustrating the author's "new political historiography," which puts the emphasis on power politics as the deciding element in international relations. Central to these studies, which range from Bismarck to World War II, is the issue of historical continuity in foreign policy.

For a challenge and critical review, see Wilhelm Alff, Materialien zum Kontinuitätsproblem der deutschen Geschichte (Frankfurt/M., 1976), pp. 142-51.

D. WEIMAR GERMANY

1. Weimar Foreign Policy

Weimar foreign policy has not received the attention Nazi foreign policy has. Scholars have addressed themselves to narrow and specific topics and only recently have they turned to broader, more general questions. No one has done for the Weimar Republic what Jacobsen has done for Nazi Germany, assessing the role of the foreign ministry on the basis of material now available and reconstructing the process of policy formulation and policymaking. Nor has anyone explored the interaction between the economy and foreign policy, as Mason and Petzina have done for the 1930s, or how foreign policy emerged from rival conceptions as these were discussed in public forums, such as the press, in parliament and within the political parties, and in the various ministries. There is no comprehensive study of the foreign policy in the Republic's final phase; there are no satisfactory biographies of the various foreign ministers or the major diplomats.

A general bibliography is Peter D. Stachura, The Weimar Era and Hitler, 1918-1933 (Oxford, 1977); an annotated list of recent articles is in ABC-Clio Information Services, The Weimar Republic: A Historical Bibliography (Santa Barbara, CA, 1984). Martin Walsdorff's Bibliographie Gustav Stresemann (Düsseldorf, 1972) lists Stresemann's own writings and covers publications through 1971. Alfons Esser's Bibliographie zu den deutsch-chinesischen Beziehungen, 1860-1945 (Munich, 1984) has a section on the Weimar period.

General

See also, Berber (no. 216); Krüger (nos. 271, 272); Michalka and Lee (no. 276); Schwendemann (no. 251); Zimmermann (no. 276).

281.   Becker, Josef. "Probleme der Aussenpolitik Brünings." In Internationale Beziehungen in der Weltwirtschaftskrise 1929-1933, edited by Josef Becker and Klaus Hildebrand. Munich, 1980, pp. 265-86.

282.   Carsten, Francis L. Britain and the Weimar Republic: The British Documents. London, 1984.

British diplomats reporting on Weimar and Weimar foreign policy, with frequent reference to conversations and interviews with officials in the German Foreign Ministry.

283.   Conze, Werner. "Deutschlands weltpolitische Sonderstellung in den zwanziger Jahren." <u>Vierteljahrshefte für Zeitgeschichte</u>, 9 (1961), 166-77.

284.   Euler, Heinrich. <u>Die Aussenpolitik der Weimarer Republik, 1918-1923</u>. Aschaffenburg, 1957.

285.   Grupp, Peter. <u>Deutsche Aussenpolitik im Schatten von Versailles, 1918-1920</u>. Paderborn, 1988.

German foreign policy between November 1918 and January 1920, as conducted by the foreign ministry. Focuses on diplomatic relations other than the peace conference (e.g., Anschluss, Eastern and Southeastern Europe), on the emerging diplomatic style, the means, and the strategic and ideological bases of policy.

286.   Hehl, Ulrich von. <u>Wilhelm Marx, 1863-1946: Eine politische Biographie</u>. Mainz, 1987.

Includes a chapter on Marx's role in foreign policy during his chancellorship, 1924-25.

287.   Hörster-Philipps, Ulrike. <u>Konservative Politik in der Endphase der Weimarer Republik: Die Regierung Franz von Papen</u>. Cologne, 1982.

Includes information on the conception and formulation of Papen's foreign policy and on various specific events (e.g., Lausanne conference).

288.   Kolb, Eberhard. "Internationale Rahmenbedingungen einer demokratischen Neuordnung in Deutschland 1918/19." In Bracher, Funke, and Jacobsen (no. 261), pp. 257-84.

289.   Krüger, Peter. "Die 'Westpolitik' in der Weimarer Republik." In <u>Deutschland und der Westen</u>, edited by Henning Köhler. Berlin, 1984, pp. 105-30.

290.   Kunz, Josef L. <u>Die Revision der Pariser Friedensverträge: Eine völkerrechtliche Untersuchung</u>. Vienna, 1932.

291.   Megerle, Klaus. "Weltwirtschaftskrise und Aussenpolitik. Zum Problem der Kontinuität der deutschen Politik in der Endphase der Weimarer Republik." In <u>Geschichte als politische Wissenschaft</u>, edited by Jürgen Bergmann, Klaus Megerle, and Peter Steinbach. Stuttgart, 1979, pp. 116-40.

292.   Michalka, Wolfgang. "Deutsche Aussenpolitik, 1920-1933." In Bracher, Funke, and Jacobsen (no. 261), pp. 303-26.

293. Weinberg, Gerhard L. "The Defeat of Germany in 1918 and the European Balance of Power." Central European History, 2 (1969), 248-60.

294. Wirth, Josef. "Die deutsche Neutralitätspolitik der Jahre 1922-32." Blätter für deutsche und internationale Politik (1960), 1013-20.

295. Zsigmond, Lázló. Zur deutschen Frage, 1918-1923: Die wirtschaftlichen und internationalen Faktoren der Wiederbelebung des deutschen Imperialismus und Militarismus. Budapest, 1964.

Foreign Ministers and the Foreign Ministry

See also, Brüning (no. 108); Stresemann (no. 75).

296. Berglar, Peter. Walther Rathenau: Seine Zeit, sein Werk, seine Persönlichkeit. Bremen, 1970.

An early work, still valuable for its insights, is Harry Kessler, Walther Rathenau: Sein Leben und sein Werk (Berlin, 1928).

297. Bretton, Henry L. Stresemann and the Revision of Versailles: A Fight for Reason. Stanford, 1953.

298. Breuning, Eleonore. "Brockdorff-Rantzau: The 'Wanderer between Two Worlds'." In Essays in Honour of E.H. Carr, edited by C. Abramsky. London, 1974, pp. 126-51.

299. Brüning, Heinrich. Reden und Aufsätze eines deutschen Staatsmannes. Edited by Wilhelm Vernekohl and Rudolf Morsey. Münster, 1968.

Includes the famous Brief of 1947, as well as several speeches on foreign policy from 1930-32.

300. Conze, Werner. "Brüning als Reichskanzler: Eine Zwischenbilanz." Historische Zeitschrift, 214 (1972), 310-34.

Conze's conclusions are challenged in Hermann Graml, "Präsidialsystem und Aussenpolitik," Vierteljahrshefte für Zeitgeschichte, 21 (1973), 134-45.

301. Cornebise, Alfred E. "Gustav Stresemann and the Ruhr Occupation: The Making of a Statesman." European Studies Review, 2 (1972), 43-67.

302. Craig, Gordon A. From Bismarck to Adenauer: Aspects of German Statecraft. Rev. ed. New York, 1965.

On "style" in foreign policy; includes essays on Rathenau, Stresemann, and Brüning.

303. Doss, Kurt. <u>Das Deutsche Auswärtige Amt im Übergang vom Kaiserreich zur Weimarer Republik</u>. Düsseldorf, 1977.

On the structural and personnel changes introduced in the foreign ministry in the transition from empire to republic, with particular emphasis on the "Schüler reforms." See also his "Vom Kaiserreich zur Weimarer Republik: Das deutsche diplomatische Korps in einer Epoche des Umbruchs." In <u>Das diplomatische Korps, 1871-1945</u>, edited by Klaus Schwabe. Boppard, 1985, pp. 81-100.

304. ———. <u>Reichsminister Adolf Köster, 1883-1930: Ein Leben für die Weimarer Republik</u>. Düsseldorf, 1978.

305. ———. <u>Zwischen Weimar und Warschau: Ulrich Rauscher, Deutscher Gesandter in Polen, 1922-1930</u>. Düsseldorf, 1984.

Concise biography of Germany's minister in Poland, one of the "outsiders" in the foreign service, and a study of his views and recommendations on German policy toward Poland.

306. Enssle, Manfred J. "Stresemann's Diplomacy Fifty Years after Locarno: Some Recent Perspectives." <u>Historical Journal</u>, 20 (1977), 937-48.

307. Freymond, Jean. "Gustav Stresemann et l'idée d'une 'Europe économique' (1925-1927)." <u>Relations internationales</u>, 8 (1976), 343-60.

308. Grathwol, Robert. "Gustav Stresemann: Reflections on His Foreign Policy." <u>Journal of Modern History</u>, 45 (1973), 52-70. (Also in Michalka and Lee [no. 316], 224-49.)

309. Gründer, Horst. <u>Walter Simons als Staatsmann, Jurist und Kirchenpolitiker</u>. Neustadt/Aisch, 1975.

Simons served in the ministry's legal department, at Versailles, and as foreign minister in the Fehrenbach cabinet (1920-21).

310. Grupp, Peter, and Jardin, Pierre. "Das Auswärtige Amt und die Entstehung der Weimarer Verfassung." <u>Francia</u>, 9 (1981), 473-93.

Opens up a new area for research.

311. Haupts, Leo. <u>Ulrich Graf von Brockdorff-Rantzau: Diplomat und Minister in Kaiserreich und Republik</u>. Göttingen, 1984.

Brief biography and assessment of Brockdorff-Rantzau's diplomatic career.

312. Helbich, Wolfgang J. "Between Stresemann and Hitler: The Foreign Policy of the Brüning Government." <u>World Politics</u>, 12 (1959), 24-44.

Brüning's foreign policy in broad strokes, now somewhat dated.

313. Hirsch, Felix. Stresemann: Ein Lebensbild. Göttingen, 1978.

Still the most recent of the "popular" biographies. Others, all entitled Stresemann, are by Heinrich Bauer (1929), Walter Görlitz (1947), Rudolf Olden (1929), Rochus von Rheinbaben (1928), and Antonina Vallentin (1930). An interpretive essay, by someone who knew him, is Theodor Eschenburg, "Gustav Stresemann," in Die improvisierte Demokratie (Munich, 1963), 143-226.

See also Wolfgang Stresemann, Mein Vater Gustav Stresemann, enl. ed., Frankfurt, 1985.

A critical review of the literature on Stresemann, still worth reading, is Hans Gatzke, "Gustav Stresemann: A Bibliographical Article," Journal of Modern History, 36 (1964), 1-13.

On the problems involved in writing a biography that would meet modern standards of scholarship, see Eberhard Kolb, "Probleme einer modernen Stresemann-Biographie," in Am Wendepunkt der europäischen Geschichte, edited by Otmar Franz (Göttingen, 1981), 107-34.

314. Krüger, Peter. "Struktur, Organisation und aussenpolitische Wirkungsmöglichkeit der leitenden Beamten des Auswärtigen Dienstes 1921-1933." In Das Diplomatische Korps, 1871-1945, edited by Klaus Schwabe. Boppard, 1985, pp. 101-169.

The first close analysis, based on research in the archives, of the foreign ministry as a bureaucratic organization and of the role and effectiveness of its leading officials.

315. ———. "Zur Bedeutung des Auswärtigen Amts für die Aussenpolitik Stresemanns." In Michalka and Lee (no. 316), 400-15.

316. Michalka, Wolfgang, and Lee, Marshall, eds. Gustav Stresemann. Darmstadt, 1982.

A collection of essays on Stresemann and his policy drawn from books and journals of the previous 25 years.

317. Rathenau, Walther. Gesammelte Schriften. 6 vols. Berlin, 1925-29; Gesammelte Reden. Berlin, 1924; Politische Briefe. Dresden, 1929; Ein preussischer Europäer: Briefe. Edited by Margarete von Eynern. Berlin, 1955.

318. Schieder, Theodor. "Walther Rathenau und die Probleme der deutschen Aussenpolitik." In Discordia Concors, edited by Marc Sieber. Basel, 1968, pp. 239-68.

See also, Eric C. Kollmann, "Walther Rathenau and German Foreign Policy: Thoughts and Actions," Journal of Modern History, 24 (1952), 127-42, and D.G. Williamson, "Walther Rathenau: Realist, Pedagogue, and Prophet, November 1918-May 1921," European Studies Review, 6 (1976), 99-121.

319.   Stresemann, Gustav. Reden und Schriften: Politik, Geschichte, Literatur, 1897-1926. 2 vols. Dresden, 1926.

A selection of Stresemann's most important speeches in the Reichstag is in Gustav Stresemann: Reichstagsreden, edited by Gerhard Zwoch (Bonn, 1972).

On a more specific topic, illustrative of Stresemann's policy in the mid-twenties, see "Eine Rede Stresemanns über seine Locarnopolitik," edited by Henry A. Turner, Jr., Vierteljahrshefte für Zeitgeschichte, 15 (1967), 412-36.

320.   Thimme, Annelise. Gustav Stresemann: Eine politische Biographie zur Geschichte der Weimarer Republik. Hanover, 1957.

A critical study, based on Stresemann's Nachlass. See also her "Gustav Stresemann: Legende und Wirklichkeit," Historische Zeitschrift, 181 (1956), 287-338.

321.   Treviranus, Gottfried Reinhold. Das Ende von Weimar: Heinrich Brüning und seine Zeit. Düsseldorf, 1968.

322.   Vietsch, Eberhard von. Wilhelm Solf: Botschafter zwischen den Zeiten. Tübingen, 1961.

323.   Weidenfeld, Werner. "Gustav Stresemann: Der Mythos vom engagierten Europäer." Geschichte in Wissenschaft und Unterricht, 24 (1973), 740-50.

324.   Wengst, Udo. Graf Brockdorff-Rantzau und die aussenpolitischen Anfänge der Weimarer Republik. Frankfurt/M., 1973.

See also, Herbert Helbig, "Graf Brockdorff-Rantzau und die Demokratie," in Zur Geschichte und Problematik der Demokratie, edited by Wilhelm Berges und Carl Hinrichs (Berlin, 1958), 577-99.

Foreign Policy and the Military

325.   Carsten, Francis L. The Reichswehr and Politics, 1918-1933. New York, 1966.

The German edition is Reichswehr und Politik, 1918-1933 (Cologne, 1964).

326.   Dülffer, Jost. Weimar, Hitler und die Marine: Reichspolitik und Flottenbau, 1920-1939. Düsseldorf, 1973.

Naval policies and strategies, disarmament and rearmament, and their implications for German foreign policy.

327. Geyer, Michael. Aufrüstung oder Sicherheit: Die Reichswehr in der Krise der Machtpolitik, 1924-1936. Wiesbaden, 1980.

Explores the relationship between rearmament, operational planning, and foreign policy, and reconstructs the military's foreign policy orientation.

328. Hansen, Ernst Willi. Reichswehr und Industrie: Rüstungswirtschaftliche Zusammenarbeit und wirtschaftliche Mobilmachungsvorbereitungen, 1923-1932. Boppard, 1978.

329. Meier-Welcker, Hans. Seeckt. Frankfurt/M., 1967.

The definitive biography. Still useful for the original material it contains is Friedrich von Rabenau, Seeckt: Aus Seinem Leben, 1918-1936 (Leipzig, 1940).

330. Post, Gaines, Jr. The Civil-Military Fabric of Weimar Foreign Policy. Princeton, 1973.

Analyzes the aims and means of German policies by examining the relationship between military planning and foreign policy.

331. Rahn, Werner. Reichsmarine und Landesverteidigung, 1919-1928. Munich, 1976.

332. Salewski, Michael. "Marineleitung und politische Führung, 1931-1935." Militärgeschichtliche Mitteilungen, 10 (1971), 113-58.

On the relations between Admiral Raeder and the government; with an appendix of documents from 1931-34.

333. Schreiber, Gerhard. Revisionismus und Weltmachtstreben: Marineführung und deutsch-italienische Beziehungen, 1919 bis 1944. Stuttgart, 1978.

Parties and Interest Groups

334. Bariéty, Jacques. "Das Zustandekommen der Internationalen Rohstahlgemeinschaft (1926) als Alternative zum misslungenen 'Schwerindustriellen Projekt' des Versailler Vertrags." In Mommsen (no. 364), 552-68.

335. Berndt, Roswitha. "Wirtschaftliche Mitteleuropapläne des deutschen Imperialismus (1926-1931); Zur Rolle des Mitteleuropäischen Wirtschaftstages und des Mitteleuropa-Institutes in den imperialistischen deutschen Expansionsplänen." In Grundfragen der deutschen Aussenpolitik seit 1871, edited by Gilbert Ziebura. Darmstadt, 1975, pp. 305-34.

336.   "Die deutschen Parteien und ihre Aussenpolitik." Europäische Gespräche, 4 (1926), 169-97, 223-38, 339-65.

Summary statements of the foreign-policy views of the different political parties, by their respective foreign-policy spokesmen.

337.   Fiedor, Karol. "Die deutschen pazifistischen Bewegungen und das Problem der deutsch-polnischen Beziehungen in der Zwischenkriegszeit." Jahrbuch für die Geschichte Mittel- und Ostdeutschlands, 24 (1975), 143-63.

See also, Rosemarie Schumann, "Initiativen deutscher Pazifisten gegen die reaktionäre Polenpolitik in der Weimarer Republik," Zeitschrift für Geschichtswissenschaft, 22 (1974), 1223-32.

338.   ———. "The Attitude of German Right-Wing Organizations to Poland in the Years 1918-1933." Polish Western Affairs, 14 (1973), 247-69.

See also, Wolfgang Ruge, "Zur chauvinistischen Propaganda gegen den Versailler Vertrag, 1919 bis 1929," Jahrbuch für Geschichte, 1 (1969), 65-106.

339.   Frommelt, Richard. Paneuropa oder Mitteleuropa: Einigungsbestrebungen im Kalkül deutscher Wirtschaft und Politik, 1925-1933. Stuttgart, 1977.

340.   Gossweiler, Kurt. Grossbanken, Industriemonopole, Staat: Ökonomie und Politik des staatsmonopolistischen Kapitalismus in Deutschland, 1914-1932. [East] Berlin, 1971.

341.   Grathwol, Robert P. Stresemann and the DNVP: Reconciliation or Revenge in German Foreign Policy, 1924-1928. Lawrence, KS, 1980.

Focuses on the influence of the DNVP in shaping the substance and conduct of Stresemann's foreign policy. Interesting material on the interaction of foreign and domestic policy, and on Stresemann's strategies in dealing with the DNVP.

342.   Hagspiel, Hermann. Verständigung zwischen Deutschland und Frankreich? Die deutsch-französische Aussenpolitik der zwanziger Jahre im innenpolitischen Kräftefeld beider Länder. Bonn, 1987.

The policy of reconciliation as it was influenced and understood by the political parties and public opinion.

343.   Hess, Jürgen C. "Das ganze Deutschland soll es sein": Demokratischer Nationalismus in der Weimarer Republik am Beispiel der Deutschen Demokratischen Partei. Stuttgart, 1978.

On the DDP and foreign policy. See also his "'Das ganze Deutschland soll es sein' -- Die republikanischen Parteien und die Deutsche Frage in der Weimarer Republik." In Die Deutsche Frage im 19. und 20. Jahrhundert, edited by Josef Becker and Andreas Hillgruber. Munich, 1983, pp. 277-317.

344. Holl, Karl. "Europapolitik im Vorfeld der deutschen Regierungspolitik: Zur Tätigkeit pro-europäischer Organisationen in der Weimarer Republik." Historische Zeitschrift, 219 (1974), 33-94.

345. Holz, Kurt. Die Diskussion um den Dawes- und Young-Plan in der deutschen Presse. Frankfurt/M., 1977.

346. Pistorius, Peter. Rudolf Breitscheid, 1874-1944. Cologne, 1970.

A biography of the SPD spokesman on foreign affairs in the Reichstag. See also, Rudolf Breitscheid: Reichstagsreden, edited by Gerhard Zwoch (Gütersloh, 1974).

347. Pohl, Karl H. "Die Finanzkrise bei Krupp und die Sicherheitspolitik Stresemanns: Ein Beitrag zum Verhältnis von Wirtschaft und Aussenpolitik in der Weimarer Republik." Vierteljahrsschrift für Sozial- und Wirtschaftsgeschichte, 61 (1974), 505-25.

348. ―――. "Die 'Stresemannsche Aussenpolitik' und das westeuropäische Eisenkartell 1926: 'Europäische Politik' oder nationales Interesse?" Vierteljahrsschrift für Sozial- und Wirtschaftsgeschichte, 65 (1978), 511-34.

349. Rieseberg, Klaus E. "Die SPD in der 'Locarnokrise,' Oktober-November 1925." Vierteljahrshefte für Zeitgeschichte, 30 (1982), 130-61.

Documentation on the position of the SPD on the Locarno agreements.

350. Spiller, Jörg-Otto. "Reformismus nach Rechts: Zur Politik des Reichsverbandes der Deutschen Industrie in den Jahren 1927-1930 am Beispiel der Reparationspolitik." In Mommsen (no. 364), 593-602.

351. Wulf, Peter. Hugo Stinnes: Wirtschaft und Politik, 1918-1924. Stuttgart, 1979.

Economics and Foreign Policy

352. Bennett, Edward W. Germany and the Diplomacy of the Financial Crisis, 1931. Cambridge, MA, 1962.

353. Born, Karl Erich. Die deutsche Bankenkrise 1931: Finanzen und Politik. Munich, 1967.

354. Büsch, Otto, and Feldman, Gerald D., eds. Historische Prozesse der deutschen Inflation 1914 bis 1924. Berlin, 1978.

Feldman, Gerald D., et al., eds. Die deutsche Inflation: Eine Zwischenbilanz. Berlin, 1982.

Feldman, Gerald D., ed. Die Nachwirkungen der Inflation auf die deutsche Geschichte, 1924-1933. Munich, 1985.

Part of a broad international research project on the causes and effects of the German inflation, these volumes include studies on German trade policy, international trade, the impact of the inflation on German foreign policy and on the international economy, and the relationship between finance and foreign policy. See also Carl-Ludwig Holtfrerich, Die deutsche Inflation, 1914-1923: Ursachen und Folgen in internationaler Perspektive, Berlin, 1980. (Trl. as The German Inflation, 1914-1923, Berlin, 1986.)

355. Dietrich, Erich. Die deutsch-französischen Wirtschaftsverhandlungen der Nachkriegszeit. Berlin, 1931.

See also, Hermann Corsten, Deutschlands Wirtschaftsverflechtung mit seinen westlichen Nachbarn (Cologne, 1940).

356. Gessner, Dieter. "Agrarprotektionismus und Welthandelskrise 1929/32: Zum Verhältnis von Agrarpolitik und Handelspolitik in der Endphase der Weimarer Republik." Zeitschrift für Agrargeschichte und Agrarsoziologie, 26 (1978/79), 161-87.

357. Habedank, Heinz. Die Reichsbank in der Weimarer Republik: Zur Rolle der Zentralbank in der Politik des deutschen Imperialismus, 1919-1933. [East] Berlin, 1981.

On the role of the Reichsbank in foreign policy (reparations, trade and credit policy in eastern Europe, the Young and Dawes plans), based on the Reichsbank documents in the archives in Potsdam. Marxist perspective.

358. Haberland, G. 11 Jahre staatliche Regelung der Ein- und Ausfuhr: Systematische Darstellung der deutschen Aussenhandelsregelung, 1914-25. Leipzig, 1927.

359. Hardach, Gerd. Weltmarktorientation und relative Stagnation: Währungspolitik in Deutschland, 1924-31. Berlin, 1976.

On the reparations transfer agreements, foreign loans and credits, and the Young plan.

360. Kroll, Gerhard. Von der Weltwirtschaftskrise zur Staatskonjunktur. Berlin, 1958.

361. Lüke, Rolf E. Von der Stabilisierung zur Krise. Zurich, 1958.

362. McNeil, William C. American Money and the Weimar Republic. New York, 1986.

Reconstructs the negotiations for American loans that enabled Germany to make its reparations payments.

363. Milward, Alan S. "Der deutsche Handel und die Weltwirtschaft, 1925-1939." In Mommsen (no. 364), 472-84.

364. Mommsen, Hans, et al., eds. Industrielles System und politische Entwicklung in der Weimarer Republik. Düsseldorf, 1974.

365. Pentzlin, Heinz. Hjalmar Schacht: Leben und Wirken einer umstrittenen Persönlichkeit. Berlin, 1980.

366. Pohl, Karl H. Weimars Wirtschaft und die Aussenpolitik der Republik, 1924-1926: Vom Dawes-Plan zum Internationalen Eisenpakt. Düsseldorf, 1979.

367. Priester, Hans Erich. Der Wiederaufbau der deutschen Handelsschiffahrt. Berlin, 1926.

The negotiations and agreements that led to the resumption of German merchant shipping in the early 1920s.

368. Radkau, Joachim. "Renovation des Imperialismus im Zeichen der 'Rationalisierung': Wirtschaftsimperialistische Strategien in Deutschland von den Stinnes-Projekten bis zum Versuch der deutsch-österreichischen Zollunion, 1922-1931." In Imperialismus im 20. Jahrhundert, edited by Joachim Radkau and Imanuel Geiss. Munich, 1976, pp. 197-264.

369. Schröter, Harm G. Aussenpolitik und Wirtschaftsinteressen: Skandinavien im aussenwirtschaftlichen Kalkül Deutschlands und Grossbritanniens, 1918-1939. Frankfurt/M., 1983.

370. Schröter, Verena. Die deutsche Industrie auf dem Weltmarkt 1929 bis 1933: Aussenwirtschaftliche Strategien unter dem Druck der Weltwirtschaftskrise. Frankfurt/M., 1984.

371. Stegmann, Dirk. "Deutsche Zoll- und Handelspolitik, 1924/5-1929, unter besonderer Berücksichtigung agrarischer und industrieller Interessen." In Mommsen (no. 364), 499-513.

372. ———. " 'Mitteleuropa' 1925-1934: Zum Problem der Kontinuität deutscher Aussenhandelspolitik von Stresemann bis Hitler." In Industrielle Gesellschaft und politisches System, edited by Dirk Stegmann, Bernd-Jürgen Wendt, and Peter-Christian Witt. Bonn, 1978, pp. 203-21.

Minority Policies

373. Blaich, Fritz. Grenzlandpolitik im Westen, 1926-1936: Die "Westhilfe" zwischen Reichspolitik und Länderinteressen. Stuttgart, 1978.

  A counterpart to Osthilfe: government support for the Rhineland and the Saar.

374. Broszat, Martin. "Aussen- und Innenpolitische Aspekte der preussisch-deutschen Minderheitenpolitik in der Ära Stresemann." In Politische Ideologien und Nationalstaatliche Ordnung, edited by Kurt Kluxen and Wolfgang J. Mommsen. Munich, 1968, pp. 393-445.

375. Bruns, Carl Georg. Gesammelte Schriften zur Minderheitenfrage. Berlin, 1934.

  Essays and memoranda by one of the most influential spokesmen for minorities in Germany.

  For a contemporary handbook of information and statistics, see Otto Boelitz, Das Grenz- und Auslandsdeutschtum (2d ed., Berlin, 1930).

376. Fink, Carole. "Stresemann's Minority Policies, 1924-29." Journal of Contemporary History, 14 (1979), 403-22. (Also in Michalka and Lee [no. 316], 375-99.)

377. Gentzen, Felix-Heinrich. "Die Rolle der deutschen Regierung beim Aufbau deutscher Minderheitenorganisationen in den an Polen abgetretenen Gebieten (1919-22)." Jahrbuch für Geschichte der UdSSR und der volksdemokratischen Länder Europas, 10 (1967), 159-82.

378. Grundmann, Karl-Heinz. Deutschtumspolitik zur Zeit der Weimarer Republik: Eine Studie am Beispiel der deutsch-baltischen Minderheit in Estland und Lettland. Hanover, 1977.

  On the dilemmas of German minority policy, on Deutschtum organizations and agencies. Complements Krekeler and Ritter (nos. 381, 384).

379. Hiden, John W. "The Weimar Republic and the Problem of the Auslandsdeutschen." Journal of Contemporary History, 12 (1977), 273-89.

  Examines the network of Deutschtum organizations and the role of the foreign ministry and the government from a perspective that distinguishes them from the Volkstumspolitik of the Nazi era.

380. Jaworski, Rudolf. <u>Vorposten oder Minderheit? Der sudetendeutsche Volkstumskampf in den Beziehungen zwischen der Weimarer Republik und der Tschechoslowakei</u>. Stuttgart, 1977.

381. Krekeler, Norbert. <u>Revisionsanspruch und geheime Ostpolitik der Weimarer Republik: Die Subventionierung der deutschen Minderheit in Polen, 1919-1933</u>. Stuttgart, 1973.

Examines the nature and extent of Germany's clandestine support of German minorities in Poland.

382. Pieper, Helmut. <u>Die Minderheitenfrage und das Deutsche Reich, 1919-1933/34</u>. Frankfurt/M., 1974.

Places German minority policies in the wider context of Germany's revisionist eastern policy.

383. Ratliff, William G. "Julius Curtius, the Minorities Question of 1930-1931, and the <u>Primat der Innenpolitik</u>." <u>German Studies Review</u>, 12 (1989), 271-88.

384. Ritter, Ernst. <u>Das Deutsche Auslands-Institut in Stuttgart, 1917-1945: Ein Beispiel deutscher Volkstumsarbeit zwischen den Weltkriegen</u>. Wiesbaden, 1976.

On the role and activities of the institute that cared for Germans living abroad, on its leadership, its orientation, and its relations with other minority organizations.

385. Schot, Bastiaan. <u>Nation oder Staat? Deutschland und der Minderheitenschutz</u>. Marburg, 1988.

On official policy (with a focus on Stresemann), on the role of the <u>Deutschtum</u> organizations, and on the public ideologies that provided the context. See also his <u>Stresemann, der deutsche Osten und der Völkerbund</u> (Wiesbaden, 1984), a lecture.

2. Armistice and Peace Conference

The literature on the Paris Peace Conference and on the Treaty of Versailles is enormous. Much of it reflects the controversies surrounding the conference and its consequences, and, especially in Germany, the emotions engendered by the lost war and bitter peace. The controversies and emotions have had a distorting effect not only on scholarship, in which the passage of time has only gradually dulled the polemical edge, but also on the published collections of documents, which in their selection and presentation tend less to inform than to advocate.

Max Gunzenhäuser, <u>Die Pariser Friedenskonferenz 1919 und die Friedensverträge 1919-1920</u> (Frankfurt/M., 1970), is a comprehensive bibliography, with a broad-ranging introduction in lieu of annotations. Alfred Diefenbach, "1918--Zusammenbruch und Waffenstillstand: Bericht und

Bibliographie der deutschen Literatur" (Jahresbibliographie der Bibliothek für Zeitgeschichte, 40 [1968], pp. 337-87), covers the German scholarship on the subject and is particularly good on contemporary works.

386.   Auswärtiges Amt, ed. Amtliche Urkunden zur Vorgeschichte des Waffenstillstandes 1918. 2d ed. Berlin, 1924. (Rpt., Frankfurt/M., 1988)

An official White Book on the events preceding Germany's capitulation. For the motives behind its publication, see The Political Education of Arnold Brecht: An Autobiography 1884-1970 (Princeton, 1970).

387.   Baumgart, Winfried. "Brest-Litovsk und Versailles: Ein Vergleich zweier Friedensschlüsse." Historische Zeitschrift, 210 (1970), 583-619.

388.   Borowsky, Peter. "Die 'bolschewistische Gefahr' und die Ostpolitik der Volksbeauftragten in der Revolution 1918/19." In Industrielle Gesellschaft und politisches System, edited by Dirk Stegmann, Bernd-Jürgen Wendt, and Peter-Christian Wendt. Bonn, 1978, pp. 389-403.

389.   Brockdorff-Rantzau, Ulrich Graf. Dokumente und Gedanken um Versailles. 3d ed. Berlin, 1925.

Papers and speeches on his policy, 1918-19. See also his Deutschlands auswärtige Politik (Berlin, 1919), in which he lays out Germany's position.

390.   Crusen, Georg, ed. Waffenstillstandsvertrag, Friedensvertrag und Rheinlandabkommen nebst Verzeichnis der zur Ausführung erlassenen Gesetze. Berlin, 1923.

Documentary record of the legislative implementation of the terms of the armistice, the peace treaty, and the occupation statutes of the Rhineland.

391.   Dickmann, Fritz. "Die Kriegsschuldfrage auf der Friedenskonferenz von Paris 1919." Historische Zeitschrift, 197 (1963), 1-101.

392.   Epstein, Fritz T. "Zwischen Compiègne und Versailles: Geheime amerikanische Militärdiplomatie in der Periode des Waffenstillstandes 1918/19." Vierteljahrshefte für Zeitgeschichte, 3 (1955), 412-45.

Unofficial contacts between the American peace delegation and the German government.

393.   Grupp, Peter. "Vom Waffenstillstand zum Versailler Vertrag: Die aussen- und friedenspolitischen Zielvorstellungen der deutschen

Reichsregierung." In Bracher, Funke, and Jacobsen (no. 261), 285-302.

394. Grupp, Peter, and Jardin, Pierre. "Une tentative de renouvellement de la diplomatie traditionelle: La 'Geschäftsstelle für die Friedensverhandlungen' (1919)." Francia, 13 (1985), 447-73.

395. Hahn, Erich J.C. "The German Foreign Ministry and the Question of War Guilt in 1918-1919." In German Nationalism and the European Response, 1890-1945, edited by Carole Fink, Isabel V. Hull, and MacGregor Knox. Norman, OK, 1985, pp. 43-70.

Deliberations within the foreign ministry on the best strategies for dealing with the accusations of war guilt raised by the allied powers.

396. Haupts, Leo. Deutsche Friedenspolitik 1918-19: Eine Alternative zur Machtpolitik des Ersten Weltkriegs. Düsseldorf, 1976.

Explores the policies put forward by political and economic liberals as alternatives to the traditional Machtpolitik.

See also his "Zur deutschen und britischen Friedenspolitik in der Krise der Pariser Friedenskonferenz: Britisch-deutsche Separatverhandlungen im April/Mai 1919," Historische Zeitschrift, 217 (1973), 54-98.

397. Kraus, Herbert, and Rödiger, Gustav, eds. Urkunden zum Friedensvertrage von Versailles vom 28. Juni 1919. 2 vols. Berlin, 1920-21.

Official documents and correspondence on the armistice and the peace conference, put together to vindicate Germany's protests.

398. Krüger, Peter. Deutschland und die Reparationen 1918/19: Die Genesis des Reparationsproblems in Deutschland zwischen Waffenstillstand und Versailler Friedensschluss. Stuttgart, 1973.

399. ————. "Die Reparationen und das Scheitern einer deutschen Verständigungspolitik auf der Pariser Friedenskonferenz im Jahre 1919," Historische Zeitschrift, 221 (1975), 326-72.

Germany's attempts at a policy of reconciliation and their consequences.

400. Low, Alfred D. Die Anschlussbewegung in Österreich und Deutschland 1918-19 und die Pariser Friedenskonferenz. Vienna, 1975.

For a more summary treatment, see Jerzy Kozenski, "The Problem of an Austro-German Union in 1918-1919," Polish Western Affairs, 8 (1967), 96-133, and Duane P. Myers, "Berlin versus Vienna:

Disagreement about Anschluss in the Winter of 1918-19," Central European History, 5 (1972), 150-75.

401. Luckau, Alma. The German Delegation at the Paris Peace Conference. New York, 1941.

Consists largely of documents, some of them otherwise unavailable.

See also, V. Schiff, So war es in Versailles (Berlin, 1929), by a member of the delegation, and the essays on Carl Melchior, another member, in Verein für Hamburgische Geschichte, ed., Carl Melchior: Ein Buch des Gedenkens und der Freundschaft (Tübingen, 1967).

402. Marhefka, E., et al., eds. Der Waffenstillstand 1918-1919: Das Dokumentenmaterial der Waffenstillstandsverhandlungen. 3 vols. Berlin, 1929.

On the negotiations and renegotiations of the armistice, compiled by several of the negotiators.

403. Mayer, Arno J. Politics and Diplomacy of Peacemaking: Containment and Counterrevolution at Versailles, 1918-1919. New York, 1967.

404. Mühleisen, Horst. "Annehmen oder Ablehnen? Das Kabinett Scheidemann, die Oberste Heeresleitung und der Vertrag von Versailles im Juni 1919." Vierteljahrshefte für Zeitgeschichte, 35 (1987), 419-81.

405. Papers Relating to the Foreign Relations of the United States: The Paris Peace Conference 1919. Edited by the Department of State. 13 vols. Washington, 1942-47.

Contains the official minutes and reports of the various commissions of the peace conference, the correspondence with Germany about the peace, and, very useful, a copy of the treaty annotated to show how the provisions were implemented, how they worked out, and how they were revised (vol. 13). This annotated treaty is available also as The Treaty of Versailles and After: Annotations of the Text of the Treaty (Washington, 1947).

406. Rakenius, Gerhard Wilhelm. Wilhelm Groener als Erster Generalquartiermeister: Die Politik der Obersten Heeresleitung 1918/19. Boppard, 1977.

Documents on the army high command's foreign policy between the armistice and the peace are in Reginald H. Phelps, "Aus den Groener-Dokumenten," Deutsche Rundschau, 76 (1950), 616-25, 830-40.

407. Renouvin, Pierre. L'Armistice de Rethondes: 11 novembre 1918. Paris, 1968.

Based on the latest research; includes extensive bibliography with reference to little-known sources and monographs. (Harry R. Rudin's Armistice 1918 [1944] is now dated.)

408. Schüddekopf, Otto-Ernst. "German Foreign Policy between Compiègne and Versailles." Journal of Contemporary History, 4 (1969), 181-97.

409. Schulze, Hagen. "Der Oststaat-Plan 1919." Vierteljahrshefte für Zeitgeschichte, 19 (1970), 123-63.

410. Schwabe, Klaus. Deutsche Revolution und Wilson-Frieden: Die amerikanische und deutsche Friedenstrategie zwischen Ideologie und Machtpolitik 1918/19. Düsseldorf, 1971.

Massive study of German strategies on the peace negotiations, critical both of Arno Mayer's views (no. 403) and of interpretations that focus on the "betrayal" of Germany's belief in Wilson. (A revised and slightly abridged version appeared in translation as Woodrow Wilson, Revolutionary Germany, and Peacemaking, 1918-1919: Missionary Diplomacy and the Realities of Power, Chapel Hill, NC, 1985.)

411. Schwengler, Walter. Völkerrecht, Versailler Vertrag und Auslieferungsfrage: Die Strafverfolgung wegen Kriegsverbrechen als Problem des Friedensschlusses 1919/20. Stuttgart, 1982.

On Germany's opposition to the peace treaty, with particular emphasis on the treaty's stipulations on war crimes trials and the extradition of war criminals. For the resolution of one particular issue subsequently, see Jürgen Heideking, "Das Ende der Sanktionspolitik: Die Alliierten Mächte und die Rückkehr des deutschen Kronprinzen im November 1923," Francia, 7 (1979), 365-400.

412. Wüest, Erich. Der Vertrag von Versailles im Licht und Schatten der Kritik: Die Kontroverse um seine wirtschaftlichen Auswirkungen. Zurich, 1962.

See also, Hans-Günther Naumann, "Über die wirtschaftlichen Auswirkungen des Versailler Vertrags," Geschichte in Wissenschaft und Unterricht, 21 (1970), 420-37.

3. Weimar and the Peace Settlement

Research on Germany's efforts to revise the peace treaty has focused primarily on three areas: reparations, territorial boundaries, disarmament and rearmament. It has thrown light on the various strategies which the government adopted and on the way it mobilized much of Germany's intellectual establishment to do its part. Among the most interesting findings have been those relating to revisionism's domestic functions and ramifications.

For contemporary bibliographies, see Gunzenhäuser (no. 206), Prinzhorn (no. 212), Reismüller and Hofmann (no. 213), and Schwab and Sveistrup (no. 214).

More recent bibliographies: Herbert Rister, ed., Schlesische Bibliographie, 1928-1957 (8 vols., Marburg, 1953-75), Max Szameitat, ed., Bibliographie des Memellandes (Würzburg, 1957), and Ernst Wermke, ed., Bibliographie der Geschichte von Ost- und Westpreussen bis 1929 (Königsberg, 1933), . . .für die Jahre 1930-1938 (Aalen, 1964), and . . .für die Jahre 1939-1961 (Marburg, 1964).

Reparations

413.   Auswärtiges Amt, ed. Material über die Konferenz von Genua. Berlin, 1922.

————. Die den Alliierten seit dem Waffenstillstand übermittelten deutschen Angebote und Vorschläge zur Lösung der Reparations- und Wiederaufbaufrage. Berlin, 1923.

————. Aktenstücke über den französisch-belgischen Einmarsch in das Ruhrgebiet. Berlin, 1923.

————. Die Londoner Konferenz, Juli-August, 1924. Berlin, 1925.

————. Die auf der Haager Konferenz getroffenen politischen und finanziellen Vereinbarungen. Berlin, 1929.

A series of government publications on reparations conferences and related matters.

414.   Baechler, Christian. "Une difficile négociation franco-allemande aux conférences de Là Haye: Le règlement de la question des sanctions (1929-1930)." Revue d'Allemagne, 12 (1980), 238-60.

415.   Bergmann, Carl. Der Weg der Reparationen: Von Versailles über den Dawesplan zum Ziel. Frankfurt/M., 1926.

A history of reparations negotiations and of German reparations policy, by one of the German experts closely involved in formulating policy and conducting negotiations.

416.   Cornebise, Alfred E. The Weimar Republic in Crisis: Cuno's Germany and the Ruhr Occupation. Washington, 1977.

For an earlier study by the same author, see "Cuno, Germany, and the Coming of the Ruhr Occupation: A Study in German-West European Relations," Proceedings of the American Philosophical Society, 116 (1972), 502-31.

417.   Favez, Jean-Claude. Le Reich devant l'occupation franco-belge de la Ruhr en 1923. Geneva, 1969.

Well-researched and careful; casts light on the antecedents of the occupation.

418.   Felix, David. Walther Rathenau and the Weimar Republic: The Politics of Reparations. Baltimore, 1971.

Rathenau's activity as minister of reconstruction and then as foreign minister; Germany's policies on reparations.

419.   Fink, Carole. The Genoa Conference: European Diplomacy, 1921-22. Chapel Hill, NC, 1984.

The diplomacy of the conference, thorough and detailed, based on extensive archival research.

420.   Glashagen, Winfried. Die Reparationspolitik Heinrich Brünings, 1930-1931: Studien zum wirtschafts- und aussenpolitischen Entscheidungsprozess in der Auflösungsphase der Weimarer Republik. Bonn, 1980.

Takes issue with Helbich (no. 423) regarding the primacy that Brüning attached to the reparations issue.

421.   Gosmann, Winfried. "Die Stellung der Reparationsfrage in der Aussenpolitik der Kabinette Brüning." In Internationale Beziehungen in der Weltwirtschaftskrise, 1929-1933, edited by Josef Becker and Klaus Hildebrand. Munich, 1980, pp. 237-63.

422.   Heilfron, Eduard, and Nassen, Paul, eds. Der Neue Plan: Young-Plan und Haager Vereinbarungen nebst den deutschen Ausführungsvorschriften. Berlin, 1931.

Official documents on the Young plan and its implementation.

423.   Helbich, Wolfgang J. Die Reparationen in der Ära Brüning: Zur Bedeutung des Young-Plans für die deutsche Politik, 1930 bis 1932. Berlin, 1962.

For a different slant, see Henning Köhler, "Arbeitsbeschaffung, Siedlung und Reparationen in der Schlussphase der Regierung Brüning," Vierteljahrshefte für Zeitgeschichte, 17 (1969), 276-307.

424.   Jones, K.P. "Stresemann, the Ruhr Crisis, and Rhenish Separatism: A Case Study of Westpolitik." European Studies Review, 7 (1977), 311-40.

425.   Krohn, Claus-Dieter. Stabilisierung und ökonomische Interessen: Die Finanzpolitik des Deutschen Reiches, 1923-1927. Düsseldorf, 1974.

Informative analysis of the Dawes negotiations and their consequences.

426.   Krüger, Peter. "Das Reparationsproblem der Weimarer Republik in fragwürdiger Sicht: Kritische Überlegungen zur neuesten Forschung." Vierteljahrshefte für Zeitgeschichte, 29 (1981), 21-47.

Critical review of research on the history of reparations between 1919 and 1924, with a close analysis of some major issues (e.g., payments transfer, implications of reparations on foreign trade). See also, Carl-Ludwig Holtfrerich, "Eine Chance für Europa: Neue Forschungen zur Reparationspolitik vor 1933," Frankfurter Allgemeine Zeitung, 14 January 1987.

427.   ———. "Die Rolle der Banken und der Industrie in den deutschen reparationspolitischen Entscheidungen nach dem Ersten Weltkrieg." In Mommsen (no. 364), 568-82.

428.   Laubach, Ernst. Die Politik der Kabinette Wirth, 1921-1922. Lübeck, 1968.

On the London ultimatum, the Genoa conference, and, in general, fulfillment policy. See also, Schulze-Bidlingmeier (above, no. 62).

429.   Marks, Sally. "Reparations Reconsidered: A Reminder." Central European History, 2 (1969), 356-65, and the criticism by David Felix, in ibid., 4 (1971), 171-79, and the rejoinder by Marks, in ibid., 5 (1972), 358-61.

Debate on the effect of reparations on Germany.

430.   Meyer, Gerd. "Die Reparationspolitik: Ihre aussen- und innenpolitischen Rückwirkungen." In Bracher, Funke, and Jacobsen (no. 261), 327-42.

431.   Piesche, Margarete. "Die Rolle des Reparationsagenten Parker Gilbert während der Weimarer Republik (1924-1930)," Jahrbuch für Geschichte, 18 (1978), 135-69.

432.   Ronde, Hans. Von Versailles bis Lausanne: Der Verlauf der Reparationsverhandlungen nach dem ersten Weltkrieg. Stuttgart, 1950.

433.   Rupieper, Hermann J. The Cuno Government and Reparations, 1922-1923: Politics and Economics. The Hague, 1979.

Efforts of the Cuno government to deal with its creditors abroad as well as with German bankers and industries in an attempt to fashion an acceptable reparations policy.

See also Rupieper's "Industrie und Reparationen: Einige Aspekte des Reparationsproblems, 1922-1924," in Mommsen (no. 364), 582-92.

434. Schmidt, Gustav, ed. Konstellationen internationaler Politik, 1924-1932: Politische und wirtschaftliche Faktoren in den Beziehungen zwischen Westeuropa und den Vereinigten Staaten. Bochum, 1983.

Proceedings of a symposium devoted to the origins and impact of the economic crisis of the 1920s. Includes essays on war debts, reparations, security issues, and disarmament.

435. Strupp, Karl. Der Vertrag von Lausanne. Berlin, 1932.

The text of the treaty with interpretative legal commentary.

436. Vogelsang, Thilo. "Papen und das aussenpolitische Erbe Brünings: Die Lausanner Konferenz, 1932." In Neue Perspektiven aus Wirtschaft und Recht, edited by Carsten Peter Claussen. Berlin, 1966, pp. 487-507.

437. Vogt, Martin, ed. Die Entstehung des Youngplans: Dargestellt vom Reichsarchiv, 1931-1933. Boppard, 1970.

A history of the Young Plan, commissioned by the government to defend its actions against the criticisms raised by Schacht (no. 248).

438. Wandel, Eckhard. Hans Schäffer: Steuermann in wirtschaftlichen und politischen Krisen. Stuttgart, 1974.

Schäffer was both in the ministry of economics and the ministry of finance, and closely involved in reparations policy. His voluminous diary is at the Institut für Zeitgeschichte.

439. Weill-Raynal, Étienne. Les réparations allemandes et la France. 3 vols. Paris, 1947-49.

Written by a member of the reparations commission, this is still the most detailed history of reparations; takes the French point of view.

Territorial Boundaries

440. Auswärtiges Amt, ed. Der Aufstand im oberschlesischen Abstimmungsgebiet, August und September 1920. Berlin, 1920.

————. Der Einspruch der deutschen Regierung gegen die Vorschriften für die Abstimmung in Oberschlesien vom 30. Dezember 1920. Berlin, 1921.

————. Amtliche Schriftstücke zur Abstimmung in Oberschlesien, Dezember 1920 bis Januar 1921. Berlin, 1921.

————. Das Saargebiet unter der Herrschaft des Waffenstill-standsabkommens und des Vertrags von Versailles. Berlin, 1921.

―――. Dokumente zur Besetzung der Rheinlande. 3 vols. Berlin, 1925.

441.   Bischof, Erwin. Rheinischer Separatismus, 1918-1924: Hans Adam Dorten's Rheinstaatsbestrebungen. Berne, 1971.

Dorten's memoirs (La tragédie rhénane [15th ed., Paris, 1945]) are abject and self-serving. A recent study of the separatist movement is Klaus Reimer, Rheinlandfrage und Rheinlandbewegung (1918-1933) (Frankfurt/M., 1979).

442.   Campbell, F. Gregory. "The Struggle for Upper Silesia, 1919-1922." Journal of Modern History, 42 (1970), 361-85.

443.   Cienciala, Anna M. "The Secret Anglo-French Agreement on Danzig and the Saar, and Its Consequences, 1919-1926." Zeitschrift für Ostforschung, 27 (1978), 434-55.

444.   Crozier, Andrew J. "The Colonial Question in Stresemann's Locarno Policy." International History Review, 4 (1982), 37-54.

See also his "The Colonial Question during the Locarno Conference and After: An Essay in Anglo-German Relations, 1924-1927." In Michalka and Lee (no. 316), 324-49.

445.   Doepgen, Heinz. Die Abtretung des Gebiets von Eupen-Malmedy im Jahre 1920. Bonn, 1966.

446.   Enssle, Manfred. Stresemann's Territorial Revisionism: Germany, Belgium, and the Eupen-Malmédy Question, 1919-1929. Wiesbaden, 1980.

See also, Robert P. Grathwol, "Germany and the Eupen-Malmédy Affair, 1924-1926: 'Here lies the Spirit of Locarno'," Central European History, 8 (1975), 221-50, and Marc Poulain, "Querelles d'Allemands entre locarnistes: La question d'Eupen-Malmédy," Revue Historique, 101 (1977), 393-439.

447.   Erdmann, Karl Dietrich. Adenauer in der Rheinlandpolitik nach dem ersten Weltkrieg. Stuttgart, 1966.

On Adenauer's role in Rhineland politics after World War I, especially on his relations with the separatists. See the review by Klaus Epstein in Review of Politics (29 [1967], 536-45).

448.   Geigenmüller, Ernst. "Botschafter von Hoesch und die Räumungsfrage." Historische Zeitschrift, 200 (1965), 606-20.

On the influence of Germany's ambassador in Paris on the formulation of policy.

449. Hirsch, Helmut. <u>Die Saar in Versailles: Die Saarfrage auf der Friedenskonferenz von 1919</u>. Bonn, 1952.

——. <u>Die Saar von Genf: Die Saarfrage während des Völker-bundregimes von 1920-35</u>. Bonn, 1954.

No more than a brief survey of the issues, written before the diplomatic documents were available.

450. Höltje, Christian. <u>Die Weimarer Republik und das Ostlocarno-Problem, 1919-1934: Revision oder Garantie der deutschen Ostgrenze von 1919</u>. Würzburg, 1958.

Reconstructs public opinion and government policy, but relies mainly on newspapers, pamphlets, and journal articles.

451. Hölzle, Erwin, et al. <u>Die deutschen Ostgebiete zur Zeit der Weimarer Republik</u>. Cologne, 1966.

Includes essays on Danzig, Memel, Upper Silesia, and on German minorities in Poland.

452. Kaeckenbeeck, Georges. <u>The International Experiment of Upper Silesia: A Study in the Working of the Upper Silesian Settlement, 1922-1937</u>. London, 1942.

Based on his experiences as president of the arbitral tribunal of Upper Silesia, 1922-37.

453. Kimmich, Christoph M. <u>The Free City: Danzig and German Foreign Policy, 1919-1934</u>. New Haven, CT, 1968.

A case study in Germany's revisionist policy, focusing on Danzig and its role in German policy.

454. Lehmann, Hans Dietrich. <u>Der "Deutsche Ausschuss" und die Abstimmungen in Schleswig, 1920</u>. Neumünster, 1969.

455. Morrow, Ian F.D. <u>The Peace Settlement in the German Polish Borderlands</u>. London, 1936.

An early but very well-informed study of the impact of the peace treaty on Germany's relations with her eastern neighbors. A similar work is John Brown Mason, <u>The Danzig Dilemma: A Study in Peacemaking by Compromise</u> (Stanford, 1946).

456. Nitsche, Peter. "Der Reichstag und die Festlegung der deutsch-polnischen Grenze nach dem Ersten Weltkrieg." <u>Historische Zeitschrift</u>, 216 (1973), 335-61.

457. Plieg, Ernst-Albrecht. <u>Das Memelland, 1920-1939</u>. Würzburg, 1962.

On the internal developments in Memel, and how these affected German-Lithuanian relations.

458. Rogge, Albrecht. Die Verfassung des Memelgebietes: Ein Kommentar zur Memelkonvention. Berlin, 1928.

Text and commentary on the Memel statute, published under the auspices of the Ausschuss für Minderheitenrecht. See also Thorsten V. Kalijarvi, The Memel Statute: Its Origin, Legal Nature, and Observation to the Present Day. London, 1937.

459. Sobczak, Janusz. "The Weimar Republic's Propaganda Concerning the Plebiscites in Warmia and Mazuria." Polish Western Affairs, 13 (1972), 334-55.

Describes the propaganda activities and the financial aid provided to prepare the plebiscite in East Prussia. For similar efforts in Upper Silesia, see Peter-Christian Witt, "Zur Finanzierung des Abstimmungskampfes und der Selbstschutzorganisationen in Oberschlesien, 1920-1922," Militärgeschichtliche Mitteilungen, 13 (1973), 59-76.

460. Wambaugh, Sarah. Plebiscites since the World War, with a Collection of Official Documents. 2 vols. Washington, 1933.

————. The Saar Plebiscite. Cambridge, MA, 1940.

The standard works on the subject.

Disarmament and Rearmament

461. Auswärtiges Amt, ed. Materialien zur Entwaffnungsnote. 2 vols. Berlin, 1925.

Correspondence between the German government and the control authorities; German legislation; directives from the ambassadors conference; etc.

462. Carroll, Bernice A. "Germany Disarmed and Rearming, 1925-1935." Journal of Peace Research, 3 (1966), 114-24.

463. Castellan, Georges. Le réarmement clandestin du Reich, 1930-1935. Paris, 1954.

An early study of Germany's secret rearmament, based on the files of French intelligence.

464. Gatzke, Hans W. Stresemann and the Rearmament of Germany. Baltimore, 1954.

Based on the Stresemann papers, which show that Stresemann was well aware of the Reichswehr's secret and illegal rearmament.

465.   Geyer, Michael. "Das zweite Rüstungsprogramm (1930-1934)." Militärgeschichtliche Mitteilungen, 17 (1975), 125-72.

Documents on the financing and construction of armaments, with a useful introduction.

466.   ———. "The Dynamics of Military Revisionism in the Interwar Years: Military Politics between Rearmament and Foreign Affairs." In The German Military in the Age of Total War, edited by Wilhelm Deist. Dover, NH, 1985.

467.   Morgan, J.H. Assize of Arms. London, 1945.

A critical survey of Germany's failure to disarm, by a member of the control commission. (A sequel to this volume is said to be in manuscript at the publishers.)

Charles M. Nollet, a French member of the control commission, published an equally critical work: Une expérience de désarmement: cinq ans de contrôle militaire en Allemagne. Paris, 1932.

468.   Salewski, Michael. Entwaffnung und Militärkontrolle in Deutschland, 1919-1927. Munich, 1966.

Comprehensive and well-researched, this will be the standard work on German disarmament and on the control commission for some time to come.

469.   Völker, Karl-Heinz. Die Entwicklung der militärischen Luftfahrt in Deutschland, 1920-1933: Planung und Massnahmen zur Schaffung einer Fliegertruppe in der Reichswehr. Stuttgart, 1962.

On the Reichswehr's secret efforts to build up an air force in violation of the disarmament terms of the peace treaty. For a collection of Reichswehr documents, edited by Karl-Heinz Völker, see Dokumente und Dokumentarfotos zur Geschichte der Deutschen Luftwaffe (Stuttgart, 1968).

War Guilt

470.   Evans, Ellen L., and Baylen, Joseph O. "History as Propaganda: The German Foreign Office and the 'Enlightenment' of American Historians on the War Guilt Question, 1930-33." Canadian Journal of History, 10 (1975), 185-208.

471.   Frauendienst, Werner. "Das Kriegsschuldreferat des Auswärtigen Amtes." Berliner Monatshefte 15 (1937).

472.   Geiss, Imanuel. "Die manipulierte Kriegsschuldfrage: Deutsche Reichspolitik in der Julikrise 1914 und deutsche Kriegsziele im Spiegel des Schuldreferats des Auswärtigen Amtes, 1919-1931." Militärgeschichtliche Mitteilungen, 2 (1983), 31-60.

473.   Heinemann, Ulrich. Die verdrängte Niederlage: Politische
        Öffentlichkeit und Kriegsschuldfrage in der Weimarer Republik.
        Göttingen, 1983.

        The efforts by the German government to keep alive the war guilt
        controversy in order to bolster the efforts to undo the peace treaty.
        Information on the Zentralstelle für Erforschung der Kriegsursachen
        and on the Arbeitsausschuss deutscher Verbände.

474.   Wittgens, Herman J. "War Guilt Propaganda Conducted by the
        German Foreign Ministry during the 1920s." Historical
        Papers/Communications Historiques, 1980, pp. 228-47.

                        4. Weimar and Collective Security

Germany's commitment to collective security, whether provided through the
League of Nations or multilateral treaties, offers insight into the ambivalence of
much of her diplomacy. Recent research illustrates some of the dilemmas of a
policy that pursued security through revision but had to operate in a system that
defined security as the preservation of the status quo. More needs to be done
on Germany's involvement in the attempts to create a European union, on the
mutually reinforcing relationships between international economic linkages and
the Locarno détente, and on the complex interrelationship of security issues,
disarmament and rearmament, international law, and League of Nations policy.

For a contemporary bibliography, see Juntke and Sveistrup (above, no. 207).

475.   Auswärtiges Amt, ed. Materialien zur Sicherheitsfrage. Berlin, 1925.

        ———. Das Schlussprotokoll von Locarno und seine Anlagen.
        Berlin, 1925.

        ———. Materialien zum Kriegsächtungspakt. 3d enl. ed. Berlin,
        1929.

        ———. Schriftstücke zum Europa-Memorandum der französischen
        Regierung. 2d ed. Berlin, 1930.

        ———. Material zur Abrüstungsfrage. Berlin, 1931.

        ———. Material zur Behandlung der Minderheitenfrage im Völker-
        bund 1932. Berlin, 1933.

476.   Bennett, Edward W. German Rearmament and the West, 1932-1933.
        Princeton, 1979.

        A prize-winning book on Germany's military plans, her policy at the
        disarmament conference, and the diplomatic response to her demand
        for equal rights.

477.   Chappius, Charles William. "Germany and the Anglo-French Accord of Confidence, July 1932." German Studies Review, 2 (1979), 211-24.

478.   Deist, Wilhelm. "Brüning, Herriot und die Abrüstungsgespräche von Bessinge 1932." Vierteljahrshefte für Zeitgeschichte, 5 (1957), 265-72.

479.   ———. "Schleicher und die deutsche Abrüstungspolitik im Juni/Juli 1932." Vierteljahrshefte für Zeitgeschichte, 7 (1959), 163-76.

480.   Dengg, Sören. Deutschlands Austritt aus dem Völkerbund und Schachts "Neuer Plan": Zum Verhältnis von Aussen- und Aussenwirtschaftspolitik in der Übergangsphase von der Weimarer Republik zum Dritten Reich (1929-1934). Frankfurt/M., 1986.

The reorientation of German foreign policy after Stresemann and the transition to Nazi policy.

481.   Deutsche Liga für Völkerbund. Memorandum zur Vertrauenskrise des Völkerbunds. Berlin, 1932.

482.   Erdmann, Karl Dietrich. "Das Problem der Ost- oder Westorientierung in der Locarno-Politik Stresemanns." Geschichte in Wissenschaft und Unterricht, 6 (1955), 133-62. (Also in Michalka and Lee [no. 316], 1-29.)

483.   Ewald, Josef W. Die deutsche Aussenpolitik und der Europaplan Briands. Marburg, 1961.

484.   Fink, Carole. "Defender of Minorities: Germany in the League of Nations, 1926-1933." Central European History, 5 (1972), 330-57.

485.   Fortuna, Ursula. Der Völkerbundsgedanke in Deutschland während des Ersten Weltkrieges. Zurich, 1974.

On German attitudes toward a league of nations between 1914 and 1920, where they came from, what they consisted of, how they evolved.

486.   Fraenkel, Ernst. "Idee und Realität des Völkerbundes im deutschen politischen Denken." Vierteljahrshefte für Zeitgeschichte, 16 (1968), 1-14.

487.   Göppert, Otto. Der Völkerbund: Organisation und Tätigkeit des Völkerbundes. Stuttgart, 1938.

Both a history and an interpretation of the League, by a member of the legal department of the foreign ministry. See also, Bülow (above, no. 234).

488. Grathwol, Robert. "Die Deutschnationale Volkspartei, Stresemann und die Einladung nach Locarno." In Tradition und Neubeginn, edited by Joachim Hütter et al. Cologne, 1975, pp. 89-99.

For an East German view of the same events, see Klaus Dichtl and Wolfgang Ruge, "Dokumentation: Zu den Auseinandersetzungen innerhalb der Reichsregierung über den Locarnopakt 1925," Zeitschrift für Geschichtswissenschaft, 22 (1974), 64-88.

489. Jacobson, Jon. Locarno Diplomacy: Germany and the West, 1925-1929. Princeton, 1972.

A major study, well-researched and well argued, on the détente of the 1920s and the relations among the great powers. See also the same author's "The Conduct of Locarno Diplomacy," Review of Politics, 34 (1972), 67-81, for an analysis of the "Locarno style" in diplomatic negotiations.

490. Kimmich, Christoph M. Germany and the League of Nations. Chicago, 1976.

An interpretation of Germany's relationship with the League between 1919 and 1933, set in the context of Weimar foreign policy as a whole.

491. Knipping, Franz. Deutschland, Frankreich und das Ende der Locarno-Ära, 1928-1931: Studien zur internationalen Politik in der Anfangsphase der Weltwirtschaftskrise. Munich, 1987.

Traces the evolution of policy from reconciliation in 1924-28 to conflict and confrontation. Covers the broad range of the Franco-German relationship: reparations, Rhineland, Saar, security and disarmament, Briand's European Union, and the proposed Austro-German Customs Union.

492. Krüger, Peter. "Ansätze zu einer europäischen Wirtschaftsgemeinschaft in Deutschland nach dem ersten Weltkrieg." In Wirtschaftliche und politische Integration in Europa im 19. und 20. Jahrhundert, edited by Helmut Berding. Göttingen, 1984, pp. 149-68.

An overview of attempts at European economic union between 1919 and 1930.

493. ———. "Der deutsch-polnische Schiedsvertrag im Rahmen der deutschen Sicherheitsinitiative von 1925." Historische Zeitschrift, 230 (1980), 577-612.

494. ———. "Friedenssicherung und deutsche Revisionspolitik: Die deutsche Aussenpolitik und die Verhandlungen über den Kellogg-Pakt." Vierteljahrshefte für Zeitgeschichte, 22 (1974), 227-57.

495. Lipgens, Walter. "Europäische Einigungsidee 1923-30 und Briands Europaplan im Urteil der deutschen Akten." Historische Zeitschrift, 203 (1966), 46-89, 316-63.

496. Luther, Hans. "Stresemann und Luther in Locarno." Politische Studien, 8 (1957), 1-15.

Some personal recollections about negotiations at Locarno. See also those by Werner von Rheinbaben, "Deutsche Ostpolitik in Locarno," Aussenpolitik, 4 (1953), 33-40.

497. Lee, Marshall. "Disarmament and Security: The German Security Proposals in the League of Nations, 1926-1930: A Study in Revisionist Aims in an International Organization." Militärgeschichtliche Mitteilungen, 1 (1979), 35-45.

498. ———. "The German Attempt to Reform the League: The Failure of German League of Nations Policy, 1930-1932." Francia, 5 (1977), 473-90.

For German policy under Stresemann, see his "Gustav Stresemann und die deutsche Völkerbundspolitik, 1925-1930," in Michalka and Lee (no. 316), 350-74.

499. Megerle, Klaus. Deutsche Aussenpolitik, 1925: Ansatz zu aktivem Revisionismus. Frankfurt/M., 1974.

Concentrates on the revisionist expectations raised between the ratification of the Dawes Plan and the conclusion of the Berlin Treaty. Good bibliographical essay.

500. Ministerium für Auswärtige Angelegenheiten der DDR, ed. Locarno-Konferenz, 1925: Eine Dokumentensammlung. Berlin, 1962.

Documents from the German foreign ministry from Jan. 1925 to Feb. 1926, of which the most important are the extensive minutes of the sessions of the conference.

501. Pohl, Karl Heinrich. "Ein sozialdemokratischer Frondeur gegen Stresemanns Aussenpolitik: Adolf Müller und Deutschlands Eintritt in den Völkerbund." In Aspekte deutscher Aussenpolitik im 20. Jahrhundert, edited by Wolfgang Benz and Hermann Graml. Stuttgart, 1976, pp. 68-86.

502. Poulain, Marc. "Zur Vorgeschichte der Thoiry-Gespräche vom 17. September 1926." In Aspekte deutscher Aussenpolitik im 20. Jahrhundert, edited by Wolfgang Benz and Hermann Graml. Stuttgart, 1976, pp. 87-120.

Another view of the antecedents of Thoiry is in Jon Jacobson and John T. Walker, "The Impulse for a Franco-German Entente: The

Origins of the Thoiry Conference, 1926." Journal of Contemporary History, 10 (1975), 157-81.

503. Ratenhof, Gabriele. Das Deutsche Reich und die internationale Krise um die Mandschurei, 1931-1933: Die deutsche Fernostpolitik als Spiegel und Instrument deutscher Revisionspolitik. Frankfurt/M., 1984.

German revisionist policy and economic interests as reflected in the Foreign Ministry's position on the Manchuria crisis.

504. Richter, Rolf. "Der Abrüstungsgedanke in Theorie und Praxis und die deutsche Politik (1920-1929)." Wehrwissenschaftliche Rundschau, 18 (1968), 442-66.

505. Ruge, Wolfgang, and Schumann, Wolfgang. "Die Reaktion des deutschen Imperialismus auf Briands Paneuropaplan, 1930." Zeitschrift für Geschichtswissenschaft, 20 (1972), 40-70.

506. Salewski, Michael. "Zur deutschen Sicherheitspolitik in der Spätzeit der Weimarer Republik." Vierteljahrshefte für Zeitgeschichte, 22 (1974), 121-47.

On the connection between security and revisionism, and the difficulties of pursuing a policy aiming at both. An important interpretation.

507. Scelle, Georges. Une crise de la Société des Nations: La réforme du Conseil et l'entrée de l'Allemagne à Genève. Paris, 1927.

508. Schücking, Walther, and Wehberg, Hans., eds. Die Satzung des Völkerbundes. 3d ed. 2 vols. Berlin, 1931.

The standard commentary on the Covenant, accepted in Germany as well as Geneva. First edition appeared in 1921; second in 1924.

509. Sharma, Shiva-Kamar. Der Völkerbund und die Grossmächte: Ein Beitrag zur Geschichte der Völkerbundspolitik Grossbritanniens, Frankreichs und Deutschlands, 1929-1933. Frankfurt/M., 1975.

Comparative study of policies on disarmament, organizational reform, and Danzig.

510. Sieburg, Heinz-Otto. "Das Gespräch zu Thoiry." In Gedenkschrift Martin Göhring, edited by Ernst Schulin. Wiesbaden, 1978, pp. 317-37.

See also his "Les entretiens de Thoiry (1926): Le sommet et la politique de rapprochement franco-allemand à l'époque Stresemann-Briand." Revue Allemagne, 4 (1972), 520-46; and Anne Orde, "Thoiry Revisited." Durham University Journal, 67 (1975), 205-18.

511. Spenz, Jürgen. Die diplomatische Vorgeschichte des Beitritts Deutschlands zum Völkerbund, 1924-1926. Göttingen, 1966.

512. Stambrook, F.G. "'Das Kind'--Lord D'Abernon and the Origins of the Locarno Pact." Central European History, 1 (1968), 233-63.

For a more recent assessment, see Angela Kaiser, "Lord D'Abernon und die Entstehungsgeschichte der Locarno-Verträge." Vierteljahrshefte für Zeitgeschichte, 34 (1986), 85-104.

513. Strupp, Karl. Das Werk von Locarno: Eine völkerrechtlich-politische Studie. Berlin, 1926.

The legal interpretation the Germans placed on Locarno, the connection between Locarno and the League, and the so-called Rückwirkungen.

514. Thimme, Annelise. "Die Locarno-Politik im Lichte des Stresemann-Nachlasses." Zeitschrift für Politik, 3 (1956), 42-63.

An interpretation of Stresemann's policy at Locarno based on the material in his Nachlass.

515. Vogelsang, Thilo. Reichswehr, Staat und NSDAP: Beiträge zur deutschen Geschichte, 1930-1932. Stuttgart, 1962.

Reconstructs the relations between the army and the state, in particular with reference to the Nazi party. Material and discussion on disarmament policy. Appendix of documents.

516. Wehberg, Hans. "Das deutsche Volk und der Völkerbund." In Les origines et l'oeuvre de la Société des Nations, edited by Peter Munch. Copenhagen, 1923, pp. 440-500.

A study of German opinion and German policy on the League between the armistice and 1923. Quotes liberally from party pamphlets, press releases, parliamentary speeches.

5. Weimar and the Powers

Of the books and articles produced on Weimar Germany's diplomatic history, those on German-Soviet relations seem to account for the largest number. The subject has long held scholarly interest, not least because the notion of two pariah powers collaborating (or, as some have argued, plotting) to overthrow the status quo fit in with certain political preconceptions. German-Polish relations have also come in for a good deal of attention, for they reflected the most burning of Germany's revisionist objectives. In contrast, Germany's relations with the western powers have seemed mundane, and they have generally been treated as part of the campaign to revise the peace treaty, as the next two chapters amply demonstrate. This balance shows signs of shifting, however, and some of the most interesting recent studies focus on Germany's policy toward the West, which, it would appear, was quite as subtle and multi-faceted as that toward the East.

Areas that deserve closer scrutiny are the relations between Weimar and Great Britain and the British Commonwealth; policy toward Latin America, the African states, and the Far East; and, in general, the effect of international financial and trade relations on the formulation and conduct of German policy.

Western and Northern Europe

517. Åhlander, Olof. Staat, Wirtschaft und Handelspolitik: Schweden und Deutschland, 1918-1921. Lund, 1983.

518. Bariéty, Jacques. "La place de la France dans la 'Westorientierung' de la République de Weimar au cours de sa phase de stabilisation, 1924-1929." Revue Allemagne, 8 (1976), 35-51. (Also in Michalka and Lee [no. 316], 304-23)

519. ———. "Le rôle d'Émile Mayrisch entre les sidérurgies allemande et française après la première guerre mondiale." Relations internationales, 1 (1974), 123-34.

520. ———. Les relations franco-allemandes après la première guerre mondiale. Paris, 1977.

On Franco-German relations between Nov. 1918 and Jan. 1925, with special emphasis on the Rhineland, the occupation of the Ruhr, and the Dawes agreement. Exhaustive research in French and German archives.

521. Bariéty, Jacques, and Bloch, Charles. "Une tentative de réconciliation franco-allemande et son échec (1932-1933)." Revue d'histoire moderne et contemporaine, 15 (1968), 433-65.

522. Boisvert, Jean-Jacques. Les relations franco-allemandes en 1920. Montreal, 1977.

523. Duroselle, Jean-Baptiste. Les relations franco-allemandes de 1914 à 1939. 4 vols. Paris, 1967.

A set of lectures delivered to a university student audience.

524. Krüger, Peter. "Deutscher Nationalismus und europäische Verständigung: Das Verhältnis Deutschlands zu Frankreich während der Weimarer Republik." Francia, 11 (1983), 509-25.

A broad overview. Similarly, Stephen Schuker, "Frankreich und die Weimarer Republik," in Die Weimarer Republik: Belagerte Civitas, edited by Michael Stürmer. Königstein, 1980, pp. 93-112.

525. L'Huillier, Fernand. Dialogues franco-allemands 1925-1933. Paris, 1971.

On the Comité franco-allemand, headed by Emil Mayrisch. See also Grimm (no. 120).

526. Maxelon, Michael-Olaf. Stresemann und Frankreich, 1914-1929: Deutsche Politik der Ost-West Balance. Düsseldorf, 1972.

Thorough study of Stresemann's views on France and on his policies toward France, set in the context of his evolving understanding of the Franco-German relationship. A careful review by Jacques Bariéty is in Francia, 3 (1975), 554-83.

527. Nelson, Keith L. "The Black Horror on the Rhine: Race as a Factor in Post-World War I Diplomacy." Journal of Modern History, 42 (1970), 606-27.

528. Recker, Marie-Luise, ed. Von der Konkurrenz zur Rivalität: Das britisch-deutsche Verhältnis in den Ländern der europäischen Peripherie, 1919-1939. Wiesbaden, 1986.

Essays on Anglo-German commercial and political rivalry in the Baltic states, southeastern Europe, Scandinavia, and Spain.

529. Soutou, Georges. "Der Einfluss der Schwerindustrie auf die Gestaltung der Frankreichpolitik Deutschlands, 1919-1921." In Mommsen (no. 364), 543-52.

530. ―――. "Problèmes concernant le rétablissement des relations économiques franco-allemandes après la première guerre mondiale." Francia, 2 (1974), 580-96.

See also his "Les mines de Silésie et la rivalité franco-allemande, 1920-1923," Relations internationales, 1 (1974), 135-54.

531. Vietsch, Eberhard von. Arnold Rechberg und das Problem der politischen West-Orientierung Deutschlands nach dem 1. Weltkrieg. Koblenz, 1958.

On unofficial attempts to bring about a Franco-German reconciliation during the Weimar years.

532. Weidenfeld, Werner. Die Englandpolitik Gustav Stresemanns: theoretische und praktische Aspekte der Aussenpolitik. Mainz, 1972.

Does for Stresemann's attitudes and policies toward Britain what Maxelon's study did for France (no. 526).

Eastern Europe and the Soviet Union

533. Alexander, Manfred. Der deutsch-tschechoslowakische Schiedsvertrag von 1925 im Rahmen der Locarno-Verträge. Munich, 1970.

534. ———. "Die erste Phase der deutsch-tschechoslowakischen diplomatischen Beziehungen, 1918-1919." In Die böhmischen Länder zwischen Ost und West, edited by Ferdinand Seibt. Munich, 1983, pp. 228-39.

On the origins of the postwar relationship between Weimar Germany and Czechoslovakia, see also Manfred Alexander, ed., Deutsche Gesandtschaftsberichte aus Prag, vol. I, Munich, 1983. This volume, the first of a projected series, deals with the period 1918-21.

535. Beitel, Werner, and Notzold, Jürgen. Deutsch-sowjetische Wirtschaftsbeziehungen in der Zeit der Weimarer Republik. Baden-Baden, 1979.

Focuses on the technical side of trade relations--on credits, concessions, treaty terms. A more general account is in Kurt Germer, Die Entwicklung der Handelsbeziehungen zwischen Deutschland und Sowjetrussland (Jena, 1931).

536. Borowsky, Peter. "Sowjetrussland in der Sicht des deutschen Auswärtigen Amts und der Reichswehrführung, 1918-1919." In Der Westen und die Sowjetunion: Einstellungen und Politik gegenüber der UdSSR in Europa und den USA seit 1917, edited by Gottfried Niedhart. Paderborn, 1983, pp. 27-51.

537. Bräutigam, Otto. "Der Berliner Vertrag vom 24. April 1926." Osteuropa, 16 (1966), 340-46.

By a German diplomat who served in the Soviet Union between 1923 and 1930.

538. Broszat, Martin. Zweihundert Jahre deutsche Polenpolitik. 2d rev. ed. Frankfurt/M., 1972.

Three of the nine chapters deal with Germany's policies between 1918 and 1945. A good introduction.

539. Brügel, Johann Wolfgang. Tschechen und Deutsche 1918-1938. Munich, 1967.

Concentrates on the relations between the Czechs and the Sudeten Germans as a background to the Munich agreement. The English translation (Czechoslovakia before Munich [New York, 1973]) is abridged.

540. Campbell, F. Gregory. Confrontation in Central Europe: Weimar Germany and Czechoslovakia. Chicago, 1975.

See also, Peter Burian, "Deutsch-Tschechoslowakische Beziehungen 1918/19," in Politische Ideologien und Nationalstaatliche Ordnung, edited by Kurt Kluxen and Wolfgang J. Mommsen (Munich, 1968), 359-76.

541. Cecil, Lamar. "The Kindermann-Wolscht Incident: An Impasse in Russo-German Relations, 1924-26." Journal of Central European Affairs, 21 (1961), 188-99.

542. Dyck, Harvey L. "German-Soviet Relations and the Anglo-Soviet Break, 1927." Slavic Review, 25 (1966), 67-83.

543. ———. Weimar Germany and Soviet Russia, 1926-1933: A Study in Diplomatic Instability. New York, 1966.

544. Erdmann, Karl Dietrich. "Deutschland, Rapallo und der Westen." Vierteljahrshefte für Zeitgeschichte, 11 (1963), 105-65.

On Germany's expectations at Genoa, the treatment of German problems at Genoa, the impact of the Rapallo treaty, its consequences on reparations negotiations.

545. Erdmann, Karl Dietrich, and Grieser, Helmut. "Die deutsch-sowjetischen Beziehungen in der Zeit der Weimarer Republik als Problem der deutschen Innenpolitik." Geschichte in Wissenschaft und Unterricht 26 (1975), 403-26.

Analyzes changing attitudes in Germany toward the Soviet Union.

546. Erickson, John. The Soviet High Command: A Military-Political History, 1918-1941. New York, 1962.

Good account of the Reichswehr's collaboration with the Red Army and of Germany's secret rearmament on Soviet soil.

547. Freund, Gerald. Unholy Alliance: Russian-German Relations from the Treaty of Brest-Litovsk to the Treaty of Berlin. New York, 1957.

548. Fuchs, Gerhard. "Die politischen Beziehungen der Weimarer Republik zur tschechoslowakischen Republik from Versailler Frieden bis zum Ende der revolutionären Nachkriegskrise." Jahrbuch für Geschichte, 9 (1973), 281-337.

549. Gasiorowski, Zygmunt. "The Russian Overture to Germany in December 1924." Journal of Modern History, 30 (1958), 99-117.

550. ———. "Stresemann and Poland after Locarno." Journal of Central European Affairs, 18 (1958), 292-317.

———. "Stresemann and Poland before Locarno." Journal of Central European Affairs, 18 (1958), 25-47.

A fairly detailed account of German-Polish relations, focusing on Stresemann and his policies. Ignores domestic determinants of these policies. Occasional careless citations and some faulty translations.

551.   Gatzke, Hans W. "Russo-German Military Collaboration during the Weimar Republic." American Historical Review, 63 (1958), 565-97.

552.   ———. "Von Rapallo nach Berlin: Stresemann und die deutsche Russlandpolitik." Vierteljahrshefte für Zeitgeschichte, 4 (1956), 1-29.

553.   Goldbach, Marie-Luise. Karl Radek und die deutsch-sowjetischen Beziehungen, 1918-1923. Bonn, 1973.

       See also, Otto-Ernst Schüddekopf, "Karl Radeks Rolle in Berlin: Ein Kapitel deutsch-russischer Beziehungen im Jahre 1919," Archiv für Sozialgeschichte, 2 (1962), 87-166.

554.   Graml, Hermann. "Die Rapallo-Politik im Urteil der westdeutschen Forschung." Vierteljahrshefte für Zeitgeschichte, 18 (1970), 366-91.

       An assessment both of the importance of Rapallo in Germany's foreign policy and of the different interpretations set forth by West German historians. Graml's own interpretation has been questioned by Peter Alter, "Rapallo: Gleichgewichtspolitik und Revisionismus," Neue Politische Literatur, 19 (1974), 509-17.

555.   Haigh, R.H, Morris, D.S, and Peters, A.R. German-Soviet Relations in the Weimar Era: Friendship from Necessity. Totowa, NJ, 1985.

       The first of two volumes on the German-Soviet relationship between 1919 and 1941: brief, concise, not based on archival research. The second volume is The Years of Triumph? German Diplomatic and Military Policy, 1933-1941 (Totowa, NJ, 1986).

556.   Helbig, Herbert. Die Träger der Rapallo-Politik. Göttingen, 1958.

       An expanded version of "Die Moskauer Mission des Grafen Brockdorff-Rantzau," Forschungen zur Osteuropäischen Geschichte, 2 (1955), 286-344.

557.   Hiden, John W. "The Baltic Germans and German Policy towards Latvia after 1918." Historical Journal, 13 (1970), 295-317.

       ———. "The Significance of Latvia: A Forgotten Aspect of Weimar Ostpolitik." Slavonic and East European Review, 53 (1975), 389-413.

       Both these articles deal with Germany's interest in Latvia as a stepping stone to Russia, and the implications of this interest for German policy and for Latvia.

558.   ———. The Baltic States and Weimar Ostpolitik. New York, 1987.

On peacemaking 1919-20, the role of the German minority in the Baltic states, trade relations 1921-23, and Randstaatenpolitik 1923-33. An earlier study is: "The 'Baltic Problem' in Weimar's Ostpolitik, 1923-32," in Germany in the Age of Total War, edited by Volker R. Berghahn and Martin Kitchen (London, 1981), 147-69.

559. Hildebrand, Klaus. Das Deutsche Reich und die Sowjetunion im internationalen System, 1918-1932: Legitimität oder Revolution? Wiesbaden, 1977. (Also in Michael Stürmer, ed., Die Weimarer Republik: Belagerte Civitas, Königstein, 1980, pp. 38-61.)

560. Himmer, Robert. "Rathenau, Russia, and Rapallo." Central European History, 9 (1976), 146-83.

See also his "Harmonicas for Lenin? The Development of German Economic Policy toward Soviet Russia, December 1918 to June 1919," Journal of Modern History, 49 (1977), abstract.

561. Hubatsch, Walther. "Die aussenpolitischen Beziehungen des Deutschen Reiches zu Lettland und Estland, 1923-1932." Deutsche Studien, 13 (1975), 305-14.

562. Jacobsen, Hans-Adolf. Misstrauische Nachbarn: Deutsche Ostpolitik 1919/1970. Düsseldorf, 1970.

Collection of documents with introductory comments; about half of them deal with the period 1919-45.

563. Korbel, Josef. Poland between East and West: Soviet and German Diplomacy toward Poland, 1919-1933. Princeton, 1963.

564. Krasuski, Jerzy. "Political Significance of the Polish-German Financial Accounting in 1919-1929." Acta Poloniae Historica, 15 (1967), 65-80.

565. Krüger, Peter. "Benes und die europäische Wirtschaftskonzeption des deutschen Staatssekretärs Carl von Schubert." Bohemia-Jahrbuch, 14 (1973), 320-40.

On Benes-Schubert discussions, May 1928, and on Schubert's ideas on economic cooperation.

566. Kruszewski, Charles. "The German-Polish Tariff War (1925-1934) and Its Aftermath." Journal of Central European Affairs, 3 (1943), 294-315.

567. Lademacher, Horst. "Von Brest-Litovsk nach Rapallo." Blätter für deutsche und internationale Politik, 6 (1961), 1037-54.

568. Laqueur, Walter. Russia and Germany: A Century of Conflict. Boston, 1965.

On what Germans and Russians have thought about each other, and on how their mutual misconceptions have affected their relations.

569. Laser, Kurt. "Der Russlandausschuss der deutschen Wirtschaft, 1928-1941." Zeitschrift für Geschichtswissenschaft, 20 (1972), 1382-1400.

For a more extensive treatment of the subject, set in the broad context of German-Soviet economic relations, see Hans Jürgen Perrey, Der Russlandausschuss der deutschen Wirtschaft: Die deutsch-sowjetischen Wirtschaftsbeziehungen der Zwischen-Kriegszeit, Munich, 1985.

570. Laubach, Ernst. "Maltzans Aufzeichnungen über die letzten Vorgänge vor dem Abschluss des Rapallo-Vertrages." Jahrbuch für Geschichte Osteuropas, 22 (1974), 556-79.

571. Linke, Horst Günther. Deutsch-sowjetische Beziehungen bis Rapallo. 2d ed. Cologne, 1972.

Thorough, well-documented account of German-Soviet relations between 1918 and 1922; focus on political, economic, and military relations.

572. Lippelt, Helmut. "Zur deutschen Politik gegenüber Polen nach Locarno." Vierteljahrshefte für Zeitgeschichte, 19 (1971), 323-73.

Stresemann's bid for the revision of the German-Polish border in the aftermath of Locarno. Supersedes Gasiorowski (no. 550).

573. Megerle, Klaus. "Danzig, Korridor und Oberschlesien: Zur deutschen Revisionspolitik gegenüber Polen in der Locarnopolitik." Jahrbuch für Geschichte Mittel- und Ostdeutschlands, 25 (1976), 145-78.

To be read in conjunction with Lippelt's piece (no. 572).

574. Mersmann-Soest, O., and Wohl, Paul. Die deutsch-russischen Verträge vom 12. Oktober 1925. Berlin, 1926.

On the commercial treaties Germany concluded with the Soviet Union in Oct. 1925: contains the texts of the treaties and supplementary material. See also, Georg Martius, "Die rechtlichen Grundzüge der deutsch-russischen Verträge vom 12. Oktober 1925," Osteuropa, 1 (1925/26), 443-52, by a member of the German negotiating team.

575. Meyer, Klaus. "Sowjetrussland und die Anfänge der Weimarer Republik." Forschungen zur Osteuropäischen Geschichte, 20 (1973), 77-91.

576. Ministerium für Auswärtige Angelegenheiten der UdSSR und der DDR, eds. Deutsch-sowjetische Beziehungen. 3 vols. [East] Berlin, 1967-78.

A collection of documents, many of them never published before, on German-Soviet relations between 1917 and Oct. 1925.

577. Morgan, Roger P. "The Political Significance of German-Soviet Trade Negotiations, 1922-25." The Historical Journal, 6 (1963), 253-71.

578. Mueller, Gordon H. "Rapallo Re-examined: A New Look at Germany's Secret Military Collaboration with Russia in 1922." Military Affairs, 40 (1976), 109-17.

Argues that the German-Soviet military contacts were far more significant and productive than has so far been assumed.

579. Niedhart, Gottfried, ed. Der Westen und die Sowjetunion: Einstellungen und Politik gegenüber der UdSSR in Europa und den USA seit 1917. Paderborn, 1983.

Includes an essay on the foreign ministry's assessment of the Soviet Union in the early years of the Weimar Republic.

580. Pogge von Strandmann, Hartmut. "Grossindustrie und Rapallopolitik: Deutsch-sowjetische Handelsbeziehungen in der Weimarer Republik." Historische Zeitschrift, 222 (1976), 265-341.

See also his "Rapallo--Strategy in Preventive Diplomacy: New Sources and New Interpretations," in Germany in the Age of Total War, edited by Volker R. Berghahn and Martin Kitchen (London, 1981), 123-46.

581. Puchert, Berthold. Der Wirtschaftskrieg des deutschen Imperialismus gegen Polen, 1925-1934. [East] Berlin, 1963.

582. ———. "Die Entwicklung der deutsch-sowjetischen Handelsbeziehungen von 1918 bis 1939." Jahrbuch für Wirtschaftsgeschichte, 14 (1973), 11-36.

583. Riekhoff, Harald von. German-Polish Relations, 1918-1933. Baltimore, 1971.

Explores the revisionist and conciliatory elements in the German-Polish relationship.

584. ———. "Pilsudski's Conciliatory Overtures to Stresemann." Canadian Slavonic Papers, 9 (1967).

585. Rodgers, Hugh I. Search for Security: A Study in Baltic Diplomacy, 1920-1934. Hamden, CT, 1975.

Contains information on Germany's relations with Latvia.

586. Rosenbaum, Kurt. Community of Fate: German-Soviet Diplomatic Relations, 1922-1928. Syracuse, NY, 1965.

German-Soviet relations during Brockdorff-Rantzau's tenure of office in Moscow.

587. Rosenfeld, Günter. Sowjetrussland und Deutschland, 1917-1922. [East] Berlin, 1960; rpt. Cologne, 1984.

————. Sowjetunion und Deutschland, 1922-1933. Cologne, 1984.

Some interesting material, especially on trade relations, but on the whole marred by political bias, especially in the first volume.

588. Rosenthal, Harry Kenneth. German and Pole: National Conflict and Modern Myth. Gainesville, FL, 1977.

A survey of German-Polish relations between 1894 and 1973.

589. Schieder, Theodor. "Die Entstehungsgeschichte des Rapallo-Vertrages." Historische Zeitschrift, 204 (1967), 545-609.

590. ————. Die Probleme des Rapallo-Vertrages: Eine Studie über die deutsch-russischen Beziehungen, 1922-1926. Cologne, 1956.

These two pieces are among the best work done on this early phase of German-Soviet relations.

591. Schüddekopf, Otto-Ernst. "Deutschland zwischen Ost und West: Karl Moor und die deutsch-sowjetischen Beziehungen in der ersten Hälfte des Jahres 1919." Archiv für Sozialgeschichte, 3 (1963), 223-63.

592. Volkmann, Hans-Erich. "Probleme des deutsch-lettischen Verhältnisses zwischen Compiègne und Versailles." Zeitschrift für Ostforschung, 14 (1974), 713-26.

593. Wagner, Gerhard. Deutschland und der polnisch-sowjetische Krieg 1920. Wiesbaden, 1979.

On German policy toward Poland and the Soviet Union in 1920 and on German-Soviet contacts during the war.

594. Walsdorff, Martin. Westorientierung und Ostpolitik: Stresemanns Russlandpolitik in der Locarno-Ära. Bremen, 1971.

Reassesses Stresemann's policy in 1924-26, and prints a number of important documents in the appendix.

595.   Zelt, Johannes.   "Die deutsch-sowjetischen Beziehungen in den Jahren 1917 bis 1921 und das Problem der Kriegsgefangenen und Internierten." <u>Zeitschrift für Geschichtswissenschaft</u>, 15 (1967), 1015-32.

Southern and Southeastern Europe

596.   Doering, Dörte.   "Deutsch-österreichische Aussenhandelsverflechtung während der Wirtschaftskrise." In Mommsen (no. 364), 514-30.

597.   Geigenmüller, Ernst.   "Botschafter von Hoesch und der deutsch-österreichische Zollunionsplan von 1931." <u>Historische Zeitschrift</u>, 195 (1962), 581-95.

598.   Goldinger, Walter.   "Das Projekt einer deutsch-österreichischen Zollunion von 1931." In <u>Oesterreich und Europa</u> (Graz, 1965), pp. 527-46.

Emphasis on the Austrian side, which has been neglected.

599.   Hauser, Oswald.   "Der Plan einer deutsch-österreichischen Zollunion von 1931 und die europäische Föderation." <u>Historische Zeitschrift</u>, 179 (1955), 45-92.

An early study, before many of the relevant documents became available.

600.   Höpfner, Hans-Paul.   <u>Deutsche Südosteuropapolitik in der Weimarer Republik</u>. Frankfurt/M., 1983.

Chapters on Hungary, Rumania, and Yugoslavia; role of German minorities in German policy.

601.   Lönne, Karl Eugen.   "Italien und das Deutschland des Versailler Vertrags." <u>Quellen und Forschungen aus italienischen Archiven und Bibliotheken</u>, 53 (1973), 318-84.

Based on the reports of Alfredo Frassati, the Italian ambassador in Berlin, 1921-22.

See also, Ludwig Förg, "Die diplomatischen Beziehungen Deutschlands zu Italien: Ihre Wiederaufnahme in der Nachkriegszeit," <u>Historisches Jahrbuch der Görresgesellschaft</u>, 57 (1937), 98-120.

602.   Luza, Radomír.   <u>Austro-German Relations in the Anschluss Era</u>. Princeton, 1975.

603.   Mitrovic, Andrej.   "Politische und wirtschaftliche Beziehungen Deutschlands und Jugoslawiens in der Zeit der Verständigungspolitik Stresemanns." In <u>Tradition und Neubeginn</u>, edited by Joachim Hütter et al. Cologne, 1975, pp. 117-40.

604. Molt, Harro. "... Wie ein Klotz inmitten Europas"; "Anschluss" und "Mitteleuropa" während der Weimarer Republik, 1925-1931. Frankfurt, 1986.

German foreign policy and foreign trade policy; trade relations between Germany and Austria; the origins of the customs union.

605. Muhr, Josef. Die deutsch-italienischen Beziehungen in der Ära des Ersten Weltkrieges (1914-1922). Göttingen, 1977.

Emphasis on the period after the armistice and on negotiations to restore relations.

606. Preradovich, Nikolaus von. Die Wilhelmstrasse und der Anschluss Österreichs, 1918-1933. Frankfurt/M., 1971.

On the foreign ministry's views and attitudes, but little on policy.

607. Schröder, Hans-Jürgen. "Deutsche Südosteuropapolitik 1929-1936: Zur Kontinuität deutscher Aussenpolitik in der Wirtschaftskrise." Geschichte und Gesellschaft, 2 (1976), 5-32.

German policies in the last years of the Weimar Republic that provided a springboard for Hitler's policy objectives. For a variant, see his "Die deutsche Südosteuropapolitik und die Reaktion der angelsächsischen Mächte, 1929-1933/34," in Internationale Beziehungen in der Weltwirtschaftskrise, 1929-1933, edited by Josef Becker and Klaus Hildebrand (Munich, 1980), pp. 343-60.

608. Spira, Thomas. German-Hungarian Relations and the Swabian Problem: From Károlyi to Gömbös, 1919-1936. New York, 1977.

609. Stambrook, F.G. "The German-Austrian Customs Union Project of 1931: A Study of German Methods and Motives." Journal of Central European Affairs, 21 (1961), 15-44.

A more recent study is Anne Orde, "The Origins of the German-Austrian Customs Union Project of 1931," Central European History, 13 (1980), 34-59.

610. Stehlin, Stewart A. Weimar and the Vatican, 1919-1933. Princeton, 1983.

Reconstructs, inter alia, German attempts to enlist the Vatican in the settlement of the Ruhr crisis and of the reparations question; new information on Weimar's ultimately unsuccessful negotiations for a concordat.

611. Sundhausen, Holm. "Die Weltwirtschaftskrise im Donau-Balkan-Raum und ihre Bedeutung für den Wandel der deutschen Aussenpolitik unter Brüning." In Aspekte deutscher Aussenpolitik

in 20. Jahrhundert, edited by Wolfgang Benz and Hermann Graml. Stuttgart, 1976, pp. 121-64.

612. Suval, Stanley. The Anschluss Question in the Weimar Era: A Study of Nationalism in Germany and Austria, 1918-1932. Baltimore, 1974.

Analyzes the extent to which nationalism in both Germany and Austria influenced foreign policy, the interrelationship of internal and external affairs in the two countries, and the importance of Anschluss for Germany's revisionist policy.

For a somewhat different view see Mary Margaret Ball, Post-War German-Austrian Relations: The Anschluss Movement, 1918-1936 (Stanford, 1937).

613. Tonch, Hans. Wirtschaft und Politik auf dem Balkan: Untersuchungen zu den deutsch-rumänischen Beziehungen in der Weimarer Republik unter besonderer Berücksichtigung der Weltwirtschaftskrise. Frankfurt/M., 1984.

Focus is on the period of the great depression.

614. Torunsky, Vera. Entente der Revisionisten: Mussolini und Stresemann, 1922-1929. Cologne, 1986.

The Locarno negotiations, German-Italian trade relations, and the question of South Tyrol.

615. Váli, Franz. Die deutsch-österreichische Zollunion vor dem Ständigen Internationalen Gerichtshof. Vienna, 1932.

The Americas

616. Berg, Peter. Deutschland und Amerika, 1918-1929: Über das deutsche Amerikabild der zwanziger Jahre. Lübeck, 1963.

617. Costigliola, Frank. "The United States and the Reconstruction of Germany in the 1920s." Business History Review, 50 (1976), 477-502.

See also, Bernard V. Burke, "American Economic Diplomacy and the Weimar Republic," Mid-America, 54 (1972), 211-33. Both authors view the subject from an American perspective.

618. Diamond, Sander A. "Ein Amerikaner in Berlin: Aus den Papieren des Botschafters Alanson B. Houghton, 1922-1925." Vierteljahrshefte für Zeitgeschichte, 27 (1979), 431-70.

See also, Hermann J. Rupieper, "Alanson B. Houghton: An American Ambassador in Germany, 1922-1925," International History Review, 1 (1979), 490-508.

619. Gottwald, Robert. Die deutsch-amerikanischen Beziehungen in der Ära Stresemann. Berlin, 1965.

620. Jones, Kenneth Paul. U.S. Diplomats in Europe, 1919-1941. Santa Barbara, CA, 1981.

Chapters on Alanson B. Houghton, Owen D. Young, and George S. Messersmith.

621. Knapp, Manfred, et al., eds. Die USA und Deutschland, 1918-1975. Munich, 1978.

A collection of essays on German-American relations, emphasizing the concurrent strains of rivalry and cooperation.

622. Link, Werner. "Der amerikanische Einfluss auf die Weimarer Republik in der Dawesplanphase (Elemente eines 'penetrierten Systems')." In Mommsen (above, no. 364), 485-98.

623. ———. Die amerikanische Stabilisierungspolitik in Deutschland, 1921-32. Düsseldorf, 1970.

On shared interests in recovery and prosperity that shaped policies in Washington and Berlin. Well-documented; thorough.

624. Marks, Sally, and Delude, Denis. "German-American Relations, 1918-1921." Mid-America, 53 (1971), 211-26.

625. Nelson, Keith L. Victors Divided: America and the Allies in Germany, 1918-1923. Berkeley, 1975.

A study primarily of American policy and of American influence in Germany, but with some useful information on the triangular relationship of the United States, her European allies, and Germany over the occupation of the Rhineland.

626. Pade, Werner. "Die Expansionspolitik des deutschen Imperialismus gegenüber Lateinamerika, 1918-1933." Zeitschrift für Geschichtswissenschaft, 22 (1974), 578-90.

627. Schröder, Ernst. Otto Wiedfeldt: Eine Biographie. Essen, 1964.

A short biography of the German ambassador in Washington, 1922-25. By the same author: "Otto Wiedfeldt als Politiker und Botschafter der Weimarer Republik," in Beiträge zur Geschichte von Stadt und Stift Essen, 86 (1971), 159-238.

628. Wandel, Eckhard. Die Bedeutung der Vereinigten Staaten von Amerika für das deutsche Reparationsproblem, 1924-1929. Tübingen, 1971.

On the war debts-reparations-credits tangle, and on the Dawes and Young plans.

Mideast and Far East

629. Brunon, Paul. "Le redressement allemand au Japon après la grande guerre (1919-1922)." Revue Historique, 256 (1976), 419-22.

630. Chi, Chen. Die Beziehungen zwischen Deutschland und China bis 1933. Hamburg, 1973.

   Emphasis on political, economic, and cultural relations between 1919 and 1933.

631. Fleury, Antoine. La pénétration allemande au Moyen-Orient 1919-1939: Le cas de la Turquie, de l'Iran et de l'Afghanistan. Leiden, 1977.

   An earlier study, focusing on the immediate postwar years, is Fleury's "La pénétration économique de l'Allemagne en Turquie et en Iran après la première guerre mondiale," Relations internationales, 1 (1974), 155-71.

632. Hirschfeld, Yair P. Deutschland und Iran im Spielfeld der Mächte: Internationale Beziehungen unter Reza Schah, 1921-1941. Düsseldorf, 1980.

   The ups and downs in the diplomatic relationship between Germany and the Shah's Iran, set in the context of international rivalries in the Middle East. For a summary, see his "German Policy towards Iran: Continuity and Change from Weimar to Hitler, 1919-1939," Jahrbuch des Instituts für Deutsche Geschichte, 1975, Beiheft 1, pp. 117-41.

633. Hirszowicz, Lukasz. "The Course of German Foreign Policy in the Middle East between the World Wars." Jahrbuch des Instituts für Deutsche Geschichte, 1975, Beiheft 1, pp. 175-90.

634. Kirby, William C. Germany and Republican China. Stanford, 1984.

   Emphasis is on economic and military relations, 1918-41.

635. Liang, Hsi-Huey. The Sino-German Connection: Alexander von Falkenhausen between China and Germany, 1900-1941. Assen, Netherlands, 1978.

636. Mahrad, Ahmad. Die deutsch-persischen Beziehungen von 1918-1933. 2d ed. Frankfurt/M., 1979.

   Mahrad's Dokumentation über die deutsch-persischen Beziehungen von 1918 bis 1933 (Frankfurt/M., 1975) consists of anti-Shah literature confiscated by the German police.

637.   Martin, Bernd. "Germany between China and Japan: German Far
        Eastern Policy of the Interwar Period." Bulletin of the Institute of
        Modern History, Academy Sinica, 7 (1978), 593-610.

        A brief overview of the dilemmas and directions of Germany's policy
        toward the Far East.

E. NAZI GERMANY

1. Nazi Foreign Policy

Studies of Nazi foreign policy reflect the uncertainties and controversies that beset studies of Nazism in general. The central question remains the interpretation of Hitler--whether one considers him a pragmatist or an ideologue, a supreme dictator or a prisoner of a social dynamic beyond his control. It is clear that he played a major role in determining and shaping policy, but it is equally clear that he did not do so in a vacuum. How was policy affected by his preference for unconventional diplomacy? By competing interest groups in the party? By the pressures generated by economic recovery and rearmament?

No less important for historians is the question of continuity and discontinuity in German foreign policy, a question that often raises others. Was the policy pursued by Weimar Germany merely a bridge between the policies of Imperial Germany and Nazi Germany? Was Nazi foreign policy in fact unique, clearly distinguishable from anything that had gone before, or merely a variant of a traditional German policy or, perhaps, of a more general fascist policy? Did Nazi policy reflect a program, and if so, was it a program consistent within itself or subject to modification as necessary; was it an amalgam of the programs put forward by other Nazi agencies; or was it merely a function of shifting domestic developments?

Some of these questions are addressed in essays by Bracher, Carr, and Milward, in Walter Laqueur, ed., Fascism: A Reader's Guide (Berkeley, 1976), and, more recently, in John Hiden and John Farquharson, Explaining Hitler's Germany: Historians and the Third Reich (Totowa, NJ, 1983); Gerhard Schreiber, Hitler: Interpretationen, 1923-1983 (Darmstadt, 1984); and Rene Schwok, Interprétations de la politique étrangère de Hitler: une analyse de l'historiographie (Paris, 1987).

Recent bibliographies: Helen Kehr and Janet Langmaid, eds., The Nazi Era, 1919-1945: A Select Bibliography of Published Works from the Early Roots to 1980 (London, 1982); Louis L. Snyder, ed., The Third Reich, 1933-1945: A Bibliographical Guide to German National Socialism (New York, 1987); and, limited to journal articles, ABC-Clio Information Services, The Third Reich, 1933-1939: A Historical Bibliography (Santa Barbara, CA, 1984).

General

See also, Weinberg (no. 274), and Wendt (no. 275).

638.   Bloch, Charles. "Die Wechselwirkung der nationalsozialistischen Innen- und Aussenpolitik, 1933-1939." In Funke (no. 643), 205-22. (Also in Relations internationales, 4 [1975], 91-109.)

639.   Bussmann, Walter. "Das Auswärtige Amt unter der nationalsozialistischen Diktatur." In Demokratie und Diktatur, edited by Manfred Funke et al. Düsseldorf, 1987, pp. 252-65.

640.   Carr, William. Arms, Autarky and Aggression: A Study in German Foreign Policy, 1933-1939. New York, 1973.

        Examines the connections between economic pressures, rearmament, and foreign policy.

641.   Döscher, Hans-Jürgen. Das Auswärtige Amt im Dritten Reich: Diplomatie im Schatten der "Endlösung." Berlin, 1987.

        Structural and staff changes in the foreign ministry (party membership, careers, Ribbentrop's innovations).

642.   Forndran, Erhard, et al. Innen- und Aussenpolitik unter nationalsozialistischer Bedrohung: Determinanten internationaler Beziehungen in historischen Fallstudien. Wiesbaden, 1977.

        Original essays on how Nazi Germany and Nazism affected various countries and their freedom of action in international affairs. Among the best work done on Nazi foreign policy.

643.   Funke, Manfred, ed. Hitler, Deutschland und die Mächte: Materialien zur Aussenpolitik des Dritten Reiches. Düsseldorf, 1976.

        A collection of essays on Nazi foreign policy, written by experts. It is divided into three parts: on foreign-policy plans and planning, on means and methods, and on relations with other states.

644.   Graml, Hermann. "Wer bestimmte die Aussenpolitik des Dritten Reiches? Ein Beitrag zur Kontroverse um Polykratie und Monokratie im NS-Herrschaftssystem." In Demokratie und Diktatur, edited by Manfred Funke et al. Düsseldorf, 1987, pp. 223-36.

        Context is provided by Gerhard Hirschfeld and Lothar Kettenacker, eds., Der "Führerstaat"--Mythos und Realität: Studien zur Struktur und Politik des Dritten Reiches, Stuttgart, 1981.

645.   Gruchmann, Lothar. Nationalsozialistische Grossraumordnung: Die Konstruktion einer "deutschen Monroe-Doktrin." Stuttgart, 1962.

646. Hildebrand, Klaus. Deutsche Aussenpolitik, 1933-1945: Kalkül oder Dogma? Stuttgart, 1971. (5th ed., Stuttgart, 1987.)

Argues that Hitler's objectives in foreign policy reflected a carefully laid-out program dating back to the 1920s, consistent with traditions alive since Bismarck. It was only Hitler's doctrinaire racism that constituted an innovation.

647. ―――. "Hitlers Ort in der Geschichte des preussisch-deutschen Nationalstaates." Historische Zeitschrift, 217 (1973), 584-632.

Charts Hitler's position in the political and diplomatic traditions of the modern German state.

See also his "Innenpolitische Antriebskräfte der nationalsozialistischen Aussenpolitik," in Funke (no. 643), 223-38.

648. Hill, Leonidas E. "The Wilhelmstrasse in the Nazi Era." Political Science Quarterly, 82 (1967), 546-70.

Disputes the claim that, in the Nazi years, the foreign ministry had declined and become nothing more than a "technical apparatus."

649. Hillgruber, Andreas. "Grundzüge der nationalsozialistischen Aussenpolitik, 1933-1945." Saeculum, 24 (1973), 328-45.

On Hitler's "grand design": a German empire on the plains of Russia, to serve as a base for the ultimate conflict with the United States.

650. Irving, David. The War Path: Hitler's Germany, 1933-1939. New York, 1978.

Focuses on events as seen "from behind the Führer's desk"--to show how Hitler led Germany to war.

651. Jacobsen, Hans-Adolf. Nationalsozialistische Aussenpolitik, 1933-1938. Frankfurt/M., 1968.

Comprehensive, heavily documented study of the structure of foreign policy in Nazi Germany. Examines organizations, decision-making processes, efforts to disseminate Nazism abroad, the role of ideology. Appendices on diplomatic personnel, finances, rearmament. Detailed chronology.

See also his "Zur Struktur der NS-Aussenpolitik, 1933-1945," in Funke (no. 643), 137-85, which extends the analysis to the end of the war and includes several organizational charts, and "Zur Rolle der Diplomatie im Dritten Reich," in Das Diplomatische Korps 1871-1945, edited by Klaus Schwabe (Boppard, 1985), pp. 171-99.

652. Kluke, Paul. Aussenpolitik und Zeitgeschichte. Wiesbaden, 1974.

Collection of his essays, including "Politische Form und Aussenpolitik des Nationalsozialismus" (pp. 159-88), on the program and style of Nazi foreign policy, and "Nationalsozialistische Europaideologie" (pp. 188-222), which deals with Hitler's hegemonial ambitions.

653.   Krüger, Peter. "'Man lässt sein Land nicht im Stich, weil es eine schlechte Regierung hat'--Die Diplomatie und die Eskalation der Gewalt." In Die deutschen Eliten und der Weg in den Zweiten Weltkrieg, edited by Martin Broszat and Klaus Schwabe. Munich, 1989, pp. 180-225.

The vulnerability of the diplomats to Hitler, their individual and collective reactions to policy in the 1930s, and the crisis created by Hitler's war policy.

654.   Leuschner, Joachim. Volk und Raum: Zum Stil der national-sozialistischen Aussenpolitik. Göttingen, 1958.

655.   Michalka, Wolfgang. "Conflicts within the German Leadership on the Objectives and Tactics of German Foreign Policy, 1933-1939." In The Fascist Challenge and the Policy of Appeasement, edited by Wolfgang J. Mommsen and Lothar Kettenacker. London, 1983, pp. 48-60.

656.   Michalka, Wolfgang, ed. Nationalsozialistische Aussenpolitik. Darmstadt, 1978.

Some twenty essays (including several original pieces), an editor's introduction on current methodological and substantive approaches, and a good bibliography.

Among the essays, Martin Broszat's "Soziale Motivation und Führer-Bindung des Nationalsozialismus," which argues that Nazi foreign policy was a function of domestic developments, and T.W. Mason's "Der Primat der Politik," which demonstrates a primacy of politics rooted in economic developments, are particularly worthy of note.

657.   Rich, Norman. Hitler's War Aims. 2 vols. New York, 1973-74.

The first volume deals with Hitler's program of expansion, its ideological premises and preconceptions; the second deals with the practical application of the program and the often necessary reformulations. Reviewed by Klaus Hildebrand in Journal of Modern History (48 [1976], 522-30).

658.   Robertson, Esmonde M. Hitler's Pre-War Policy and Military Plans, 1933-1939. London, 1963.

659.   Schmädeke, Jürgen, and Steinbach, Peter, eds. Der Widerstand gegen den Nationalsozialismus: Die deutsche Gesellschaft und der Widerstand gegen Hitler. Munich, 1985.

Includes essays on the contacts between members of the opposition (Weizsäcker, the Kordt brothers, Adam von Trott zu Solz) and foreign governments, and on their plans for a new foreign policy.

660. Seabury, Paul. The Wilhelmstrasse: A Study of German Diplomats under the Nazi Regime. Berkeley, 1954.

See also Seabury's "Ribbentrop and the German Foreign Office," Political Science Quarterly, 66 (1951), 532-55, which, though dated, has not been entirely superseded.

661. Sywottek, Jutta. Mobilmachung für den totalen Krieg: Die propagandistische Vorbereitung der deutschen Bevölkerung auf den Zweiten Weltkrieg. Opladen, 1976.

A careful, thorough study, both of Nazi ideas and of the institutions which disseminated them at home and abroad. See also, Gerhard Weinberg, "Friedenspropaganda und Kriegsvorbereitung," in Deutschland 1933, edited by Wolfgang Treue and Jürgen Schmädeke (Berlin, 1984), 119-35.

Hitler

662. Aigner, Dietrich. "Hitler und die Weltherrschaft." In Michalka (no. 656), 49-69; and in Aspects of the Third Reich, edited by H. W. Koch (New York, 1985), pp. 251-66.

Hitler's objectives in foreign policy, their meaning, and their consistency throughout the Nazi era.

663. Binion, Rudolph. Hitler among the Germans. New York, 1976.

A psychohistorical study that shows that Hitler framed his war program in response to Germany's national trauma of 1918, and that he intended to use his power to refight the lost war of 1914-18. See also, Rudolph Binion, "Hitler Looks East," History of Childhood Quarterly, 3 (1975), 82-102.

664. Bullock, Alan. Hitler: A Study in Tyranny. Rev. ed. New York, 1964.

665. Dickmann, Fritz. "Machtwille und Ideologie in Hitler's aussenpolitischen Zielsetzungen vor 1933." In Spiegel der Geschichte, edited by Konrad Repgen and Stephan Skalweit. Münster, 1964, pp. 915-41.

666. Fest, Joachim C. Hitler: Eine Biographie. Berlin, 1973.

A massive and very detailed biography, but not a "new" Hitler. See the review by Hermann Graml in Vierteljahrshefte für Zeitgeschichte (22 [1974], 76-92).

667.   Hitler, Adolf. Adolf Hitler: My New Order. Edited by Raoul de
       Roussy de Sales. New York, 1941.

       ————. "Es spricht der Führer": 7 exemplarische Hitler-Reden.
       Edited by Hildegard von Kotze and Helmut Krausnick. Gütersloh,
       1966.

       ————. Hitler: Reden und Proklamationen, 1932-1945. Edited by
       Max Domarus. 2 vols. Neustadt/Aisch, 1962.

       ————. Hitler's Words. Edited by Gordon W. Prange.
       Washington, 1944.

       ————. The Speeches of Adolf Hitler. Edited by Norman H.
       Baynes. 2 vols. London, 1942.

668.   ————. Hitlers Zweites Buch: Ein Dokument aus dem Jahre 1928.
       Edited by Gerhard L. Weinberg. Stuttgart, 1961.

       A treatise on foreign affairs, not published during Hitler's lifetime.
       For an assessment of its historical importance, see Martin Broszat,
       "Betrachtungen zu 'Hitlers Zweitem Buch'," Vierteljahrshefte für
       Zeitgeschichte, 9 (1961), 417-29.

669.   ————. Mein Kampf. 2 vols. Munich, 1925-27 (and many
       subsequent editions).

       Remains important as a statement of Hitler's ideas, but must be treated
       with due caution.

       On the significance of the work, see Karl Lange, Hitlers unbeachtete
       Maximen: "Mein Kampf" und die Öffentlichkeit, Stuttgart, 1968.

670.   Jäckel, Eberhard. Hitlers Herrschaft: Vollzug einer Weltanschauung.
       Stuttgart, 1986.

       A sequel to no. 671; emphasizes the central importance of Hitler's
       expansionist ideology.

671.   ————. Hitlers Weltanschauung: Entwurf einer Herrschaft. 2d ed.
       Tübingen, 1981.

       The chapter on Hitler's objectives in foreign policy has been translated
       and published in Henry A. Turner, Jr., ed., Nazism and the Third
       Reich (New York, 1972), pp. 201-17.

672.   Kuhn, Axel. Hitlers aussenpolitisches Programm: Entstehung und
       Entwicklung, 1919-1939. Stuttgart, 1970.

       Essentially two parts: the development of Hitler's policy ideas in the
       period before 1933, and the central position of Great Britain in his
       policy after 1933.

See also, John Hiden, "National Socialism and Foreign Policy, 1919-1933," in The Nazi Machtergreifung, edited by Peter D. Stachura, London, 1983, pp. 146-61.

673. Michaelis, Meir. "World Power Status or World Dominion? A Survey of the Literature on Hitler's 'Plan of World Dominion' (1937-1970)." Historical Journal, 15 (1972), 331-60.

A more recent assessment is Milan Hauner, "Did Hitler Want a World Dominion?" Journal of Contemporary History, 13 (1978), 15-32.

674. Moltmann, Günter. "Weltherrschaftsideen Hitlers." In Europa und Übersee, edited by Otto Brunner and Dietrich Gerhard. Hamburg, 1961, pp. 197-240.

675. Rauschning, Hermann. Gespräche mit Hitler. Zurich, 1940.

On the historical authenticity of this source, see Theodor Schieder, Hermann Rauschnings "Gespräche mit Hitler" als Geschichtsquelle, Opladen, 1972.

676. Schubert, Günter. Anfänge nationalsozialistischer Aussenpolitik. Cologne, 1963.

On the evolution of Hitler's "grand design," which took shape in the mid-twenties. On the earlier period, see Geoffrey Stoakes, "The Evolution of Hitler's Ideas on Foreign Policy, 1919-1925," in The Shaping of the Nazi State, edited by Peter D. Stachura (New York, 1978).

677. Stoakes, Geoffrey. Hitler and the Quest for World Dominion. Leamington Spa, 1986.

Hitler's views on foreign policy in the context of views held by other party spokesmen and by leading right-wing agitators in the 1920s.

678. Thies, Jochen. Architekt der Weltherrschaft: Die "Endziele" Hitlers. Düsseldorf, 1976.

Draws on Hitler's speeches and on his architectural plans to argue that Hitler had global ambitions. See also Thies's "Hitlers 'Endziele': Zielloser Aktionismus, Kontinentalimperium oder Weltherrschaft?" in Michalka (no. 656), 70-91; and in Bracher, Funke, and Jacobsen (no. 260), 390-406.

679. Zipfel, Friedrich. "Hitlers Konzept einer 'Neuordnung' Europas." In Aus Theorie und Praxis der Geschichtswissenschaft, edited by Dietrich Kurze. Berlin, 1972, pp. 154-74.

Ministers and Envoys

See also, Goebbels (no. 119), Ribbentrop (no. 154), and Rosenberg (no. 158).

680. Bewley, Charles H. Hermann Göring and the Third Reich. Toronto, 1962.

A biography based both on official and family papers, by the former Irish minister in Berlin who knew Göring personally. See also, with caution, David Irving, Göring: A Biography (New York, 1989).

681. Goebbels Reden, 1932-1945. Edited by Helmut Heiber. 2 vols. Düsseldorf, 1971-72.

682. Göring, Hermann. Reden und Aufsätze. Edited by Erich Gritzbach. Munich, 1939.

Gritzbach also wrote an authorized biography: Hermann Göring: Werk und Mensch. Munich, 1937.

683. Heineman, John L. Hitler's First Foreign Minister: Constantin Freiherr von Neurath. Berkeley, 1979.

Especially good on the early years of Nazi policy and on the conflict between the traditionalists in the foreign ministry and the party.

684. Himmler, Heinrich. Geheimreden 1933 bis 1945 und andere Ansprachen. Edited by Bradley F. Smith and Agnes F. Peterson. Frankfurt/M., 1974.

685. Kempner, Robert M. W. Das Dritte Reich im Kreuzverhör: Aus den unveröffentlichten Vernehmungsprotokollen des Anklägers. Munich, 1969.

Interrogations of Weizsäcker, Ritter, Rahn, Woermann, and others. See also his memoirs Ankläger einer Epoche: Lebenserinnerungen, Frankfurt/M., 1983.

686. Kube, Alfred. Pour le mérite und Hakenkreuz: Hermann Göring im Dritten Reich. 2d ed. Munich, 1987.

687. Kuusisto, Seppo. Alfred Rosenberg in der nationalsozialistischen Aussenpolitik, 1933-1939. Helsinki, 1984.

On Rosenberg's ideology, the Aussenpolitisches Amt, the efforts to shape policy, and activities in Scandinavia and Eastern Europe.

688. Martens, Stefan. Hermann Göring: "Erster Paladin des Führers" und "Zweiter Mann im Reich." Paderborn, 1985.

Focuses on Göring's role as diplomat and "European statesman." Has been challenged for being too uncritical of Göring's own carefully cultivated image as a moderate. See also his "Hermann Göring: der 'zweite' Mann im Dritten Reich?" Francia, 12 (1985), 473-90.

689. Michalka, Wolfgang. Ribbentrop und die deutsche Weltpolitik, 1933-1940. Munich, 1980.

A short survey is F. L'Huillier, "Joachim von Ribbentrop," Revue d'histoire de la deuxième guerre mondiale, 22 (1956), 1-9.

690. Overy, Richard J. Goering: The "Iron" Man. London, 1984.

Part of a larger argument, developed in a series of articles, to the effect that Germany was preparing for "total war," to be launched in the 1940s. Much interesting information on the Reichswerke Hermann Göring.

691. Ribbentrop, Joachim von. Die alleinige Kriegsschuld Englands. Berlin, 1939.

————. Vierjahresplan und Welthandel. Berlin, 1937.

Two of Ribbentrop's major speeches, the first made on 24 Oct. 1939, the second on 1 Mar. 1937.

692. Rosar, Wolfgang. Deutsche Gemeinschaft: Seyss-Inquart und der Anschluss. Frankfurt/M., 1971.

Another biography, concentrating more on the Dutch period, is H.J. Neumann, Arthur Seyss-Inquart (Cologne, 1970).

693. Rosenberg, Alfred. Grossdeutschland: Traum und Tragödie. Edited by Heinrich Härtle. Munich, 1970.

————. Gestaltung der Idee: Reden und Aufsätze, 1933-1935. Munich, 1936.

————. Tradition und Gegenwart: Reden und Aufsätze, 1936-1940. Munich, 1941.

————. Der Zukunftsweg der deutschen Aussenpolitik. Munich, 1927.

Rosenberg's ideas on the reorganization of the European continent and on the role of National Socialism in the world. See also, Hans-Jürgen Lutzhöft, Der Nordische Gedanke in Deutschland, 1920-1940 (Stuttgart, 1971), with an interesting chapter on Rosenberg, and Reinhard Bollmus, Das Amt Rosenberg und seine Gegner (Stuttgart, 1970), which deals with the APA and Einsatzstab Rosenberg.

694. Sommer, Erich F. Botschafter Graf Schulenburg: Der letzte Vertreter des Deutschen Reiches in Moskau. Asendorf, 1987.

On Schulenburg the diplomat, within the context of German-Soviet relations between the wars, by a former member of the German foreign service personally acquainted with his subject. Complements Herwarth (no. 129).

695. Vogelsang, Reinhard. Der Freundeskreis Himmler. Göttingen, 1972.

Information on Wilhelm Keppler, Hitler's roving ambassador.

Subversion

See also, Ritter (no. 384).

696. Bischoff, Ralph F. Nazi Conquest through Nazi Culture. Cambridge, MA, 1942.

697. Broszat, Martin. "Die Memeldeutschen Organisationen und der Nationalsozialismus, 1933-1939." Vierteljahrshefte für Zeitgeschichte, 5 (1957), 273-78.

698. Brown, Macalister. "The Third Reich's Mobilization of the German Fifth Column in Eastern Europe." Journal of Central European Affairs, 19 (1959), 128-48.

699. Burleigh, Michael. Germany turns Eastwards: A Study of "Ostforschung" in the Third Reich. New York, 1989.

On the role of German intellectuals in the preparation and defense of Nazi Germany's conquest of Eastern Europe.

700. César, Jaroslav, and Cerný, Bohumil. "The Nazi Fifth Column in Czechoslovakia." Historica, 4 (1962), 191-255.

Similarly, see also Georges Castellan, "The Germans in Rumania," Journal of Contemporary History, 6 (1971), 51-75.

701. Dankelmann, Otfried. "Aus der Praxis auswärtiger Kulturpolitik des deutschen Imperialismus, 1937-1945." Zeitschrift für Geschichtswissenschaft, 20 (1972), 719-37.

702. Delfiner, Henry. Vienna Broadcasts to Slovakia, 1938-1939: A Case Study in Subversion. New York, 1974.

Transcripts of broadcasts beamed at Slovakia in an attempt to undermine the relationship between Slovaks and Czechs.

703. Hauner, Milan. "The Professionals and the Amateurs in National Socialist Foreign Policy: Revolution and Subversion in the Islamic and Indian World." In Der "Führerstaat"--Mythos und Realität: Studien zur Struktur und Politik des Dritten Reiches, edited by Gerhard Hirschfeld and Lothar Kettenacker. Stuttgart, 1981, pp. 305-28.

704. Jacobsen, Hans-Adolf, ed. Hans Steinacher, Bundesleiter des VDA, 1933-1937; Erinnerungen und Dokumente. Boppard, 1970.

705. Johnson, Ronald W. "The German-American Bund and Nazi Germany, 1936-1941." Studies in History and Society, 6 (1975), 31-45.

706. Kipphan, Klaus. Deutsche Propaganda in den Vereinigten Staaten, 1933-1945. Heidelberg, 1971.

   A thorough examination of Germany's propaganda and propaganda agencies in the United States, based on materials in the National Archives.

707. Komjathy, Anthony, and Stockwell, Rebecca. German Minorities and the Third Reich: Ethnic Germans of East Central Europe between the Wars. New York, 1979.

   The German minorities in Poland, Czechoslovakia, Rumania, Hungary, and Yugoslavia, their activities, and their relationship with Nazi Germany.

708. Kühne, Horst. "Die fünfte Kolonne des faschistischen deutschen Imperialismus in Südwestafrika (1933-1939)." Zeitschrift für Geschichtswissenschaft, 8 (1960), 765-90.

709. Kupferman, Alfred. "Le Bureau Ribbentrop et les campagnes pour le rapprochement franco-allemand, 1934-1937." In Les relations franco-allemandes, 1933-1939. Paris, 1976.

   By the same author: "Diplomatie parallèle et guerre psychologique: le rôle de la Ribbentrop Dienststelle dans les tentatives d'actions sur l'opinion française, 1934-1939." Relations internationales, 3 (1975), 79-95; and in Revue Allemagne, 10 (1978), 507-27.

710. Lachmann, Günter. Der Nationalsozialismus in der Schweiz, 1931-1945: Ein Beitrag zur Geschichte der Auslandsorganisation der NSDAP. Berlin, 1962.

711. McKale, Donald M. "The Nazi Party in the Far East, 1931-1945." Journal of Contemporary History, 12 (1977), 291-311.

   See also his "Hitlerism for Export: The Nazi Attempt to Control Schools and Youth Clubs outside Germany," Journal of European Studies, 5 (1975), 239-53.

712. ———. The Swastika outside Germany. N.p., 1977.

   On Bohle and the Auslandsorganisation, and on the many organizations formed by the Nazis in foreign countries in the 1930s.

See also, Arthur L. Smith, "Hitlers Gau Ausland," Politische Studien, 14 (1966), 90-95.

713. Milge, Wolfgang. Das Dritte Reich und die deutsche Volksgruppe in Rumänien, 1933-38: Ein Beitrag zur nationalsozialistischen Volkstumspolitik. Frankfurt/ M., 1972.

Shows that the Gleichschaltung of the German minorities became effective only in 1938-39, and that until then the Nazis had to compete with the older, more traditional minority organizations.

714. Orlow, Dietrich. The Nazis in the Balkans: A Case Study of Totalitarian Politics. Pittsburgh, 1968.

715. Rimscha, Hans von. "Zur Gleichschaltung der deutschen Volksgruppen durch das Dritte Reich: Am Beispiel der deutschbaltischen Volksgruppe in Lettland." Historische Zeitschrift, 182 (1956), 29-63.

716. Smelser, Ronald M. "The Betrayal of a Myth: National Socialism and the Financing of Middle-Class Socialism in the Sudetenland." Central European History, 5 (1972), 256-77.

717. Smith, Arthur L. The Deutschtum of Nazi Germany and the United States. The Hague, 1965.

See also, with a narrower focus, Smith's "The Kameradschaft USA," Journal of Modern History, 34 (1962), 398-408.

718. Tägil, Sven. Deutschland und die deutsche Minderheit in Nordschleswig: Eine Studie zur deutschen Grenzpolitik, 1933-1939. Stockholm, 1970.

Rearmament and Economic Mobilization

See also, Dülffer (no. 326), and Geyer (no. 327).

719. Bagel-Bohlan, Anja E. Hitlers industrielle Kriegsvorbereitung, 1936 bis 1939. Koblenz, 1975.

Complements studies on the war economy (Milward, Wagenführ), and shows that the German economy fell short of what has been generally assumed.

720. Bensel, Rolf. Die deutsche Flottenpolitik von 1933 bis 1939: Eine Studie über die Rolle des Flottenbaus in Hitlers Aussenpolitik. Berlin, 1958.

721. Bernhardt, Walter. Die deutsche Aufrüstung, 1934-39: Militärische und politische Konzeptionen und ihre Einschätzung durch die Alliierten. Frankfurt/M., 1969.

722. Blaich, Fritz. <u>Wirtschaft und Rüstung im "Dritten Reich."</u> Düsseldorf, 1987.

Collection of documents with introduction on the economic preparation of the war in the 1930s and the economic basis for conducting the war.

723. Carroll, Berenice A. <u>Design for Total War: Arms and Economics in the Third Reich.</u> The Hague, 1968.

Argues that by 1938 Germany had a war economy, but that it was not fully geared to war until 1942.

724. Deist, Wilhelm. <u>The Wehrmacht and German Rearmament.</u> Toronto, 1981.

A summary, brief and concise, of the rapid expansion of the armed forces between 1933 and 1939; well-documented. See also his "Zum Problem der deutschen Aufrüstung, 1933-1936," <u>Francia</u>, 5 (1977), 539-65.

725. Doering, Dörte. <u>Deutsche Aussenwirtschaftspolitik, 1933-1935: Die Gleichschaltung der Aussenwirtschaft in der Frühphase des nationalsozialistischen Regimes.</u> Berlin, 1969.

726. Esenwein-Rothe, Ingeborg. <u>Die Wirtschaftsverbände von 1933 bis 1945.</u> Berlin, 1965.

Explains the development, organization, and role in the economy of business and industrial associations, the Four-Year Plan, and the like.

727. Forstmeier, Friedrich, and Volkmann, Hans-Erich, eds. <u>Wirtschaft und Rüstung am Vorabend des Zweiten Weltkrieges.</u> 2d ed. Düsseldorf, 1981.

A symposium on the influence of German rearmament on government and industry, and on their interest in expansion. Includes essays on the rearmament industry (Karl-Heinz Ludwig), the Four-Year Plan (Dieter Petzina), foreign trade (Hans-Erich Volkmann, Alice Teichova).

728. Gemzell, Carl-Axel. <u>Organization, Conflict and Innovation: A Study of German Naval Strategic Planning, 1888-1940.</u> Lund, 1973.

729. Geyer, Michael. "Militär, Rüstung und Aussenpolitik--Aspekte militärischer Revisionspolitik in der Zwischenkriegszeit." In Funke (no. 643), 239-68.

730. Jäger, Jörg-Johannes. <u>Die wirtschaftliche Abhängigkeit des 3. Reichs vom Ausland, dargestellt am Beispiel der Stahlindustrie.</u> Berlin, 1969.

731. Klein, Burton. Germany's Economic Preparations for War. Cambridge, MA, 1959.

Both his data and his conclusions have been disputed. See Carroll (no. 723) and Arthur Schweitzer, "Die wirtschaftliche Wieder-aufrüstung Deutschlands von 1934-1936," Zeitschrift für die gesamte Staatswissenschaft, 114 (1958), 594-637.

732. Meinck, Gerhard. Hitler und die deutsche Aufrüstung, 1933-1937. Wiesbaden, 1959.

733. Müller, Klaus-Jürgen. Das Heer und Hitler: Armee und nationalsozialistisches Regime, 1933-1940. Stuttgart, 1969.

A well-documented study on the political relations between Hitler and the armed forces; in effect a sequel to Carsten (no. 325). See also his General Ludwig Beck: Studien und Dokumente zur politisch-militärischen Vorstellungswelt und Tätigkeit des Generalstabschefs des deutschen Heeres, 1933-1938, Boppard, 1980.

734. Neal, Larry. "The Economics and Finances of Bilateral Clearing Agreements: Germany, 1934-1938." Economic History Review, 32 (1979), 391-404.

735. Overy, R.J. "Transportation and Rearmament in the Third Reich." Historical Journal, 16 (1973), 389-409.

Arrives at interesting conclusions about the level of Germany's war preparations and plans. See also his "The German Pre-War Aircraft Production Plans: November 1936-April 1939," English Historical Review (1975), 778-93, for clues to the development of Nazi policy.

736. Petzina, Dieter. Autarkiepolitik im Dritten Reich: Der nationalsozialistische Vierjahresplan. Stuttgart, 1968.

The only study to cover the various facets of the Four-Year Plan.

737. Radkau, Joachim. "Entscheidungsprozesse und Entscheidungs-defizite in der deutschen Aussenwirtschaftspolitik, 1933-1940." Geschichte und Gesellschaft, 2 (1976), 33-65.

Analyzes the dynamics of Nazi Germany's trade relations with other countries, and how they influenced decisions in foreign policy.

738. Riedel, Matthias. Eisen und Kohle für das Deutsche Reich: Paul Pleigers Stellung in der NS-Wirtschaft. Göttingen, 1973.

A study of the Reichswerke Hermann Göring and their role in the German economy before and during the war.

739. Salewski, Michael, et al. Wehrmacht und Nationalsozialismus, 1933-1939. Munich, 1979.

740.   Schweitzer, Arthur. Big Business in the Third Reich. Bloomington, IN, 1964.

On rearmament, the Four-Year Plan, and the involvement of business in government policies. See also, by the same author, "Plans and Markets: Nazi Style," Kyklos, 30 (1977), 88-115.

741.   Teichert, Eckart. Autarkie und Grossraumwirtschaft in Deutschland, 1930-1939: Aussenwirtschaftliche Konzeptionen zwischen Wirtschaftskrise und Zweitem Weltkrieg. Munich, 1984.

The attitudes of the National Socialists and of members of the traditional elites about Germany's external economic relations in the 1930s. Role of the government ministries and the trade associations.

See also, Ludolf Herbst, "Der Krieg und die Unternehmens-Strategie deutscher Industrie-Konzerne in der Zwischenkriegszeit," in Die deutschen Eliten und der Weg in den Zweiten Weltkrieg, edited by Martin Broszat and Klaus Schwabe (Munich, 1989), pp. 72-134.

742.   Thomas, Georg. Geschichte der deutschen Wehr- und Rüstungswirtschaft (1918-1943/45). Edited by Wolfgang Birkenfeld. Boppard, 1966.

By the general who headed the armed force's economic and armaments office.

743.   Volkmann, Hans-Erich. "Politik, Wirtschaft und Aufrüstung unter dem Nationalsozialismus." In Funke (no. 643), 269-91.

Colonial Ambitions

744.   Ageron, Charles-Robert. "L'idée d'Eurafrique et le débat colonial franco-allemand de l'entre-deux-guerres." Revue d'histoire moderne et contemporaine, 22 (1977), 446-75.

745.   Hildebrand, Klaus. Vom Reich zum Weltreich: Hitler, NSDAP und koloniale Frage, 1919-1945. Munich, 1969.

Comprehensive study of the importance of colonial questions for Hitler and the Nazis, which throws light on Hitler's plans and strategies. Exhaustively researched, with a massive bibliography.

See also his "Deutschland, die Westmächte und das Kolonialproblem: Ein Beitrag über Hitlers Aussenpolitik vom Ende der Münchner Konferenz bis zum 'Griff nach Prag'," Aus Politik und Zeitgeschichte, 31 May 1969, pp. 23-40.

746.   Kühne, Horst. Faschistische Kolonialideologie und zweiter Weltkrieg. [East] Berlin, 1962.

An East German study of Nazi colonialism, supplemented by the author's "Zur Kolonialpolitik des faschistischen deutschen Imperialismus (1933-1939)," Zeitschrift für Geschichtswissenschaft, 9 (1961), 514-37, and by Olaf Groehler's "Kolonialforderungen als Teil der faschistischen Kriegszielplanung," Zeitschrift für Militärgeschichte, 4 (1965), 547-73.

747.   Schmokel, Wolfe W. Dream of Empire: German Colonialism, 1919-1945. New Haven, CT, 1964.

        Largely superseded by Hildebrand (no. 745).

748.   Weinberg, Gerhard. "German Colonial Plans and Policies, 1938-1942." In Geschichte und Gegenwartsbewusstsein, edited by Wolfgang Besson and Friedrich Hiller von Gaertringen. Göttingen, 1963, pp. 462-91.

2. Policy in Transition, 1933-34

The transition period from Weimar policy to Nazi policy raises some obvious problems of definition. Hitler took a hand in foreign policy right from the start, but he only gradually abandoned the policies of his predecessors. For some time, therefore, old and new policies ran parallel, overlapping here and there and occasionally coming into conflict. This parallelism, part necessity, part intent, produced confusion at the time, and it is still not fully and satisfactorily sorted out. See also, Bennett (no. 476), and Geyer (no. 327).

749.   Aretin, Karl Otmar von. "Prälat Kaas, Franz von Papen und das Reichskonkordat von 1933." Vierteljahrshefte für Zeitgeschichte, 14 (1966), 252-79.

750.   Backlund, Lawrence. "The German-Finnish Commercial Conflict of 1933-1934." Journal of Baltic Studies, 8 (1977), 324-53.

751.   Bloch, Charles. Hitler und die europäischen Mächte 1933/34: Kontinuität oder Bruch. Frankfurt/M., 1966.

        A good introduction to the problem, but should be read in conjunction with Wollstein (no. 764).

752.   Bracher, Karl Dietrich. "Das Anfangsstadium der Hitlerschen Aussenpolitik." Vierteljahrshefte für Zeitgeschichte, 5 (1957), 63-76.

753.   Celovsky, Boris. "Pilsudskis Präventivkrieg gegen das nationalsozialistische Deutschland: Entstehung, Verbreitung und Wiederlegung einer Legende." Welt als Geschichte, 14 (1954), 53-70.

        Argues against the existence of such plans, in contrast to Hans Roos, "Die 'Präventivkriegspläne' Pilsudskis von 1933," Vierteljahrshefte für Zeitgeschichte, 3 (1955), 344-63, who says that such plans indeed existed.

Zygmunt Gasiorowski, "Did Pilsudski attempt to initiate a Preventive War in 1933?" Journal of Modern History, 27 (1955), 135-51, concludes that the rumors of war were part of a carefully calculated diplomatic maneuver, and Waclaw Jedrzejewicz, "The Polish Plan for a 'Preventive War' against Germany in 1933," Polish Review, 11 (1966), 62-91, summarizes the issue and reviews everything that has been said about it in print.

754. Cienciala, Anna. "The Significance of the Declaration of Nonaggression of January 26, 1934, in Polish-German and International Relations: A Reappraisal." East European Quarterly, 1 (1967), 1-30.

For an earlier view, see Zygmunt Gasiorowski, "The German-Polish Non-Aggression Pact of 1934," Journal of Central European Affairs, 15 (1955), 3-29.

755. Heineman, John L. "Constantin von Neurath and German Policy at the London Economic Conference of 1933: Background to the Resignation of Alfred Hugenberg." Journal of Modern History, 41 (1969), 160-88.

756. Jarausch, Konrad H. The Four Power Pact 1933. Madison, WI, 1965.

Includes a synoptic table of the various drafts of the pact.

757. Krüger, Peter. "Hitlers Machtergreifung und der Verfall der Diplomatie." Bohemia, 25 (1984), 279-94.

A brief overview of the role and perception of diplomacy in both the Weimar and the Nazi years.

758. Krüger, Peter, and Hahn, Erich J.C. "Der Loyalitätskonflikt des Staatssekretärs Bernhard Wilhelm von Bülow im Frühjahr 1933." Vierteljahrshefte für Zeitgeschichte, 20 (1972), 376-410.

Bülow's assessment of German policy in the spring of 1933, summarized by Neurath in the cabinet on 7 Apr. 1933 (ADAP, Series C, I, no. 142), is in "Eine Denkschrift des Staatssekretärs Bernhard von Bülow vom März 1933," Militärgeschichtliche Mitteilungen, 13 (1973), 77-94.

759. McKale, Donald M. "The Aggressive Diplomacy of a Totalitarian Party: The Nazi Seizure of Power Abroad, 1933-1934." International Review of History and Politics, 10 (1973), 22-38.

760. Nadolny, Sten. Abrüstungsdiplomatie 1932/33: Deutschland auf der Genfer Konferenz im Übergang von Weimar zu Hitler. Munich, 1978.

761. Scholder, Klaus. Die Kirchen und das Dritte Reich. Vol. 1. Enl. ed. Frankfurt/M., 1986. (Trl. as The Churches and the Third Reich, London, 1987.)

Covers the period 1918-34, and is excellent on 1933 and the negotiations of the concordat. Supersedes all previous works. For a critical reaction see Konrad Repgen's review in Vierteljahrshefte für Zeitgeschichte, 26 (1978), 499-534, to which Scholder responded at length in the same journal, pp. 535-70.

762. Volk, Ludwig. Das Reichskonkordat vom 20. Juli 1933. Mainz, 1972.

A thorough account, with documents; from its origins in the Weimar Republic to its ratification in Sept. 1933.

A collection of documents on the concordat is in Alfons Kupper, ed., Staatliche Akten über die Reichskonkordatsverhandlungen 1933 (Mainz, 1969).

763. Winkel, Harald. "Boycott und Gegenboycott: Zu den deutsch-englischen Handelsbeziehungen im Jahre 1933." In Preussen, Deutschland und der Westen, edited by Heinrich Bodensieck. Göttingen, 1980, pp. 179-202.

764. Wollstein, Günter. Vom Weimarer Revisionismus zu Hitler: Das Deutsche Reich und die Grossmächte in der Anfangsphase der nationalsozialistischen Herrschaft in Deutschland. Bonn, 1973.

A detailed, well-documented account of the transition from Weimar policy to Nazi policy.

3. Nazi Germany and the Powers

Listed below are works on Germany's diplomatic and economic relations with other states, 1933-39. Research has focused primarily on (a) Britain, not only because she played an important role in Germany's efforts to remove the final restrictions of Versailles but also because she was central to Hitler's thinking and planning, (b) the United States and Latin America, where the Nazi AO clashed with German diplomats and local authorities alike, and (c) Southeastern Europe, which was exploited economically and subverted politically. The list does not include works on Germany's relations with the fascist states (Italy and Spain) and on the course of German territorial expansion. These are cited in the following two chapters.

Western Europe

See also, Michalka (no. 689).

765. Adamthwaite, Anthony P. "The Franco-German Declaration of 6 December 1938." In Les relations franco-allemandes, 1933-1939, published under the auspices of the Centre National de la Recherche Scientifique. Paris, 1976, pp. 395-409.

For an East German assessment, see Heinz Lindner, "Die deutsch-französische Erklärung vom 6. Dezember 1938: Zur diplomatischen Vorgeschichte des zweiten Weltkrieges." Zeitschrift für Geschichtswissenschaft, 16 (1968), 884-93.

766. Aigner, Dietrich. Das Ringen um England: Das deutsch-britische Verhältnis; die öffentliche Meinung, 1933-1939; Tragödie zweier Völker. Munich, 1969.

767. Bloch, Charles. "La Grande-Bretagne face au réarmement allemand et l'accord naval de 1935." Revue d'histoire de la deuxième guerre mondiale, 16 (1966), 41-68.

768. ———. "La place de la France dans les différents stades de la politique extérieure du troisième Reich (1933-1940)." In Les relations franco-allemandes, 1933-1939, published under the auspices of the Centre National de la Recherche Scientifique. Paris, 1976, pp. 15-31.

769. ———. "Les relations anglo-allemandes de l'accord de Munich à la dénonciation du traité naval de 1935." Revue d'histoire de la deuxième guerre mondiale, 5 (1955), 51-65.

770. Brundu Olla, Paola. Le origini diplomatiche dell'accordo navale anglo-tedesco del giugno 1935. Milan, 1974.

A brief survey, with an appendix of documents.

771. Burdick, Charles B. "German Military Planning and France, 1930-1938." World Affairs Quarterly, 30 (1959), 299-313.

772. Dickel, Horst. Die deutsche Aussenpolitik und die irische Frage von 1932 bis 1944. Wiesbaden, 1983.

Better than John P. Duggan, Neutral Ireland and the Third Reich (Totowa, NJ, 1985), which suffers from poor documentation, archival research notwithstanding.

773. Dülffer, Jost. "Das deutsch-englische Flottenabkommen vom 18. Juni 1935." In Michalka (no. 656), 244-76. (Originally in Marine-Rundschau, 69 [1972], 641-59.)

See also, Wolfgang Malanowski, "Das deutsch-englische Flottenabkommen vom 18. Juni 1935 als Ausgangspunkt für Hitlers doktrinäre Bündnispolitik," Wehrwissenschaftliche Rundschau, 5 (1955), 408-20; D.C. Watt, "The Anglo-German Naval Agreement of 1935: An Interim Judgment," Journal of Modern History, 28 (1956), 155-75; and Dülffer (no. 326).

774.   Emmerson, James Thomas. The Rhineland Crisis, 7 March 1936: A Study in Multilateral Diplomacy. Ames, IA, 1977.

The first detailed account on the origins, the course, and the consequences of the crisis. Broadly conceived, touches on diplomatic, military, and domestic concerns. Similarly, Eva H. Haraszti, The Invaders: Hitler Occupies the Rhineland, Budapest, 1983.

775.   Fitz Randolph, Sigismond-Sizzo. Der Frühstücks-Attaché aus London. Stuttgart, 1954.

On Anglo-German relations, mainly after Ribbentrop became ambassador in London, by the German embassy's press attaché (1933-39).

776.   La France et l'Allemagne, 1932-1936. Paris, 1980.

Deutschland und Frankreich, 1936-1939. Edited by Klaus Hildebrand and Karl Ferdinand Werner. Munich, 1981.

Proceedings of French-German colloquia held, respectively, in 1977 and 1979, under the auspices of the Comité d'Histoire de la 2e Guerre Mondiale. The first volume includes essays on German foreign policy by Becker (15-26), Knipping (213-32), and Hildebrand (339-71), the second by Niedhart (475-92) and Dülffer (409-25).

777.   Funke, Manfred. "7. März 1936: Studie zum aussenpolitischen Führungsstil Hitlers." Aus Politik und Zeitgeschichte, 3 Oct. 1970, pp. 3-34. (A condensed version is in Michalka [no. 656], 277-324.)

778.   Geyr von Schweppenburg, Leo. Erinnerungen eines Militärattachés: London, 1933-1937. Stuttgart, 1949.

779.   Haraszti, Eva H. Treaty-Breakers or "Realpolitiker?" The Anglo-German Naval Agreement of June 1935. Boppard, 1974.

Focuses on Britain and rather slights the German side. Appendix with diplomatic documents.

780.   Hauser, Oswald. England und das Dritte Reich: Eine dokumentierte Geschichte der englisch-deutschen Beziehungen von 1933 bis 1939 auf Grund unveröffentlicher Akten aus dem Britischen Staatsarchiv.

Vol. 1 (1933-36). Stuttgart, 1972. Vol. 2 (1936-38). Göttingen, 1982.

See also his "Lord Halifax und Hitler, November 1937," in Staat und Gesellschaft im politischen Wandel, edited by Werner Pöls (Stuttgart, 1979), pp. 492-522.

781.   Henke, Josef. England in Hitlers politischem Kalkül: Vom Scheitern der Bündniskonzeption bis zu Kriegsbeginn (1935-1939). Boppard, 1973.

On the central significance of relations with Britain in the 1930s, and on Hitler's changing views on Britain.

See also Henke's "Hitlers England-Konzeptionen: Formulierung und Realisierungsversuche," in Funke (no. 643), 584-603.

782.   Hillgruber, Andreas. "England in Hitlers aussenpolitischer Konzeption." Historische Zeitschrift, 218 (1974), 65-84.

Analyzes Hitler's views of before 1933 and then his policies toward Britain, 1933-45, and concludes that Hitler was consistent throughout.

783.   Klefisch, Peter. Das Dritte Reich und Belgien, 1933-1939. Frankfurt/M., 1988.

784.   Robertson, Esmonde M., ed. "Zur Wiederbesetzung des Rheinlandes, 1936." Vierteljahrshefte für Zeitgeschichte, 10 (1962), 178-205.

Documents from the foreign ministry on the reoccupation of the Rhineland.

In an important comment, D.C. Watt challenged the view that German troops would have been withdrawn if France had called Germany's bluff. Evidence in the German naval archives suggests that the troops were under orders to fight if attacked. See his "German Plans for the Reoccupation of the Rhineland: A Note," Journal of Contemporary History, 1 (1966), 193-99.

785.   Schramm, Wilhelm von. ...sprich vom Frieden, wenn du den Krieg willst: Die psychologischen Offensiven Hitlers gegen die Franzosen, 1933 bis 1939. Mainz, 1973. (2d edition entitled Hitler und die Franzosen, Mainz, 1980.)

On a more limited scale, see his "Frankreich und die psychologische Offensive Hitlers 1933/38: Geschichte eines Modellfalls," Wehrkunde, 9 (1960), 234-40.

786.   Schwoerer, Lois G. "Lord Halifax's Visit to Germany, November 1937." Historian, 32 (1970), 353-75.

787. Weinberg, Gerhard. "Hitler and England, 1933-1945: Pretense and Reality." German Studies Review, 8 (1985), 299-309.

788. Woerden, A.V.N. van. "Hitler Faces England: Theories, Images, and Policies." Acta Historiae Neerlandica, 3 (1968), 141-59 (also in Michalka [no. 656], 220-43).

Eastern Europe and the Soviet Union

See also, Erickson (no. 546), Jacobsen (no. 562), Haigh et al. (no. 555), Laqueur (no. 568), and Laser and Perrey (no. 569).

789. Bosl, Karl, ed. Gleichgewicht-Revision-Restauration. Munich, 1976.

A symposium on the history of Czechoslovakia, including papers by Peter Krüger (on German policy toward Czechoslovakia in the 1930s) and by Stephan Dolezel (on German-Czechoslovak relations between Munich and Prague).

790. Brandes, Detlef. "Die Politik des Dritten Reiches gegenüber der Tschechoslowakei." In Funke (no. 643), 508-23.

791. Breyer, Richard. Das Deutsche Reich und Polen, 1932-1937: Aussenpolitik und Volksgruppenrecht. Würzburg, 1955.

An early work, still worth reading.

792. Denne, Ludwig. Das Danzig-Problem in der deutschen Aussenpolitik, 1934-39. Bonn, 1959.

793. Fabry, Philipp W. Die Sowjetunion und das Dritte Reich: Eine dokumentierte Geschichte der deutsch-sowjetischen Beziehungen von 1933 bis 1941. Stuttgart, 1971.

Survey with some dubious conclusions.

794. Finger, Gerhard. "Deutsches Generalkonsulat Thorn: Aus den Jahren 1937-1939." Westpreussen-Jahrbuch, 24 (1974), 126-35.

795. Fleischhauer, Ingeborg. Das Dritte Reich und die Deutschen in der Sowjetunion. Stuttgart, 1983.

Use of the German minority as a pawn in relations with the Soviet Union.

796. Higgins, Trumbull. Hitler and Russia: The Third Reich in a Two-Front War, 1937-1943. New York, 1966.

797. Hitchens, Marilynn Giroux. Germany, Russia, and the Balkans: Prelude to the Nazi-Soviet Non-Aggression Pact. New York, 1983.

798. Ilnytzkyj, Roman. Deutschland und die Ukraine, 1934-1945: Tatsachen europäischer Ostpolitik. 2 vols. Munich, 1955-56.

See also, Wolodymyr Kosyk, ed., Das Dritte Reich und die ukrainische Frage: Dokumente 1934-1944, Munich, 1985. Documents on German policy toward the Ukraine, from the Nuremberg Trials and from various German archives.

799. Kuhn, Axel. "Das nationalsozialistische Deutschland und die Sowjetunion." In Funke (no. 643), 639-53.

800. Levine, Herbert S. Hitler's Free City: A History of the Nazi Party in Danzig, 1925-39. Chicago, 1973.

Supersedes Hans L. Leonhardt, Nazi Conquest of Danzig (Chicago, 1942).

801. Marczewski, Jerzy. "The Nazi Concept of Drang nach Osten and the Basic Premises of the Occupation Policy in the 'Polish Question.' " Polish Western Affairs, 8 (1967), 289-324.

802. McMurry, Dean Scott. Deutschland und die Sowjetunion, 1933-1936: Ideologie, Machtpolitik und Wirtschaftsbeziehungen. Cologne, 1979.

Hitler's policy objectives in the Soviet Union, the role of the foreign ministry and other agencies.

803. Müller, Rolf-Dieter. Das Tor zur Weltmacht: Die Bedeutung der Sowjetunion für die deutsche Wirtschafts- und Rüstungspolitik zwischen den Weltkriegen. Boppard, 1984.

804. Niclauss, Karlheinz. Die Sowjetunion und Hitlers Machtergreifung: Eine Studie über die deutsch-russischen Beziehungen der Jahre 1929 bis 1935. Bonn, 1966.

For a study that focuses more on the Soviet Union, see Thomas Weingartner, Stalin und der Aufstieg Hitlers: Die Deutschlandpolitik der Sowjetunion und der kommunistischen Internationale, 1929-1934 (Berlin, 1970).

805. Puchert, Berthold. "Die deutsch-polnische Nichtangriffserklärung und die Aussenwirtschaftspolitik des deutschen Imperialismus gegenüber Polen bis 1939." Jahrbuch für Geschichte der UdSSR und der Volksdemokratischen Länder Europas, 12 (1968), 339-54.

806. Roos, Hans. Polen und Europa: Studien zur polnischen Aussenpolitik, 1931-1939. Tübingen, 1957.

A solid, well-researched study, mainly on Poland's evolving relationship with Germany.

807. Smelser, Ronald M. The Sudeten Problem, 1933-1938: Volkstumspolitik and the Formulation of Nazi Foreign Policy. Middletown, CT, 1974.

See also, Radomír Luza, The Transfer of the Sudeten Germans: A Study of Czech-German Relations, 1933-1962 (New York, 1964).

808. Stein, George H. "Russo-German Military Collaboration: The Last Phase, 1933." Political Science Quarterly, 77 (1962), 54-71.

809. Szymanski, Antoni. "Als polnischer Militärattaché in Berlin (1932-1939)." Politische Studien, 13 (1962), 42-51, 176-85, 313-20.

Recollections on German-Polish relations in the 1930s, by the Polish military attaché.

810. Vehviläinen, O. Nationalsozialistisches Deutschland und Sowjetunion: Die Geschichte ihrer diplomatischen Beziehungen, 1933-1939. Wiesbaden, 1970.

811. Volkmann, Hans-Erich. "Ökonomie und Machtpolitik: Lettland und Estland im politisch-ökonomischen Kalkül des Dritten Reiches (1933-1940)." Geschichte und Gesellschaft, 2 (1976), 471-500.

812. Weinberg, Gerhard. "Secret Hitler-Benes Negotiations in 1936-1937." Journal of Central European Affairs, 19 (1960), 366-74.

813. Wojciechowski, Marian. Die polnisch-deutschen Beziehungen, 1933-1938. Leiden, 1971.

Based on both German and Polish sources.

814. Wollstein, Günter. "Die Politik des nationalsozialistischen Deutschland gegenüber Polen, 1933-1939/45." In Funke (no. 643), 795-810.

Southeastern Europe

815. Adám, Magda. "Les Pays danubiens et Hitler (1933-1936)." Revue d'histoire de la deuxième guerre mondiale, 98 (1975), 1-26.

816. Adám, Magda, et al., eds. Allianz Hitler-Horthy-Mussolini: Dokumente zur ungarischen Aussenpolitik, 1933-1944. Budapest, 1966.

Documents from the Hungarian foreign ministry. For further such documents, see Elek Karsai, ed., "The Meeting of Gömbös and Hitler in 1933," New Hungarian Quarterly, 3 (1962), 170-96, and Miklos Szinai and László Szücs, eds., "Horthy's Secret Correspondence with Hitler," ibid., 4 (1963), 174-91.

817.   Basch, Antonín. The Danube Basin and the German Economic Sphere. New York, 1943.

An early but still valuable work on the growth of Germany's economic presence in southeastern Europe.

818.   Berend, Iván, and Ránki, György. "German-Hungarian Relations following Hitler's Rise to Power." Acta Historica, 8 (1961), 313-46.

See also, János Tihany, "Deutsch-ungarische Aussenhandels-beziehungen im Dienste der faschistischen Aggressionspolitik 1933 bis 1944," Jahrbuch für Wirtschaftsgeschichte (1972), 65-73.

819.   Broszat, Martin. "Deutschland-Ungarn-Rumänien: Entwicklung und Grundfaktoren nationalsozialistischer Hegemonial- und Bündnispolitik, 1938-1941." Historische Zeitschrift, 206 (1968), 45-96. (Also in Funke [no. 643], 524-64.)

820.   ———. "Faschismus und Kollaboration in Ostmitteleuropa zwischen den Weltkriegen." Vierteljahrshefte für Zeitgeschichte, 14 (1966), 225-51.

On the impact of Nazism and Nazi policy. See also his "Der Nationalsozialismus und Ostmitteleuropa," in Die Deutschen und ihre östlichen Nachbarn, edited by V. Aschenbrenner et al. (Frankfurt, 1967), 528-61.

821.   Hillgruber, Andreas. "Deutschland und Ungarn, 1933-1944: Ein Überblick über die politischen und militärischen Beziehungen im Rahmen der europäischen Politik." Wehrwissenschaftliche Rundschau, 9 (1959), 651-76.

822.   ———. Hitler, König Carol und Marschall Antonescu: Die deutsch-rumänischen Beziehungen, 1938-1944. 2d ed. Wiesbaden, 1965.

823.   Institute for Contemporary History, Belgrade, ed. The Third Reich and Yugoslavia, 1933-1945. Belgrade, 1977.

A massive volume, with nearly 40 essays on Germany's economic, diplomatic, and annexationist and occupation policies toward Yugoslavia.

824.   Kube, Alfred. "Aussenpolitik und 'Grossraumwirtschaft': Die deutsche Politik zur wirtschaftlichen Integration Südosteuropas 1933 bis 1939." In Wirtschaftliche und politische Integration in Europa im 19. und 20. Jahrhundert, edited by Helmut Berding. Göttingen, 1984, pp. 185-211.

825.   Littlefield, Frank C. Germany and Yugoslavia, 1933-1941: The German Conquest of Yugoslavia. New York, 1988.

826. Marguerat, Philippe. Le IIIe Reich et le pétrole roumain, 1938-1940: étude de la pénétration allemande dans les Balkans. The Hague, 1977.

Thorough, well-researched study of Germany's economic penetration of the Balkans (commercial, trade, and financial relations).

See also, his "L'Allemagne et la Roumanie à l'automne 1938: Économie et diplomatie," Relations internationales, 1 (1974), 173-79, and Eliza Campus, "Die Hitlerfaschistische Infiltration Rumäniens, 1939-1940," Zeitschrift für Geschichtswissenschaft, 5 (1957), 213-28.

827. Sakmyster, Thomas L. Hungary, the Great Powers, and the Danubian Crisis, 1936-1939. Athens, GA, 1979.

828. Schröder, Hans-Jürgen. "Südosteuropa als 'Informal Empire' Deutschlands, 1933-39: Das Beispiel Jugoslawien." Jahrbücher für Geschichte Osteuropas, 23 (1975), 70-96.

See also, Schröder's "Der Aufbau der deutschen Hegemonialstellung in Südosteuropa, 1933-1936," in Funke (no. 643), 757-73, and his article cited above (no. 607).

829. Wendt, Bernd Jürgen. "England und der deutsche 'Drang nach Südosten': Kapitalbeziehungen und Warenverkehr in Südosteuropa zwischen den Weltkriegen." In Deutschland in der Weltpolitik des 19. und 20. Jahrhunderts, edited by Imanuel Geiss and Bernd Jürgen Wendt. Düsseldorf, 1973, pp. 483-512.

On Germany's aggressive foreign trade policy and its collision with British interests in the Balkans, 1936-41.

830. Wuescht, Johann. Jugoslawien und das Dritte Reich: Eine dokumentierte Geschichte der deutsch-jugoslawischen Beziehungen von 1933 bis 1945. Stuttgart, 1969.

A source of information; controversial conclusions and interpretations.

The Extra-European Powers

See also, Jahrbuch (no. 54).

831. Bloss, Hartmut. "Die Zweigleisigkeit der deutschen Fernostpolitik und Hitlers Option für Japan 1938." Militärgeschichtliche Mitteilungen, 29 (1980), 55-92.

832. Boelcke, Willi A. "Deutschlands politische und wirtschaftliche Beziehungen zu Afghanistan bis zum zweiten Weltkrieg." Tradition, 14 (1969), 153-88.

833.   Boyd, Carl. <u>The Extraordinary Envoy: General Hiroshi Oshima and Diplomacy in the Third Reich, 1934-1939</u>. Washington, 1980.

Oshima was influential in forging German-Japanese ties in the 1930s. Further on Oshima, see Boyd's "The Berlin-Tokyo Axis and Japanese Military Initiative," <u>Modern Asian Studies</u>, 15 (1981), 311-38.

834.   Compton, James V. <u>The Swastika and the Eagle: Hitler, the United States, and the Origins of World War II</u>. Boston, 1967.

On Hitler's attitudes and policies toward the United States before 1941. Based largely on the files of the German embassy in Washington.

835.   Drechsler, Karl. <u>Deutschland-China-Japan, 1933-1939: Das Dilemma der deutschen Fernostpolitik</u>. [East] Berlin, 1964.

836.   Ebel, Arnold. <u>Das Dritte Reich und Argentinien: Die diplomatischen Beziehungen unter besonderer Berücksichtigung der Handelspolitik (1933-1939)</u>. Cologne, 1971.

Examines Nazi Germany's political and ideological aims in Argentina as well as her economic policies. An introductory chapter surveys the relations between Weimar Germany and Argentina.

837.   El Dessouki, Mohamed-Kamal. <u>Hitler und der Nahe Osten</u>. Berlin, 1963.

838.   Fox, John P. <u>Germany and the Far Eastern Crisis, 1931-1938</u>. London, 1981.

The different origins and different aspects of Germany's Far East policy (seen from the perspective of the foreign ministry). Set against the background of Germany's internal developments.

839.   Frye, Alton. <u>Nazi Germany and the American Hemisphere, 1933-1941</u>. New Haven, CT, 1967.

On the activities of the AO, interpreted as an attempt to soften up the United States for conquest.

840.   Harms-Baltzer, Käte. <u>Die Nationalisierung der deutschen Einwanderer und ihrer Nachkommen in Brasilien als Problem der deutsch-brasilianischen Beziehungen, 1930-1938</u>. Berlin, 1970.

A study of German policy built around the problems raised by Brazil's efforts to integrate German immigrants into Brazilian society. See also, Rainer Pommerin, "Überlegungen des 'Dritten Reiches' zur Rückholung deutscher Auswanderer aus Lateinamerika," <u>Jahrbuch für Geschichte von Staat, Wirtschaft und Gesellschaft Lateinamerikas</u>, 16 (1979), 365-77.

841. Hauner, Milan. "Das nationalsozialistische Deutschland und Indien." In Funke (no. 643), 430-53.

842. Hirszowicz, Lukasz. The Third Reich and the Arab East. Toronto, 1966.

843. Iklé, Frank William. German-Japanese Relations, 1936-1940. New York, 1956.

844. Kienzle, William. "German-South African Trade Relations in the Nazi Era." African Affairs, 78 (1979), 81-90.

845. Kossok, Manfred. " 'Sonderauftrag Südamerika': Zur deutschen Politik gegenüber Lateinamerika, 1938-1942." In Lateinamerika zwischen Emanzipation und Liberalismus, 1810-1960. [East] Berlin, 1961, pp. 234-55.

846. Kum'a N'dumbe III, Alexandre. Hitler voulait Afrique: Les plans secrets pour une Afrique fasciste, 1933-1945. Paris, 1980.

847. Martin, Bernd. "Die deutsch-japanischen Beziehungen während des Dritten Reiches." In Funke (no. 643), 454-70; and in Bracher, Funke, and Jacobsen (no. 260), 370-89.

848. Martin, Bernd, ed. Die deutsche Beraterschaft in China, 1927-1938: Militär, Wirtschaft, Aussenpolitik. Düsseldorf, 1981.

The German advisory group in China and diplomatic, military, and economic issues in Sino-German relations. See also his "Das Deutsche Reich und Guomindang-China, 1927-1941," in Von der Kolonialpolitik zur Kooperation, edited by Kuo Heng-yü (Munich, 1986), pp. 325-75.

849. Menzel, Johanna M. "Der geheime deutsch-japanische Notenaustausch zum Dreimächtepakt." Vierteljahrshefte für Zeitgeschichte, 5 (1957), 182-93.

850. Moss, Kenneth. "George S. Messersmith and Nazi Germany: The Diplomacy of Limits in Central Europe." In Jones (no. 620), 113-26.

Messersmith served as consul in the U.S. embassy in Berlin in the 1930s.

851. Nicosia, Francis R. The Third Reich and the Palestine Question. Austin, TX, 1985.

Nazi attitudes toward Zionism and the role of Palestine in Hitler's policy toward England. For an earlier account, see David Yisraeli, "The Third Reich and Palestine," Middle Eastern Studies, 7 (1971), 343-53, as well as R. Melka, "Nazi Germany and the Palestine Question," ibid., 5 (1969), 221-33.

852. Presseisen, Ernst L. Germany and Japan: A Study in Totalitarian Diplomacy, 1933-1941. The Hague, 1958.

Complements Iklé (no. 843) by relying more on German sources and concentrating more on German policy.

853. Ratenhof, Udo. Die Chinapolitik des Deutschen Reiches 1871 bis 1945: Wirtschaft, Rüstung, Militär. Boppard, 1987.

Emphasizes the military and armaments elements of German policy in China.

854. Sanke, Heinz, ed. Der deutsche Faschismus in Lateinamerika, 1933-1943. [East] Berlin, 1966.

Essays on Nazi policy in Argentina, Brazil, Colombia, and Central America, by East German historians.

855. Schröder, Hans-Jürgen. Deutschland und die Vereinigten Staaten, 1933-1939: Wirtschaft und Politik in der Entwicklung des deutsch-amerikanischen Gegensatzes. Wiesbaden, 1970.

Especially good on German-American economic relations and rivalries, but goes too far in interpreting Hitler's program as economically motivated.

856. ———. "Das Dritte Reich, die USA und Lateinamerika, 1933-1941." In Funke (no. 643), 339-64.

857. ———. "Die 'Neue Deutsche Südamerikapolitik': Dokumente zur nationalsozialistischen Wirtschaftspolitik in Lateinamerika von 1933 bis 1936." Jahrbuch für Geschichte von Staat, Wirtschaft und Gesellschaft Lateinamerikas, 6 (1969), 337-450.

———. "Die Vereinigten Staaten und die nationalsozialistische Handelspolitik gegenüber Lateinamerika 1937/38." Ibid., 7 (1970), 309-70.

858. Schröder, Josef. "Die Beziehungen der Achsenmächte zur arabischen Welt." In Funke (no. 643), 365-82. (Also in Zeitschrift für Politik, 18 [1971], 80-95.)

On the dilemmas of Axis policy in North Africa and the Middle East.

859. Sommer, Theo. Deutschland und Japan zwischen den Mächten, 1935-1940: Vom Antikominternpakt zum Dreimächtepakt. Tübingen, 1962.

860. Voigt, Johannes. "Hitler und Indien." Vierteljahrshefte für Zeitgeschichte, 19 (1971), 33-63.

861. Volberg, Heinrich. Auslandsdeutschtum und Drittes Reich: Der Fall Argentinien. Cologne, 1981.

The author writes from firsthand knowledge of the activities of the National Socialists in Argentina.

862. Volland, Klaus. Das Dritte Reich und Mexiko: Studien zur Entwicklung des deutsch-mexikanischen Verhältnisses 1933-1942 unter besonderer Berücksichtigung der Ölpolitik. Frankfurt/M., 1976.

863. Weinberg, Gerhard L. "Deutsch-japanische Verhandlungen über das Südseemandat, 1937-1938." Vierteljahrshefte für Zeitgeschichte, 4 (1956), 390-98.

————. "Die geheimen Abkommen zum Antikominternpakt." Ibid., 2 (1954), 193-201.

————. "German Recognition of Manchoukuo." World Affairs Quarterly, 28 (1957), 149-64.

864. ————. "Hitler's Image of the United States." American Historical Review, 69 (1964), 1006-21.

————. "Schachts Besuch in den USA im Jahre 1933." Vierteljahrshefte für Zeitgeschichte, 11 (1963), 166-80.

865. Yisraeli, David. "The Third Reich and the Transfer Agreement." Journal of Contemporary History, 6 (1971), 129-48.

On the negotiations leading up to the transfer agreement, see Edwin Black, The Transfer Agreement: The Untold Story of the Secret Agreement between the Third Reich and Jewish Palestine, New York, 1984.

The Smaller Powers

866. Bourgeois, Daniel. Le Troisième Reich et la Suisse, 1933-1941. Neuchatel, 1974.

867. Fink, Jürgen. Die Schweiz aus der Sicht des Dritten Reiches, 1933-1945. Zurich, 1985.

868. Harrigan, William H. "Nazi Germany and the Holy See, 1933-1936: The Historical Background of Mit brennender Sorge." Catholic Historical Review, 47 (1961), 164-73.

A more broadly conceived study is George O. Kent, "Pope Pius XII and Germany: Some Aspects of German-Vatican Relations, 1933-1943," American Historical Review, 69 (1964), 59-78. See also, Dieter Albrecht, "Die Politische Klausel des Reichskonkordats in den deutsch-vatikanischen Beziehungen, 1936-1943," in Festschrift für

Max Spindler, edited by Dieter Albrecht et al. Munich, 1969, pp. 793-829.

869. Loock, Hans-Dietrich. "Nordeuropa zwischen Aussenpolitik und 'grossgermanischer' Innenpolitik." In Funke (no. 643), 684-706.

870. Wittmann, Klaus. Schwedens Wirtschaftsbeziehungen zum Dritten Reich, 1933-1945. Munich, 1978.

An analysis of Germany's foreign trade policy, which aimed at (a) establishing bilateral relations which would benefit Germany's armaments economy, and (b) integrating Sweden into a larger economic union in central Europe.

4. Hitler, Franco, Mussolini

The course of German-Italian and of German-Spanish relations has been examined in detail, especially for 1936, when the outbreak of the Spanish Civil War drew Hitler and Mussolini closer together. But more needs to be done on the structure of the German-Italian relationship, for there is still no satisfactory explanation of its weaknesses and contradictions. This has been less of a problem in the German-Spanish relationship, since Franco, unlike Mussolini, was able to stand up to Hitler, and while he accepted German aid, he never pledged more than benevolent neutrality in return. The structure of the triangular relationship has not been examined at all.

Italy

See also, Schreiber (no. 333).

871. Funke, Manfred. "Die deutsch-italienischen Beziehungen: Antibolschewismus und aussenpolitische Interessenkonkurrenz als Strukturprinzip der 'Achse.' " In Funke (no. 643), 823-46; and in Bracher, Funke, and Jacobsen (no. 260), 345-69.

See also his "Brutale Freundschaft im Legendenschleier: Marginalie zur Vorgeschichte der 'Achse,' " Geschichte in Wissenschaft und Unterricht, 23 (1972), 713-24.

872. ———. Sanktionen und Kanonen: Hitler, Mussolini und der italienische Abessinienkonflikt, 1934-36. Düsseldorf, 1970.

Demonstrates that Germany did not back Italy in this conflict (and, in fact, supplied arms to Abyssinia) and that the assumption that the Axis alliance emerged from this conflict is wrong.

For the opposite view, see Giovanni Buccianti, "Hitler, Mussolini et il conflitto italo-etiopico," Il Politico, 37 (1972), 415-29.

873. Michaelis, Meir. Mussolini and the Jews: German-Italian Relations and the Jewish Question in Italy, 1922-1945. Oxford, 1979.

Examines the impact of the Axis alliance on Italy's racial policy.

874.   Petersen, Jens. Hitler-Mussolini: Die Entstehung der Achse Berlin-Rom, 1933-1936. Tübingen, 1973.

Argues that an alliance between the two fascist leaders was virtually inevitable (contrary to Funke [no. 872]).

See also Petersen's "Deutschland und Italien im Sommer 1935: Der Wechsel des italienischen Botschafters in Berlin." Geschichte in Wissenschaft und Unterricht, 20 (1969), 330-41.

875.   ———. "Italien in der aussenpolitischen Konzeption Hitlers." In Historisch-Politische Streiflichter, edited by Kurt Jürgensen and Reimer Hansen. Neumünster, 1971, pp. 200-20.

Covering an earlier phase of Hitler's views in some detail is Walter Pese, "Hitler und Italien, 1920-1926," Vierteljahrshefte für Zeitgeschichte, 3 (1955), 113-26.

876.   Poulain, Marc. "Deutschlands Drang nach Südosten contra Mussolini's Hinterlandpolitik, 1931-1934." Donauraum, 22 (1977), 129-53.

877.   Robertson, Esmonde M. "Hitler and Sanctions: Mussolini and the Rhineland." European Studies Review, 7 (1977), 409-35. (Reprinted, in translation, in Vierteljahrshefte für Zeitgeschichte, 26 [1978], 237-64.)

878.   Schröder, Josef, ed. Brief- und Telegrammwechsel zwischen Hitler und Mussolini, 1931-1945. Göttingen, 1976.

A collection of letters exchanged between the two in the period 1940-43 is in Hitler e Mussolini: Lettere e documenti (Milan, 1946).

879.   Schütt, Werner. "Der Stahlpakt und Italiens 'Nonbelligeranza,' 1938-1940." Wehrwissenschaftliche Rundschau, 8 (1958), 498-521.

See also, Ettore Anchieri, "Dal convegno di Salisburgo alla non belligeranza italiana," Il Politico, 1 (1954), 23-43.

880.   Siebert, Ferdinand. "Der deutsch-italienische Stahlpakt." Vierteljahrshefte für Zeitgeschichte, 7 (1959), 372-95.

881.   Toscano, Mario. "Italy and the Nazi-Soviet Accords of August, 1939," in Designs in Diplomacy. Baltimore, 1970, pp. 48-123.

882.   ———. "Le origine del 'Testamento politico' di Hitler per la frontiera del Brennero," in Pagine di storia diplomatica contemporanea. Milan, 1963, pp. 161-86.

See also, Winfried Schmitz-Esser, "Hitler-Mussolini: Das Südtiroler Abkommen von 1939," Aussenpolitik, 13 (1962), 397-409.

883. ———. The Origins of the Pact of Steel. Baltimore, 1967. (A translation of the second edition of the Italian original, published in 1956.)

Vinicio Araldi's Il patto d'acciaio (Rome, 1962) adds little to Toscano's interpretation.

884. Watt, D.C. "Hitler's Visit to Rome and the May Weekend Crisis: A Study in Hitler's Response to External Stimuli." Journal of Contemporary History, 9 (1974), 23-32.

Analyzes the reasons why Hitler made his decision to attack Czechoslovakia in connection with his visit to Rome.

See also, D.C. Watt, "An Earlier Model for the Pact of Steel: The Draft Treaties Exchanged between Germany and Italy during Hitler's Visit to Rome in May, 1938," International Affairs, 33 (1957), 185-97.

885. ———. "The Rome-Berlin Axis, 1936-1940: Myth and Reality." Review of Politics, 22 (1960), 519-43.

886. Wiskemann, Elizabeth. The Rome-Berlin Axis: A Study of the Relations between Hitler and Mussolini. 2d ed. London, 1966.

Spain

887. Abendroth, Hans-Henning. Hitler in der spanischen Arena: Die deutsch-spanischen Beziehungen im Spannungsfeld der euro-päischen Interessenpolitik vom Ausbruch des Bürgerkrieges bis zum Ausbruch des Weltkrieges, 1936-1939. Paderborn, 1973.

Examines Germany's intervention in its international setting, and stresses the improved and defensive quality of Hitler's policy.

See also, Hans-Henning Abendroth, "Deutschlands Rolle im Spanischen Bürgerkrieg," in Funke (no. 643), 471-88, and his "Die deutsche Intervention im Spanischen Bürgerkrieg," Vierteljahrshefte für Zeitgeschichte, 30 (1982) 117-29.

888. Abendroth, Hans-Henning, ed. Mittelsmann zwischen Franco und Hitler: Johannes Bernhardt erinnert 1936. Marktheidenfeld, 1980.

Reminiscences of a member of the AO in Spain, who participated in the first phase of Germany's intervention in the civil war.

889. Einhorn, Marion. Die ökonomischen Hintergründe der faschistischen deutschen Intervention in Spanien, 1936-1939. [East] Berlin, 1962.

890. Dankelmann, Otfried. <u>Franco zwischen Hitler und den Westmächten</u>. [East] Berlin, 1970.

891. Harper, Glenn T. <u>German Economic Policy in Spain during the Spanish Civil War, 1936-1939</u>. The Hague, 1967.

Based purely on published sources, deals with the economic motives and benefits of Germany's intervention.

892. Maier, Klaus M. <u>Guernica, 26.4.1937: Die deutsche Intervention in Spanien und der "Fall Guernica."</u> Freiburg i.B., 1975.

893. Merkes, Manfred. <u>Die deutsche Politik gegenüber dem spanischen Bürgerkrieg, 1936-1939</u>. Rev. enl. ed. Bonn, 1969.

A comprehensive, well-documented work; one of the best treatments of the subject.

894. Ruhl, Klaus Jörg. "L'Alliance à distance: Les relations économiques germano-espagnoles de 1936 à 1945." <u>Revue d'histoire de la deuxième guerre mondiale</u>, 30 (1980), 69-102.

895. Schieder, Wolfgang, and Dipper, Christof, eds. <u>Der Spanische Bürgerkrieg in der internationalen Politik (1936-1939)</u>. Munich, 1976.

A dozen essays, reflective of the current state of research. Includes essays by Abendroth and Einhorn, drawn from their respective books, as well as a piece by Schieder ("Spanischer Bürgerkrieg und Vierjahresplan: Zur Struktur nationalsozialistischer Aussenpolitik") that casts light on Nazi policymaking. Schieder's essay is reprinted in Michalka (no. 656), 325-59.

5. The Road to War, 1937-39

The works that follow deal with German policy and German diplomacy in the two years before the outbreak of the war in September 1939. They are concerned with the three big crises--Anschluss, Munich and Prague, and Danzig--insofar as these were initiated and affected by Hitler's decisions.

For general works on the origins of the war and on the international events of summer 1939, see below, pp. 219-25.

General

896. Bullock, Alan. <u>Hitler and the Origins of the Second World War</u>. Oxford, 1967.

A superb assessment of the evidence, taking into account all recent findings and arguments. Reprinted in Hans W. Gatzke, ed., <u>European Diplomacy between Two Wars, 1919-1939</u> (Chicago,

1972), pp. 221-46, in Esmonde M. Robertson, ed., The Origins of the Second World War (London, 1971), pp. 188-224, and in Niedhart (no. 955).

897.   Carr, William.   "Rüstung, Wirtschaft und Politik am Vorabend des zweiten Weltkrieges." In Michalka (no. 656), 437-54.

898.   Deutsch, Harold C.   Hitler and His Generals: The Hidden Crisis, January-June 1938. Minneapolis, 1974.

————. The Conspiracy against Hitler in the Twilight War. Minneapolis, 1968.

Includes information on the military's position on Hitler's foreign policy and on the opposition in the foreign ministry.

899.   Eichholtz, Dietrich.   "Zum Anteil des IG-Farben Konzerns an der Vorbereitung des Zweiten Weltkriegs." Jahrbuch für Wirtschaftsgeschichte (1969), 83-105.

See also, Dietrich Eichholtz and Wolfgang Schumann, eds. Anatomie des Krieges: Neue Dokumente über die Rolle des deutschen Monopolkapitals bei der Vorbereitung und Durchführung des zweiten Weltkrieges (Berlin, 1969), which reproduces documents to demonstrate that banks and industries penetrated deeply into the economies of southeastern Europe before and after the invasion.

900.   Eisenbach, Artur.   "Nazi Foreign Policy on the Eve of World War II and the Jewish Question." Acta Poloniae Historica, 5 (1962), 107-39.

901.   Gackenholz, Hermann.   "Reichskanzlei, 5. November 1937: Bemerkungen über 'Politik und Kriegführung' im Dritten Reich." In Forschungen zu Staat und Verfassung, edited by Richard Dietrich and Gerhard Oestreich. Berlin, 1958, pp. 459-84.

Gackenholz was the first to subject the so-called Hossbach memorandum to close textual and contextual analysis (see above, p. 53, and Hossbach [no. 132]).

Subsequent analyses include:

Kielmannsegg, Peter Graf. "Die militärisch-politische Tragweite der Hossbach Besprechung." Vierteljahrshefte für Zeitgeschichte, 8 (1960), 268-75.

Bussmann, Walter. "Zur Entstehung und Überlieferung der 'Hossbach-Niederschrift.'" Vierteljahrshefte für Zeitgeschichte, 16 (1968), 373-84. (Reprinted in Werner Pöls, ed., Walter Bussmann: Wandel und Kontinuität in Politik und Geschichte, Boppard, 1973, pp. 229-40.)

Henrikson, Göran. "Das Nürnberger Dokument 386-PS (Das 'Hossbach-Protokoll'): Eine Untersuchung seines Wertes als Quelle." Probleme deutscher Zeitgeschichte (Stockholm, 1970), 151-94.

902. Knipping, Franz, and Müller, Klaus-Jürgen, eds. Machtbewusstsein in Deutschland am Vorabend des Zweiten Weltkrieges. Paderborn, 1984.

The results of a collaborative research project on the realities and illusions of power on the eve of World War II. Includes essays on German policy in 1938 (Niedhart), Göring's role in policymaking (Martens), eastern policy 1937-38 (Müller), Weizsäcker (Blasius), and ambassador Schulenburg (Wollstein).

903. Mason, Timothy W. Arbeiterklasse und Volksgemeinschaft: Dokumente und Materialien zur deutschen Arbeiterpolitik, 1936-1939. Opladen, 1975.

An interesting thesis (and documents to back it up) on the economic considerations of German foreign policy, 1938-39, especially as they affected the timing of hostilities. A revised version of the introduction to this volume was published as Sozialpolitik im Dritten Reich (Opladen, 1977). For a review, see Vierteljahrshefte für Zeitgeschichte, 26 (1978), 347-92.

904. ———. "Innere Krise und Angriffskrieg, 1938-1939." In Forstmeier and Volkmann (no. 727), 158-88.

905. Michalka, Wolfgang. "Vom Antikominternpakt zum Euro-Asiatischen Kontinentalblock: Ribbentrops Alternativkonzeption zu Hitlers aussenpolitischen Programm." In Michalka (no. 656), 471-92.

906. Murray, Williamson. The Change in the European Balance of Power, 1938-1939: The Path to Ruin. Princeton, 1984.

German diplomatic and military policy in the context of the larger European situation in the late 1930s. Emphasis on the evolution of policy and the stages of policymaking; on military strategies and perceptions.

907. Niedhart, Gottfried. "Deutsche Aussenpolitik und internationales System im Krisenjahr 1937." In Michalka (no. 656), 360-76.

908. Overy, Richard J. "Hitler's War and the German Economy: A Reinterpretation." Economic History Review, 35 (1982), 272-91.

Disagrees with Mason (no. 903). Argues that the outbreak of war caught Hitler by surprise, before his plans for war were complete.

909. Seraphim, Hans Günther. "Nachkriegsprozesse und zeitgeschichtliche Forschung." In Mensch und Staat in Recht und

Geschichte, edited by Hans Krause and Hans Günther Seraphim. Kitzingen/M., 1954, pp. 436-55.

Analyzes four of Hitler's prewar conferences and their documentation. See also, H.W. Koch, "Hitler and the Origins of the Second World War: Second Thoughts on the Status of Some of the Documents," Historical Journal, 11 (1968), 125-43.

910. Weinberg, Gerhard L. "The German Generals and the Outbreak of War, 1938-1939." In General Staffs and Diplomacy before the Second World War, edited by Adrian Preston. Totowa, NJ, 1978, pp. 24-40.

Anschluss

See also, Luza (no. 602), Rosar (no. 692).

911. Botz, Gerhard. Die Eingliederung Österreichs in das Deutsche Reich: Planung und Verwirklichung des politischen-administrativen Anschlusses, 1938-1940. Vienna, 1972.

On the planning and measures taken to integrate Austria into Germany. See also, Maurice Williams, "German Imperialism and Austria, 1938," Journal of Contemporary History, 14 (1979), 139-53.

912. Eichstädt, Ulrich. Von Dollfuss zu Hitler: Geschichte des Anschlusses Österreichs, 1933-1938. Wiesbaden, 1955.

913. Gehl, Jürgen. Austria, Germany, and the Anschluss, 1931-1938. New York, 1963.

German-Austrian relations, beginning with the abortive customs union, through the July putsch and the crises over Abyssinia and the Spanish Civil War, to merger in 1938.

914. Jedlicka, Ludwig, and Neck, Rudolf, eds. Das Juliabkommen von 1936: Vorgeschichte, Hintergründe und Folgen. Munich, 1977.

Symposium on the Austro-German agreement of July 1936, with interesting contributions on the economic background and the economic penetration of Austria.

915. Kindermann, Gottfried-Karl. Hitlers Niederlage in Österreich: Bewaffneter NS-Putsch, Kanzler-Mord und Österreichs Abwehrsieg von 1934. Hamburg, 1984.

Dollfuss's assassination, its background and aftermath. Has been criticized for overestimating Hitler's control of policy and strategy at the expense of a more careful analysis of the internal conflict among German policymakers.

916. Koerner, Ralf R. So haben sie es damals gemacht: Die Propagandavorbereitung zum Österreich-Anschluss durch das Hitlerregime, 1933-1938. Vienna, 1958.

917. Otruba, Gustav. "Hitlers 'Tausend-Mark-Sperre' und Österreichs Fremdenverkehr 1933." In Beiträge zur Zeitgeschichte, edited by Rudolf Neck and Adam Wandruszka. Vienna, 1976, pp. 113-62.

918. Ross, Dieter. Hitler und Dollfuss: Die deutsche Österreichpolitik, 1933-1934. Hamburg, 1966.

919. Schausberger, Norbert. Der Griff nach Österreich: Der Anschluss. Vienna, 1978.

   See also the same author's "Österreich und die nationalsozialistische Anschluss-Politik," in Funke (no. 643), 728-56, and "Österreich und die deutsche Wirtschaftsexpansion nach dem Donauraum," Österreich in Geschichte und Literatur, 16 (1972), 196-213.

920. Stuhlpfarrer, Karl, and Steurer, Leopold. "Die Ossa in Österreich," in Vom Justizpalast zum Heldenplatz, edited by Ludwig Jedlicka and Rudolf Neck. Vienna, 1975, pp. 35-64.

921. Vosske, Heinz. "Diplomatische Berichte über die Vorbereitung der Annexion Österreichs." Zeitschrift für Geschichtswissenschaft, 16 (1968), 906-20.

Munich and Prague

See also, Bosl (no. 789).

922. Blasius, Rainer A. Für Grossdeutschland--wider den grossen Krieg: Ernst von Weizsäcker in den Krisen um die Tschechoslowakei und Polen. Cologne, 1981.

   Unlike Thielenhaus (no. 937), focuses largely on Weizsäcker and his activities in the context of his views on policy and Hitler's policy objectives. Destroys some of the Weizsäcker legends.

923. Bodensieck, Heinrich. "Der Plan eines 'Freundschaftsvertrags' zwischen dem Reich und der Tschechoslowakei im Jahre 1938." Zeitschrift für Ostforschung, 10 (1961), 462-76.

   Prints a number of important documents on the "friendship treaty" of Dec. 1938. Supersedes Hans Schiefer, "Deutschland und die Tschechoslowakei von September 1938 bis März 1939," Zeitschrift für Ostforschung 4 (1955), 48-66.

924. ———. "Volksgruppenrecht und nationalsozialistische Aussenpolitik nach dem Münchner Abkommen 1938." Zeitschrift für Ostforschung, 7 (1958), 502-18.

925. ———. "Zur Vorgeschichte des 'Protektorats Böhmen und Mähren.'" Geschichte in Wissenschaft und Unterricht, 19 (1968), 713-32.

926. Braddick, Henderson B. Germany, Czechoslovakia and the "Grand Alliance" in the May Crisis, 1938. Denver, CO, 1969.

927. Brügel, Johann W. "German Diplomacy in the Sudeten Question before 1938." International Affairs, 37 (1961), 323-31.

928. Celovsky, Boris. Das Münchner Abkommen von 1938. Stuttgart, 1958.

One of the most thorough studies, ranks with Rönnefarth (no. 935) and Taylor (no. 936).

929. Hill, Leonidas. "Three Crises, 1938-39." Journal of Contemporary History, 3 (1968), 113-44.

On Munich, Prague, and September 1939, based on the Weizsäcker papers and interviews. Argues that Hitler's military timetable was of preeminent importance in these crises.

930. Hoensch, Jörg Konrad. Die Slowakei und Hitlers Ostpolitik: Hlinkas Slowakische Volkspartei zwischen Autonomie und Separation 1938/39. Cologne, 1965.

A study of the Slovak autonomy movement and of Hitler's success in undermining Czechoslovakian integrity. See also, Ferdinand Durcanský, "Mit Tiso bei Hitler: Die Entstehung der Slowakischen Republik, 1939," Politische Studien, 7 (1956), 1-10.

931. ———. "Revision und Expansion: Überlegungen zur Zielsetzung, Methode und Planung der Tschechoslowakei-Politik Hitlers." Bohemia 1968 (1969), 208-28.

932. Komjathy, Anthony. "The First Vienna Award (November 2, 1938)." Austrian History Yearbook, 15/16 (1979-80), 131-56.

933. Král, Václav, ed. Das Abkommen von München: Tschechoslowakische Dokumente, 1937-1939. Prague, 1968.

———. Die Deutschen in der Tschechoslowakei, 1933-1947. Prague, 1964.

Collections of documents from Czech archives, many of them of German origin, which offer a rather one-sided view of events.

934. Mastny, Vojtech. "Design or Improvisation: The Origins of the German Protectorate of Bohemia and Moravia." In Columbia Essays in International Affairs, 1965, edited by Andrew W. Cordier. New York, 1966, pp. 127-53.

935.   Rönnefarth, Helmut K.G. Die Sudetenkrise in der internationalen Politik: Entstehung. Verlauf. Auswirkung. 2 vols. Wiesbaden, 1961.

Massive, detailed, reliable, along with Celovsky (no. 928) and Taylor (no. 936) the best work on the conference.

936.   Taylor, Telford. Munich: The Price of Peace. New York, 1979.

An earlier reassessment, written more from a British perspective, is Keith Robbins, Munich 1938 (London, 1968).

937.   Thielenhaus, Marion. Zwischen Anpassung und Widerstand: Deutsche Diplomaten, 1938-1941. 2d ed. Paderborn, 1985.

The political activities of the German diplomats around Weizsäcker and the Kordt brothers, their efforts to moderate Hitler's policies, and their failure, first, to preserve and, then, to reestablish peace.

938.   Weinberg, Gerhard L. "The May Crisis, 1938." Journal of Modern History, 29 (1957), 213-25.

See also, W.V. Wallace, "The Making of the May Crisis of 1938," Slavonic and East European Review, 41 (1963), 368-90.

939.   Wendt, Bernd-Jürgen. München 1938: England zwischen Hitler und Preussen. Frankfurt/M., 1965.

————. Appeasement 1938: Wirtschaftliche Rezession und Mitteleuropa. Frankfurt/M., 1966.

The first volume deals with the attempts by members of the German opposition to get British help for overthrowing Hitler, the second picks up where the first leaves off and concentrates on Anglo-German trade rivalries in southeastern Europe.

Summer 1939

940.   Benz, Wolfgang, and Graml, Hermann, eds. Sommer 1939: Die Grossmächte und der europäische Krieg. Stuttgart, 1979.

Collection of essays, including Gerhard Weinberg on international relations 1937-39, Fritz Blaich on German rearmament and economic mobilization between 1933 and 1939, and Ludolf Herbst on the government's conflict with business and industry in 1938-39.

941.   Baumgart, Winfried. "Zur Ansprache Hitlers vor den Führern der Wehrmacht am 22. August 1939: Eine quellenkritische Untersuchung." Vierteljahrshefte für Zeitgeschichte, 16 (1968), 120-49.

Demonstrates that Hitler made two speeches that day and engaged in discussion with a smaller group of generals as well. For additional comment on the issue, see Vierteljahrshefte für Zeitgeschichte, 19 (1971), 294-304.

942. Brügel, Johann W. Stalin und Hitler: Pakt gegen Europa. Vienna, 1973.

943. Chanaday, A., and Jensen, J. "Germany, Rumania, and the British Guarantee of March-April 1939." Australian Journal of Politics and History, 16 (1970), 201-17.

944. Dahlerus, Birger. The Last Attempt. London, 1948 (rpt. 1973).

See also Johann W. Brügel, "Dahlerus als Zwischenträger nach Kriegsausbruch," Historische Zeitschrift, 228 (1979), 70-97, which reconstructs the attempts at intermediation.

945. Douglas-Hamilton, James. "Ribbentrop and War." Journal of Contemporary History, 5 (1970), 45-63.

Reproduces and comments on a memorandum by Ernest Tennant on his conversation with Ribbentrop in July 1939.

946. Dülffer, Jost. "Der Beginn des Krieges 1939: Hitler, die innere Krise und das Mächtesystem." Geschichte und Gesellschaft, 2 (1976), 443-70; and in Bracher, Funke, and Jacobsen (no. 260), 317-44.

Examines the four major interpretations on Nazi policy in 1939, and concludes that both the international situation and the internal crisis must be taken into account.

947. Fabry, Philipp W. Der Hitler-Stalin Pakt, 1939-1941: Ein Beitrag zur Methode sowjetischer Aussenpolitik. Darmstadt, 1962.

Conclusions as dubious as those in his first book (no. 793)--that Stalin signed a pact with Hitler in order to embroil Germany in a war with the West and that Hitler invaded the USSR as a preventive measure.

948. Hehn, J. von. "Zum deutsch-lettischen Verhältnis im Jahr 1939." Zeitschrift für Ostforschung, 23 (1974), 661-75.

949. Hillgruber, Andreas. "Der Hitler-Stalin-Pakt und die Entfesselung des Zweiten Weltkrieges: Situationsanalyse und Machtkalkül der beiden Pakt-Partner." Historische Zeitschrift, 230 (1980), 339-61.

950. Hubatsch, Walther. "Die Rückkehr des Memelgebiets, 1939." Deutsche Studien, 7 (1969), 256-64.

See also, Felix-Heinrich Gentzen, "Die Rolle der 'Deutschen Stiftung' bei der Vorbereitung der Annexion des Memellandes im März 1939,"

Jahrbuch für Geschichte der UdSSR und der Volksdemokratischen Länder, 5 (1961), 71-94.

951. Kessel, Albrecht von. "Der Weg in die Katastrophe: 25. bis 31. August 1939," in Aus der Schule der Diplomatie, edited by Walter J. Schütz. Düsseldorf, 1965, pp. 565-75.

Recollections, written late in 1944, by a young diplomat who was on the scene in Berlin. For a close reconstruction of events on the last day, see Henryk Batowski, "August 31st, 1939 in Berlin," Polish Western Affairs, 4 (1963), 20-50.

952. Levine, Herbert S. "The Mediator: Carl J. Burckhardt's Efforts to Avert a Second World War." Journal of Modern History, 45 (1973), 439-55.

953. Loeber, Dietrich A. "Deutsche Politik gegenüber Estland und Lettland--Die Umsiedlung der deutsch-baltischen Volksgruppe im Zeichen der Geheimabsprache mit der Sowjetunion 1939." In Funke (no. 643), 675-83.

954. Metzmacher, Helmut. "Deutsch-englische Ausgleichsbemühungen im Sommer 1939." Vierteljahrshefte für Zeitgeschichte, 14 (1966), 369-412.

See also, Josef Henke, "Hitler und England Mitte August 1939," Vierteljahrshefte für Zeitgeschichte, 21 (1973), 231-42.

955. Niedhart, Gottfried, ed. Kriegsbeginn 1939: Entfesselung oder Ausbruch des Zweiten Weltkriegs? Darmstadt, 1976.

Brings together previously published essays on German policy and on the central issue of Anglo-German antagonisms. A useful compendium.

956. Watt, D.C. "The Initiation of the Negotiations Leading to the Nazi-Soviet Pact: A Historical Problem." In Essays in Honour of E.H. Carr, edited by C. Abramsky, London, 1974, pp. 152-70. (Also in Michalka [no. 656], 414-36.)

See also an earlier interpretation: Max Braubach, Hitlers Weg zur Verständigung mit Russland im Jahre 1939 (Cologne, 1960).

957. Weber, Reinhold W. Die Entstehungsgeschichte des Hitler-Stalin-Paktes 1939. Frankfurt/M., 1980.

Straightforward, detailed account of the negotiations leading to the pact in August 1939.

958. Weinberg, Gerhard L. "A Proposed Compromise over Danzig in 1939." Journal of Central European Affairs, 14 (1955), 334-38.

F. WORLD WAR II

1. Origins and Conduct of the War

This chapter comprises general works. It lists the most important interpretations of the diplomatic origins and military conduct of the war. These treat Germany's role as part of a larger context, and they are useful for background and comparisons. It also lists primary sources and secondary literature on the war as the Germans saw and experienced it, and here, again, it is usually Hitler who is the central figure.

There are several bibliographies on the war. A.G.S. Enser, ed., A Subject Bibliography of the Second World War: Books in English, 1939-1974 (London, 1977), is the most recent. Gwyn M. Bayliss, Bibliographic Guide to the Two World Wars: An Annotated Survey of English-Language Reference Materials (New York, 1977), is a bibliography of bibliographies. Andreas Hillgruber, Zur Entstehung des Zweiten Weltkrieges: Forschungsstand und Literatur (Düsseldorf, 1980), assesses current research and surveys the literature. ABC-Clio Information Services, The Third Reich at War: A Historical Bibliography (Santa Barbara, CA, 1984), lists more than a thousand references to articles in books and journals.

General

959.　Baumont, Maurice. The Origins of the Second World War. New Haven, CT, 1978.

960.　Bell, P.M.H. The Origins of the Second World War in Europe. London, 1986.

Examines the ideological, economic, and strategic context for the coming of war, 1932-41, and traces the course of events in those years.

961.　Bosl, Karl, ed. Das Jahr 1941 in der europäischen Politik. Munich, 1972.

Essays include Peter Krüger on Germany's diplomatic and military policies, Klaus Reinhardt on the failure of Hitler's strategy in Russia, and Hans Lemberg on collaboration regimes--all in 1941.

962.   Calvocoressi, Peter, and Wint, Guy. Total War: Causes and Courses of the Second World War. 2d ed., London, 1989.

Treats the origins of the war, Germany's military successes and failures, and Nazi Europe.

963.   Hillgruber, Andreas. Der Zenit des Zweiten Weltkrieges: Juli 1941. Wiesbaden, 1977.

964.   ———. Der Zweite Weltkrieg, 1939-1945: Kriegsziele und Strategie der grossen Mächte. 4th ed. Stuttgart, 1985.

965.   Hillgruber, Andreas, ed. Probleme des Zweiten Weltkrieges. Cologne, 1967.

Essays by various experts on problems of the war; useful bibliography.

966.   Hillgruber, Andreas, and Hümmelchen, Gerhard. Chronik des Zweiten Weltkrieges: Kalendarium militärischer und politischer Ereignisse, 1939-1945. Düsseldorf, 1978.

A useful chronology of events. The Royal Institute of International Affairs in London compiled a similar calendar during the war: Chronology of the Second World War (London, 1947).

967.   Hofer, Walther. Die Entfesselung des Zweiten Weltkrieges: Eine Studie über die internationalen Beziehungen im Sommer 1939. Rev. ed. Frankfurt/M., 1960.

Focus is on the last ten days before the outbreak of war; includes documents from various published sources.

968.   Hoggan, David L. Der erzwungene Krieg: Die Ursachen und Urheber des 2. Weltkriegs. Tübingen, 1961.

The most notorious revisionist interpretation of the origins of the war, which sees Hitler as the victim of Anglo-American intrigues and Italian treachery.

For reviews, see Geschichte in Wissenschaft und Unterricht, 14 (1963), 492-514, and Vierteljahrshefte für Zeitgeschichte, 10 (1962), 311-40.

969.   Howard, Michael. History of the Second World War. London, 1971.

By a British military historian. See also, B.H. Liddell Hart, History of the Second World War (New York, 1971), by another military historian, a comprehensive survey.

970.   Jacobsen, Hans-Adolf. Der Weg zur Teilung der Welt: Politik und Strategie, 1939-1945. Bonn, 1977.

A German history of the war, covering both the military and the political aspects. For an older German view, see Helmuth G. Dahms, Geschichte des Zweiten Weltkriegs (rev. ed., Tübingen, 1965).

971.   Kaiser, David E. Economic Diplomacy and the Origins of the Second World War: Germany, Britain, France, and Eastern Europe, 1930-1939. Princeton, 1980.

The rivalry of the great powers for economic (and hence political) influence in Eastern Europe in the 1930s. Emphasizes the key role of Germany's trade policy after 1936 and Germany's ability to achieve her policy goals by linking economic objectives and foreign policy.

972.   Michel, Henri. La seconde guerre mondiale. 2 vols. Paris, 1968-69.

The standard French account, written by the long-time editor of Revue d'histoire de la deuxième guerre mondiale.

973.   Robertson, Esmonde M., ed. The Origins of the Second World War. London, 1971.

Historical interpretations, mainly by British historians, with an introduction by the editor. A collection of more recent interpretations, originally conceived as a second edition of Robertson's volume, is Robert Boyce and Esmonde M. Robertson, eds., Paths to War: New Essays on the Origins of the Second World War, London, 1989, with essays on Hitler's war plans and the German economy (Richard Overy), German mobilization and the German-Soviet pact of 1939 (E.M. Robertson), and Hitler's decision to turn against the West in 1940 (E.M. Robertson).

974.   Taylor, A.J.P. The Origins of the Second World War. Rev. ed. London, 1963.

Has become a classic. A provocative challenge to orthodox views, not without its flaws and internal contradictions, but also not without its effect.

Reviews are in Past and Present, 29 (1964), 67-87, and in Vierteljahrshefte für Zeitgeschichte, 10 (1962), 311-40. The current state of the "Taylor debate" is reflected in the essays collected in Gordon Martel, ed., The Origins of the Second World War Reconsidered, Boston, 1986.

975.   Thorne, Christopher. The Approach of War 1938-39. London, 1967.

976.   Watt, Donald Cameron. How War Came: The Immediate Origins of the Second World War, 1938-1939. New York, 1989.

Examines policy and policymakers in the countries involved and argues that Hitler and his accomplices "willed" the war to happen.

977. ———. Too Serious a Business: European Armed Forces and the Approach to the Second World War. Berkeley, 1975.

978. Weinberg, Gerhard. World in Balance: Behind the Scenes of World War II. Hanover, NH, 1981.

A collection of lectures and previously published essays, on Hitler's policy toward the United States, Axis diplomacy in 1939-41, German colonial policies, etc.

Hitler's War

979. Ansel, Walter. Hitler Confronts England. Durham, NC, 1960.

A study of Hitler's plans for the invasion of Britain in the summer of 1940. For Hitler's plans for the Balkans and the Mediterranean, see the author's Hitler and the Middle Sea (Durham, NC, 1972).

980. Boelcke, Willi A., ed. Deutschlands Rüstung im zweiten Weltkrieg: Hitlers Konferenzen mit Albert Speer, 1942 bis 1945. Frankfurt/M., 1969.

Records of the conferences between Hitler and Speer on the war economy. Casts light on military and political decisions, the conduct of war, successes and failures.

981. Eichholtz, Dieter. Geschichte der deutschen Kriegswirtschaft. Vol. 1 (1939-41). Berlin, 1969.

The focus is on IG Farben and other industrial giants, not on Hitler. Should be read in conjunction with Milward (no. 995).

982. Forstmeier, Friedrich, and Volkmann, Hans-Erich, eds. Kriegswirtschaft und Rüstung, 1939-1945. Düsseldorf, 1977.

Something of a sequel to their earlier volume (no. 727), with essays on foreign trade (Volkmann), trade relations with Italy (Schinzinger) and Sweden (Wittmann), and the exploitation of occupied territories (Winkel, Dlugoborski and Madajczyk).

983. Freymond, Jean. Le troisième Reich et la réorganisation économique de l'Europe, 1940-1942: origines et projets. Leiden, 1974.

984. Herbst, Ludolf. Der totale Krieg und die Ordnung der Wirtschaft: Die Kriegswirtschaft im Spannungsfeld von Politik, Ideologie und Propaganda, 1939-1945. Stuttgart, 1982.

Hitler's ideas and plans for the political economy of his New Order during and after the war; the ideological and practical mobilization of the economy and society to meet wartime exigencies.

985. Hitlers Lagebesprechungen: Die Protokollfragmente seiner militärischen Konferenzen, 1942-1945. Edited by Helmut Heiber. Stuttgart, 1962.

The surviving stenographic records of Hitler's daily war conferences. Provide insight into Hitler's views and his approach to the war. A selection of these records was published by Felix Gilbert as Hitler Directs His War: The Secret Records of His Daily Military Conferences (New York, 1950).

986. Hitlers Tischgespräche im Führerhauptquartier, 1941-42. Edited by Henry Picker. Bonn, 1951. (Second edition, by Percy E. Schramm et al., Stuttgart, 1963.)

Hitler's Table Talk, 1941-1944: His Private Conversations. Edited by Hugh R. Trevor-Roper. London, 1973. (First published 1953.)

Adolf Hitler: Monologe im Führerhauptquartier 1941-1944, Die Aufzeichnungen Heinrich Heims. Edited by Werner Jochmann. Hamburg, 1980.

Three versions of Hitler's wartime monologues, which cover a wide range of subjects and merit serious scholarly consideration.

Picker's edition (very ably reedited by Schramm et al.) reproduces notes taken by Picker at Bormann's request. Trevor-Roper's edition is based on the "Bormann Vermerke," notes made by Bormann. Jochmann's edition consists of the notes kept by Heim, Bormann's adjutant. (A third, completely revised edition of the first version, again edited by Picker, contains some additional commentary by the editor and a few personal recollections [Stuttgart, 1976].)

987. Hitlers Weisungen für die Kriegsführung, 1939-1945: Dokumente des Oberkommandos der Wehrmacht. Edited by Walther Hubatsch. 2d ed. Koblenz, 1983.

Hitler's directives and instructions to his army commanders. This edition supersedes the English version: Fuehrer Directives and Other Top-Level Directives of the German Armed Forces (2 vols., Washington, 1948).

988. Irving, David. Hitler's War. New York, 1977.

A sequel to Irving above (no. 650), again with much new and unfamiliar source material but as controversial in its conclusions as the other.

989. Klee, Karl. Das Unternehmen "Seelöwe". Göttingen, 1958.

A detailed account of Hitler's plans to invade Britain. For a companion volume of documents, see Karl Klee, ed., Dokumente zum Unternehmen "Seelöwe" (Göttingen, 1958).

990.   Kriegstagebuch des Oberkommandos der Wehrmacht, 1940-1945. Edited by Percy E. Schramm et al. 4 vols. Frankfurt/M., 1961-65.

The official war diary of the armed forces high command during World War II, with useful notes and appendixes.

991.   Lagevorträge des Oberbefehlshabers der Kriegsmarine vor Hitler, 1939-1945. Edited by Gerhard Wagner. Munich, 1972.

Minutes of the meetings between Hitler and his naval commanders; records Hitler's views on military, political, diplomatic matters; with extensive editorial comment.

The English version (Fuehrer Conferences on Matters Dealing with the German Navy, 1939-1945 [7 vols., Washington, 1946-47]), available also on microfilm, is not as complete.

992.   Leach, Barry A. German Strategy against Russia, 1939-1941. Oxford, 1973.

See also, Alan Clark, Barbarossa: The Russian-German Conflict, 1941-1945 (London, 1965).

993.   Messerschmidt, Manfred. "La stratégie allemande (1939-1945): conception, objectif, commandement, réussite." Revue d'histoire de la deuxième guerre mondiale, 25 (1975), 1-26.

994.   Militärgeschichtliches Forschungsamt, ed. Das Deutsche Reich und der Zweite Weltkrieg. Stuttgart, 1979-.

A major piece of collaborative research, projected to consist of ten volumes, prepared under the auspices of the Militärgeschichtliches Forschungsamt in Freiburg. It offers new information on a broad range of subjects related to the war (origins, diplomacy, social and economic issues, strategy, allies, occupation issues, etc.).

Volumes to date:

Vol. I. Wilhelm Deist et al. Ursachen und Voraussetzungen der deutschen Kriegspolitik. Stuttgart, 1979 (rev. ed., Frankfurt/M., 1989). The background to war; ideology and propaganda; economic preparations; rearmament; diplomatic developments.

Vol. II. Klaus A. Maier et al. Die Errichtung der Hegemonie auf dem europäischen Kontinent. Stuttgart, 1979. The outbreak and conduct of war, 1939-40; the conquest of Western Europe; military occupation and administration.

Vol. III. Gerhard Schreiber et al. Der Mittelmeerraum und Südosteuropa. Stuttgart, 1984. The war in the Balkans, 1939-41; the politics of the Axis powers, their conflicting aims and complex interrelationships.

Vol. IV. Horst Boog et al. Der Angriff auf die Sowjetunion. Stuttgart, 1983. The invasion of the Soviet Union and the conduct of war, 1941-42.

Vol. V/1. Bernhard R. Kroener et al. Organisation und Mobilmachung des deutschen Machtbereichs, 1939-1941. Stuttgart, 1988. Control and domination of the continent; the mobilization and exploitation of its resources.

995.   Milward, Alan S. The German Economy at War. London, 1965.

An outstanding work of analysis, based heavily on the records of the Speer Ministry. Traces the political and economic factors underlying Hitler's strategies. See also, Hans-Erich Volkmann, "Zum Verhältnis von Grosswirtschaft und NS-Regime im Zweiten Weltkrieg," in Bracher, Funke, and Jacobsen (no. 260), 480-508.

996.   Salewski, Michael. Die deutsche Seekriegsleitung, 1935-1945. 3 vols. Frankfurt/M., 1970-75.

On the war in general and on the war at sea in particular, with interesting information on Germany's relations with Britain and on Hitler's plans of Weltpolitik. The first two volumes are text; the third is documents.

997.   Schumann, Wolfgang, and Hass, Gerhart, eds. Deutschland im Zweiten Weltkrieg. 6 vols. Cologne, 1974-85.

A collaborative East German work on the origins and conduct of the war, with special emphasis on domestic developments. A Marxist counterpart to no. 994.

998.   Taylor, Telford. The Breaking Wave: World War II in the Summer of 1940. New York, 1967.

————. The March of Conquest: The German Victories in Western Europe, 1940. New York, 1958.

2. The Secret War

During the war, intelligence services and propaganda offices took over many of the tasks ordinarily discharged by the foreign service. Books on their activities tend to focus on episodes and exploits, not least because serious research is hampered by the lack of source material. Most of the files of the Abwehr are missing, as are those of the Sicherheitsdienst (SD), which made policy and conducted negotiations on its own.

There is a long bibliography, with a critical introduction, in Max Gunzenhäuser, Geschichte des geheimen Nachrichtendienstes (Spionage, Sabotage und Abwehr): Literaturbericht und Bibliographie (Frankfurt/M., 1968). Paul W. Blackstock and Frank L. Schaf, Jr., eds., Intelligence, Espionage, Counterespionage, and Covert Operations: A Guide to Information Sources (Detroit, 1978), is selective.

Intelligence and Espionage

999. Abshagen, Karl Heinz. Canaris: Patriot und Weltbürger. 2d ed. Stuttgart, 1950.

The first of many books on Canaris, most of them based on the same skimpy documentation.

See: Cestmir Amort and I.M. Jedlicka, The Canaris File (London, 1970); André Brissaud, Canaris: Le "petit amiral," prince de l'espionnage allemand (Paris, 1970); Ian Colvin, Chief of Intelligence (London, 1951).

1000. Bartz, Karl. Die Tragödie der deutschen Abwehr. Oldendorf, 1972.

1001. Brissaud, André. The Nazi Secret Service. London, 1974.

1002. Farago, Ladislas. The Game of the Foxes: The Untold Story of German Espionage in the United States and Great Britain during World War II. New York, 1971.

Focuses on the war, but with background narrative on the 1920s and 1930s. Based on German documents from an Abwehr outpost.

1003. Gehlen, Reinhard. Der Dienst: Erinnerungen, 1942-1971. Mainz, 1971.

Early chapters on his service on the eastern front; not reliable. See David Thomas, "Foreign Armies East and German Military Intelligence in Russia, 1941-45," Journal of Contemporary History, 22 (1987), 261-301.

1004. Hagen, Walter (pseud. of Wilhelm Hoettl). Die Geheime Front: Organisationen, Personen und Aktionen des deutschen Geheimdienstes. Linz, 1950.

Written by a former member of the SD, deals with intelligence affairs in southeastern Europe. Of doubtful accuracy. See also his Hitler's Paper Weapon (London, 1955), written under his real name, on the secret service, 1938-45.

1005. Höhne, Heinz. Canaris: Patriot im Zwielicht. Munich, 1976.

A good biography, with many new details and no use for myth and legend, based on intensive research and interviews. See also his more

general account: <u>Der Orden unter dem Totenkopf: Die Geschichte der</u>
<u>SS</u> (Gütersloh, 1967), which has chapters on intelligence and foreign
policy.

1006. Jong, Louis de. <u>The German Fifth Column in the Second World</u>
<u>War</u>. Chicago, 1956.

Argues that the significance of the fifth column has been overestimated
and that its role has been exaggerated. Similarly, Alfred Schickel,
"Entschied Verrat den Zweiten Weltkrieg?" <u>Geschichte in</u>
<u>Wissenschaft und Unterricht</u>, 19 (1968), 608-31.

1007. Kahn, David. <u>Hitler's Spies: German Military Intelligence in World</u>
<u>War II</u>. New York, 1978.

A massive work, based on captured documents, on the organization of
Germany's intelligence services, their personnel, missions, successes
and failures.

1008. Leverkühn, Paul. <u>Der geheime Nachrichtendienst der deutschen</u>
<u>Wehrmacht im Kriege</u>. Frankfurt/M., 1957.

1009. Mader, Julius. <u>Hitlers Spionagegenerale sagen aus: Ein</u>
<u>Dokumentarbericht über Aufbau, Struktur und Operationen des</u>
<u>OKW-Geheimdienstes Ausland/Abwehr mit einer Chronologie</u>
<u>seiner Einsätze von 1933 bis 1944</u>. 2d ed. [East] Berlin, 1971.

Based on reports by a number of former intelligence officers.

1010. Moyzisch, L.C. <u>Operation Cicero</u>. New York, 1950.

An account of one of the most famous German espionage missions,
by a "police attaché" in the German embassy at Ankara. For Cicero's
own account, see Elyesa Bazna, with Hans Nogly, <u>Ich war Cicero</u>
(Munich, 1962); adds some few details to Moyzisch's story.

1011. Reile, Oscar. <u>Geheime Ostfront: Die deutsche Abwehr im Osten,</u>
<u>1921-1945</u>. Munich, 1963.

————. <u>Geheime Westfront: Die deutsche Abwehr im Westen, 1921-</u>
<u>1945</u>. Munich, 1962.

Material on military intelligence, based largely on the secondary
literature and on Reile's own experiences.

1012. Rogge, O. John. <u>The Official German Report: Nazi Penetration,</u>
<u>1924-1942</u>. New York, 1961.

On Nazi activities in the United States, based on a report of the
Department of Justice.

1013. Schramm, Wilhelm von. Geheimdienst im Zweiten Weltkrieg: Organisation, Methoden, Erfolge. 4th ed. Munich, 1983.

On military intelligence in the various branches of the armed forces and on the Nachrichtentruppen.

1014. Tillmann, Heinz. "Tätigkeit und Ziele der Fünften Kolonne in Südafrika während des zweiten Weltkrieges." Zeitschrift für Geschichtswissenschaft, 9 (1961), 182-209.

1015. Wighton, Charles, and Peis, Günter. Hitler's Spies and Saboteurs: Based on the German Secret Service War Diary of General Lahousen. New York, 1958.

Lahousen was a section head in the Abwehr under Canaris.

Wartime Propaganda

1016. Baird, Jay W. The Mythical World of Nazi War Propaganda, 1939-1945. Minneapolis, MN, 1974.

See also, Jay W. Baird, "La campagne de propagande nazie en 1945," Revue d'histoire de la deuxième guerre mondiale, 19 (1969), 71-92.

1017. Balfour, Michael L.G. Propaganda in War, 1939-1945: Organisations, Policies and Publics in Britain and Germany. London, 1979.

On the propaganda ministry and its activities, on broadcasting to the enemy, and the like.

1018. Boelcke, Willi A. Die Macht des Radios: Weltpolitik und Auslandsrundfunk, 1924-1976. Frankfurt/M., 1977.

On the institutional setting, aims, and content of German radio propaganda, largely during the war.

See also, Heinz Pohle, Der Rundfunk als Instrument der Politik (Hamburg, 1955), which devotes some chapters to the use of radio in foreign relations in the 1920s and 1930s.

1019. Boelcke, Willi A., ed. Kriegspropaganda 1939-1941: Geheime Ministerkonferenzen im Reichspropagandaministerium. Stuttgart, 1966.

———. "Wollt Ihr den totalen Krieg?" Die geheimen Goebbels-Konferenzen, 1939-1943. Stuttgart, 1967.

1020. Bramstedt, Ernest K. Goebbels and National Socialist Propaganda, 1925-1945. East Lansing, MI, 1965.

1021. Buchbender, Ortwin. Das tönende Erz: Deutsche Propaganda gegen die Rote Armee im Zweiten Weltkrieg. Stuttgart, 1978.

On the methods and accomplishments of Wehrmacht propaganda in the East, 1941-45.

See also, J. Defrasne, "L'Organisation et l'emploi de l'arme psychologique dans la Wehrmacht," Revue d'histoire de la deuxième guerre mondiale, 18 (1968), 41-48.

1022. Herzstein, Robert Edwin. The War that Hitler Won. New York, 1978.

The propaganda war; good bibliography.

1023. Liss, Ulrich. Westfront 1939/40: Erinnerungen des Feindbearbeiters im O.K.H. Neckargemünd, 1959.

Memoirs by the general responsible for gathering and interpreting information on enemy plans and intentions.

1024. Pevsner, Max. "Les thèmes de la propagande allemande avant le 22 juin 1941." Revue d'histoire de la deuxième guerre mondiale, 16 (1966), 29-38.

And the follow-up article: Pierre Mermet and Yves Maxime Danan, "Les thèmes de la propagande allemande après le 22 juin 1941," ibid., 16 (1966), 39-62.

1025. Schnabel, Reimund, ed. Missbrauchte Mikrofone: Deutsche Rundfunkpropaganda im Zweiten Weltkrieg. Vienna, 1967.

A collection of documents on Germany's foreign-language broadcasts during World War II.

1026. Wortschlacht im Äther: Der deutsche Auslandsrundfunk im Zweiten Weltkrieg. Edited by Deutsche Welle, Köln. Berlin, 1971.

1027. Zeman, Zbynek A.B. Nazi Propaganda. 2d ed., London, 1973.

3. The Politics of War

Hitler's war aims remain in dispute. Disagreement exists on whether these aims reflected a longstanding design, put into effect during the war, or mere improvisations dictated by opportunity. Research on the subject has made use of Hitler's speeches and writings, his wartime table talk (no. 986), and many of the war diaries (nos. 985, 990-91), which are the best records of his views after 1939.

German policy in the occupied territories indicates, at least on one level, that aims were being put into practice. The policy varied from country to country, from agency to agency. There is abundant material, both published and unpublished, and the subject has proved a fertile field of research. The list below includes only the more important studies. For a bibliography and guide to holdings in various repositories, see Alexander Dallin, ed., The German Occupation of the USSR in World War II (New York, 1955).

War Aims

See also, Hildebrand (nos. 646, 745), Kühne (no. 746), Rich (no. 657), Thies (no. 678).

1028.   Cecil, Robert. Hitler's Decision to Invade Russia, 1941. London, 1975.

   Pulls together all the available evidence to arrive at an assessment of Hitler's motives and intentions.

   See also, Gerhard L. Weinberg, "Der deutsche Entschluss zum Angriff auf die Sowjetunion," Vierteljahrshefte für Zeitgeschichte, 1 (1953), 301-18, and a rejoinder by Hans-Günther Seraphim and Andreas Hillgruber in ibid., 2 (1954), 240-54.

1029.   Creveld, Martin L. van. Hitler's Strategy 1940-1941: The Balkan Clue. London, 1973.

   Examines military strategy for evidence of Hitler's aims.

1030.   Hass, Gerhart, and Schumann, Wolfgang, eds. Anatomie der Aggression: Neue Dokumente zu den Kriegszielen des faschistischen deutschen Imperialismus im zweiten Weltkrieg. Berlin, 1972.

   Documents on German economic expansion and exploitation during the war, with an overly dogmatic introduction.

   A similar volume is Wolfgang Schumann, ed., Griff nach Südosteuropa: Neue Dokumente über die Politik des deutschen Imperialismus und Militarismus gegenüber Südosteuropa im Zweiten Weltkrieg (Berlin, 1973).

1031.   Hildebrand, Klaus. "Hitlers 'Programm' und seine Realisierung 1939-1942." In Funke (no. 643), 63-93, and in Niedhart (no. 955), 178-224.

1032.   Hillgruber, Andreas. "Die 'Endlösung' und das deutsche Ostimperium als Kernstück des rassenideologischen Programms des Nationalsozialismus." In Funke (no. 643), 94-114.

1033.   ———. Hitlers Strategie: Politik und Kriegführung, 1940-1941. 2d ed. Munich, 1982.

   Examines Hitler's strategies and policies in the twelve months between the fall of France and the attack on Russia, analyzes the political, military, and economic problems facing Germany, and concludes that Hitler aimed first at European hegemony and then at world supremacy. Superb piece of scholarship; heavily documented.

1034. Jacobsen, Hans-Adolf. "Les buts et la politique de guerre de Hitler de 1939 à 1943." Revue d'histoire de la deuxième guerre mondiale, 16 (1966), 23-40.

1035. Kum'a N'dumbe III, Alexandre. "Les buts de guerre de l'Allemagne Hitlérienne en Afrique." Revue d'histoire de la deuxième guerre mondiale, 27 (1977), 37-60.

1036. Koch, H. W. "Hitler's 'Programme' and the Genesis of Operation 'Barbarossa.' " In Aspects of the Third Reich, edited by H. W. Koch. New York, 1985, pp. 285-322.

1037. Krausnick, Helmut. "Zu Hitlers Ostpolitik im Sommer 1943." Vierteljahrshefte für Zeitgeschichte, 2 (1954), 305-12.

1038. Schröder, Josef. "La Germania e i suoi alleati nella seconda guerra mondiale." Storia Contemporanea, 7 (1976), 751-81.

1039. Stegmann, Dirk. "Hitlers Ziele im ersten Kriegsjahr 1939/40: Ein Beitrag zur Quellenkritik." Militärgeschichtliche Mitteilungen, 29 (1980), 73-105.

1040. Trevor-Roper, Hugh R. "Hitlers Kriegsziele." Vierteljahrshefte für Zeitgeschichte, 8 (1960), 121-33. Reprinted in Michalka (no. 656), 31-48; and in H. W. Koch, ed., Aspects of the Third Reich (New York, 1985), pp. 235-50.

Occupation Policy

See also, Forstmeier and Volkmann (no. 982), Rich (no. 657).

1041. Böhme, Hermann. Der deutsch-französische Waffenstillstand im Zweiten Weltkrieg. Stuttgart, 1966.

On the armistice negotiations in June 1940 and on the period that followed, by a German army officer who helped draft the terms. For the memoirs of a French general on the armistice commission, see Marcel Vernoux, Wiesbaden, 1940-1944 (Paris, 1954).

1042. Brajovic, Petar, et al., eds. Les systèmes d'occupation en Yougoslavie, 1941-1945. Belgrade, 1963.

1043. Brandes, Detlef. Die Tschechen unter deutschem Protektorat. Vol. 1 (1939-42), Munich, 1969; Vol. 2 (1942-45), Munich, 1975.

1044. Broszat, Martin. Nationalsozialistische Polenpolitik. Frankfurt/M., 1961.

A comprehensive and reliable account of Nazi rule in Poland. Reviewed in <u>Polish Western Affairs</u> 3 (1962), 378-87. See also, Waclaw Dlugoborski, "Die deutsche Besatzungspolitik gegenüber Polen," in Bracher, Funke, and Jacobsen (no. 260), 572-90.

1045. Brügel, Johann W. <u>Tschechen und Deutsche, 1939-1946</u>. Munich, 1974.

1046. Collotti, Enzo. <u>L'amministrazione tedesca dell'Italia occupata, 1943-1945: studio e documenti</u>. Milan, 1963.

1047. Collotti, Enzo, ed. <u>L'occupazione nazista in Europa</u>. Rome, 1964.

Introduction to the political and economic aspects of Nazi occupation, by various non-German historians.

1048. Dallin, Alexander. <u>German Rule in Russia, 1941-1945: A Study of Occupation Policies</u>. 2d ed. London, 1981.

1049. <u>Documenta Occupationes</u>. Edited by Institut Zachodni, Poznan. 7 vols. Poznan, 1945-59.

1050. Eisenblätter, Gerhard. <u>Grundlinien der Politik des Reiches gegenüber dem Generalgouvernement, 1939-1945</u>. Frankfurt/M., 1969.

1051. Fletcher, William A. "The German Administration of Luxemburg, 1940-1942: Toward a 'de facto' Annexation." <u>Historical Journal</u>, 13 (1970), 533-44.

On the Nazi administration, which prepared the way for outright annexation.

1052. Frank, Ernst. <u>Karl Hermann Frank: Staatsminister im Protektorat</u>. Heusenstamm, 1971.

Part autobiography (written in prison in Prague), part biography (by a brother), offered in explanation of his role in the Protectorate.

See also, Gustav von Schmoller, "Heydrich im Protektorat Böhmen und Mähren," <u>Vierteljahrshefte für Zeitgeschichte</u>, 27 (1979), 626-45.

1053. Geschke, Günter. <u>Die deutsche Frankreichpolitik 1940 von Compiègne bis Montoire: Das Problem einer deutsch-französischen Annäherung nach dem Frankreichfeldzug</u>. Frankfurt/M., 1960.

1054. Gross, Jan Tomasz. <u>Polish Society under German Occupation: The Generalgouvernement, 1939-1944</u>. Princeton, 1979.

German occupation in theory and practice; military and police control; terror; collaboration; resistance and the underground movements.

1055. Hayes, Paul M. Quisling: The Career and Political Ideas of Vidkun Quisling, 1887-1945. London, 1972.

1056. Hirschfeld, Gerhard. Fremdherrschaft und Kollaboration: Die Niederlande unter deutscher Besatzung, 1940-1945. Munich, 1984. (Trl. as Nazi Rule and Dutch Collaboration: The Netherlands under German Occupation, 1940-1945, New York, 1988.)

Seyss-Inquart's Reichskommissariat; occupation policies and forms of collaboration. The translation omits some of the source material and references of the original.

1057. Hoffmann, Gabriele. NS-Propaganda in den Niederlanden: Organisation und Lenkung der Publizistik unter deutscher Besatzung, 1940-1945. Munich, 1972.

1058. Jäckel, Eberhard. Frankreich in Hitlers Europa: Die deutsche Frankreichpolitik im Zweiten Weltkrieg. Stuttgart, 1966.

A thorough, well-documented study of Germany's policy, based on German documents.

See also, Hermann Böhme, "Deutschland und Frankreich im Zweiten Weltkrieg, 1940-1944," Aus Politik und Zeitgeschichte, 3 and 17 Aug. 1966; and Pétain et les allemands: Mémorandum d'Abetz sur les rapports franco-allemands (Paris, 1948), a number of dispatches written by Abetz between 1940 and 1942.

1059. Kamenetsky, Ihor. Secret Nazi Plans for Eastern Europe: A Study of Lebensraum Policies. New York, 1961.

On the occupation, colonization, germanization, etc. of eastern Europe by Himmler's SS.

1060. Kettenacker, Lothar. Nationalsozialistische Volkstumspolitik im Elsass. Stuttgart, 1973.

1061. Klessmann, Christoph. Die Selbstbehauptung einer Nation: National-sozialistische Kulturpolitik und polnische Widerstandsbewegung im Generalgouvernement, 1939-1945. Düsseldorf, 1971.

And by the same author: "Der Generalgouverneur Hans Frank," Vierteljahrshefte für Zeitgeschichte, 19 (1971), 245-60; "NS-Kirchenpolitik und Nationalitätenfrage im Generalgouvernement (1939-1945)," Jahrbücher für Geschichte Osteuropas, 18 (1970), 575-600.

1062. Kluke, Paul. "Nationalsozialistische Volkstumspolitik in Elsass-Lothringen, 1940 bis 1945." In Aussenpolitik und Zeitgeschichte. Wiesbaden, 1974, pp. 222-37.

See also, D. Wolfanger, Die nationalsozialistische Politik in Lothringen (1940-1945), Saarbrücken, 1977.

1063.   Král, Václav, ed. Die Vergangenheit warnt: Dokumente über die Germanisierungs- und Austilgungspolitik der Naziokkupanten in der Tschechoslowakei. Prague, 1960.

1064.   Kwiet, Konrad. Reichskommissariat Niederlande: Versuch und Scheitern nationalsozialistischer Neuordnung. Stuttgart, 1968.

1065.   Lampe, David. The Last Ditch. New York, 1968.

Examines Nazi plans for the occupation of Britain, and British plans of resistance.

1066.   Lemkin, Raphaël. Axis Rule in Occupied Europe: Laws of Occupation, Analysis of Government, Proposals for Redress. New York, 1944.

A compilation and analysis of German laws, decrees, and ordinances put into effect in the occupied territories.

1067.   Loock, Hans-Dietrich. Quisling, Rosenberg und Terboven: Zur Vorgeschichte und Geschichte der nationalsozialistischen Revolution in Norwegen. Stuttgart, 1970.

1068.   Madajczyk, Czeslaw. Die deutsche Besatzungspolitik in Polen (1939-1945). Wiesbaden, 1967. (An abridged version was published as Die Okkupationspolitik Nazideutschlands in Polen, 1939-1945, Cologne, 1988.)

1069.   Mastny, Vojtech. The Czechs under Nazi Rule: The Failure of National Resistance, 1939-1942. New York, 1971.

For a wartime assessment, see Shiela Grant Duff, A German Protectorate: The Czechs under Nazi Rule (London, 1970; originally, 1942).

1070.   Milward, Alan S. The Fascist Economy in Norway. London, 1972.

On the Nazi attempt to reorient the Norwegian economy and integrate it with that of Germany; throws light on Nazi economic policy in general.

1071.   ———. The New Order and the French Economy. London, 1970.

See also the author's shorter piece: "German Economic Policy towards France, 1942-1944," in Studies in International History, edited by K. Bourne and D.C. Watt (London, 1967), 423-43.

1072. Mühlen, Patrick von zur. Zwischen Hakenkreuz und Sowjetstern: Der Nationalismus der sowjetischen Orientvölker im Zweiten Weltkrieg. Düsseldorf, 1971.

On German policies toward the Caucasian and Turkic ethnic groups in Soviet Russia.

1073. Müller, Norbert. Wehrmacht und Okkupation, 1941-44: Zur Rolle der Wehrmacht und ihrer Führungsorgane im Okkupationsregime des faschistischen deutschen Imperialismus auf sowjetischem Territorium. [East] Berlin, 1971.

1074. Mulligan, Timothy Patrick. The Politics of Illusion and Empire: German Occupation Policy in the Soviet Union, 1942-43. New York, 1988.

The various conceptions of occupation policy, the various institutions involved in implementing policy, and the impact   of the war on both conceptions and institutions. Supplements and in part corrects the works of Buchbender (no. 1021), Dallin (no. 1048), and Reitlinger (no. 1081) by reconstructing the flexibility, even subtlety, of German policy.

1075. Myllyniemi, Seppo. Die Neuordnung der baltischen Länder, 1941-1944: Zum nationalsozialistischen Inhalt der deutschen Besatzungspolitik. Helsinki, 1973.

1076. Olshausen, Klaus. Zwischenspiel auf dem Balkan: Die deutsche Politik gegenüber Jugoslawien und Griechenland von März bis Juli 1941. Stuttgart, 1973.

See also his "Die deutsche Balkan-Politik 1940-1941," in Funke (no. 643), 707-27.

1077. Petrow, Richard. The Bitter Years: The Invasion and Occupation of Denmark and Norway, April 1940-May 1945. New York, 1974.

1078. Präg, Werner, and Jacobmeyer, Wolfgang, eds. Das Diensttagebuch des deutschen Generalgouverneurs in Polen, 1939-1945. Stuttgart, 1975.

Hans Frank's official diary, introduced at the Nuremberg trials and available on microfilm at the National Achives. A basic source, with a great deal of information on occupation policies.

A handbook on the Government General, with a full list of offices and staff, is Max Du Prel, ed., Das Generalgouvernement (2d ed., Würzburg, 1942), by a member of Frank's retinue.

1079. Ramme, Alwin. Der Sicherheitsdienst der SS. [East] Berlin, 1970.

The role of the SD in the occupation of Poland; with an appendix of some official documents.

1080. Ránki, György. "The German Occupation of Hungary." Acta Historica, 11 (1965), 261-83.

Based on German diplomatic and military records; covers the period between 19 Mar. and 15 Oct. 1944.

1081. Reitlinger, Gerald. The House Built on Sand: The Conflicts of German Policy in Russia, 1939-1945. London, 1960.

Critical of Dallin (no. 1048), but supersedes it only in part.

1082. Rhode, Gotthold. "Das Protektorat Böhmen und Mähren, 1939-1945." In Das deutsch-tschechische Verhältnis, edited by Eugen Lemberg and Gotthold Rhode. Stuttgart, 1969, pp. 59-91.

1083. Rings, Werner. Leben mit dem Feind: Anpassung und Widerstand in Hitlers Europa, 1939-1945. Munich, 1979. (Trl. as Life with the Enemy: Collaboration and Resistance in Hitler's Europe, 1939-1945, Garden City, NY, 1982.)

A synthesis of the secondary literature by a Swiss journalist.

1084. Ritter, Harry. "German Policy in Occupied Greece and Its Economic Impact, 1941-1944." In Germany and Europe in the Era of the Two World Wars, edited by F.X.J. Homer and Larry Wilcox. Charlottesville, VA, 1986, pp. 157-82.

1085. Schärer, Martin R. Deutsche Annexionspolitik im Westen: Die Wiedereingliederung Eupen-Malmedys im Zweiten Weltkrieg. 2d ed. Frankfurt/M., 1978.

1086. Streit, Christian. Keine Kameraden: Die Wehrmacht und die sowjetischen Kriegsgefangenen, 1941-1945. 2d ed., Stuttgart, 1980.

Policy toward prisoners of war in the occupied areas in Eastern Europe.

1087. Szarota, Tomasz. Warschau unter dem Hakenkreuz. Paderborn, 1985.

1088. Thomsen, Erich. Deutsche Besatzungspolitik in Dänemark, 1940-1945. Düsseldorf, 1971.

See also, Harald Winkel, "Die wirtschaftlichen Beziehungen Deutschlands zu Dänemark in den Jahren der Besatzung, 1940-1945," in Probleme der nationalsozialistischen Wirtschaftspolitik, edited by Friedrich-Wilhelm Henning (Berlin, 1976), pp. 119-74, which concludes that the relationship was not purely one-sided. For a collection of documents, see Wolfgang Schumann, "Das Scheitern einer Zoll- und Währungsunion zwischen dem faschistischen Deutschland und Dänemark, 1940," Jahrbuch für Geschichte, 9 (1973), 515-66.

1089. Umbreit, Hans. Der Militärbefehlshaber in Frankreich, 1940-1944. Boppard, 1968.

————. Deutsche Militärverwaltungen 1938/39: Die militärische Besetzung der Tschechoslowakei und Polens. Stuttgart, 1977.

Two well-researched monographs on German military government, illustrating administrative rivalries and muddled policies. The second of the two is a fine contribution especially to the history of the occupation of Poland. For an overview, see Umbreit's "Nationalsozialistische Expansion, 1938-1941: Strukturen der deutschen Besatzungsverwaltungen im Zweiten Weltkrieg," in Dienst für die Geschichte, edited by Michael Salewski and Josef Schröder (Göttingen, 1985), pp. 163-86.

1090. United States Office of Military Government for Germany, Finance Division. Report on the Investigation of the Deutsche Bank. 4 vols. OMGUS, 1946; Annex, OMGUS, 1947.

An investigative report, using documents seized by the Allies, on the role of Germany's banking system in contributing to the war and to the exploitation of conquered areas.

See also, Dresdner und Deutsche Banks (1947), published by the same office; a summary of the findings on the history of these two banks during the Nazi era.

1091. Vegesack, Siegfried von. Als Dolmetscher im Osten: Ein Erlebnisbericht aus den Jahren 1942-43. Hanover, 1965.

1092. Wagner, Wilfried. Belgien in der deutschen Politik während des Zweiten Weltkrieges. Boppard, 1974.

Careful examination of the Falkenhausen regime, based on military files and Belgian sources.

1093. Warmbrunn, Werner. The Dutch under German Occupation, 1940-1945. Stanford, 1963.

1094. Weber, Wolfram. Die innere Sicherheit im besetzten Belgien und Nordfrankreich, 1940-44. Düsseldorf, 1978.

1095. Wehler, Hans Ulrich. " 'Reichsfestung Belgrad': Nationalsozialistische 'Raumordnung' in Südosteuropa." Vierteljahrshefte für Zeitgeschichte, 11 (1963), 72-84.

Resettlement and Genocide

1096. Adam, Uwe Dietrich. Judenpolitik im Dritten Reich. Düsseldorf, 1972.

Examines the "final solution" in the context of Hitler's overall policy. Useful information on the SS and on Volkstumspolitik.

1097. Ben-Elissar, Eliahu. La diplomatie du IIIe Reich et les juifs, 1933-1939. Paris, 1969.

1098. Browning, Christopher R. The Final Solution and the German Foreign Office: A Study of Referat D III of Abteilung Deutschland, 1940-1943. New York, 1978.

The contributions made to anti-Jewish policies by the foreign ministry, especially by under state secretary Luther. See also his "Referat Deutschland, Jewish Policy, and the German Foreign Office, 1933-40," Yad Vashem Studies, 12 (1977), 37-74.

1099. Dawidowicz, Lucy S. The War against the Jews, 1933-1945. New York, 1975.

1100. Hecker, Hellmuth. Die Umsiedlungsverträge des Dritten Reiches während des Zweiten Weltkriegs. Hamburg, 1971.

A collection of treaties, between Germany and various East European countries, on the resettlement of German minority groups.

1101. Heiber, Helmut. "Der Generalplan Ost." Vierteljahrshefte für Zeitgeschichte, 6 (1958), 281-325.

Documentation on Germany's plans to expel the inhabitants of Eastern Europe. See also, Czeslaw Madajczyk, ed., "Generalplan Ost," Polish Western Affairs, 3 (1962), 391-442; and Rolf-Dieter Müller, "Industrielle Interessenpolitik im Rahmen des 'Gesamtplans Ost'," Militärgeschichtliche Mitteilungen, 30 (1981), 101-41, a selection of documents.

1102. Hilberg, Raul. The Destruction of the European Jews. Rev. ed., New York, 1985 (originally, Chicago, 1967).

1103. Koehl, Robert L. RKFDV: German Resettlement and Population Policy, 1939-1945. Cambridge, MA, 1957.

A history of the SS agency for "strengthening Germandom" and a useful survey of Volkstumspolitik.

1104. Kroeger, Erhard. Der Auszug aus der alten Heimat: Die Umsiedlung der Baltendeutschen. Tübingen, 1967.

Memoirs by a leader of the resettlement movement in the Baltic states.

1105. Loeber, Dietrich A., ed. <u>Diktierte Option: Die Umsiedlung der Deutsch-Balten aus Estland und Lettland, 1939-1941</u>. Neumünster, 1972.

Huge collection of documents on the resettlement of Baltic Germans in Germany and German-occupied Poland.

See also, Hans von Rimscha, "Zur Umsiedlung der Deutschen aus den baltischen Staaten während des zweiten Weltkriegs," <u>Osteuropa</u>, 11 (1961), 134-36, a brief summary with statistics.

1106. Poliakov, Leon, and Wulf, Josef, eds. <u>Das Dritte Reich und seine Diener: Dokumente</u>. Berlin, 1956.

Includes a section on the foreign ministry and its involvement in anti-Jewish policy during the war, especially in southeastern Europe.

1107. Sobczak, Janusz. "Ethnic Germans as the Subject of the Nazi Resettlement Campaign during the Second World War." <u>Polish Western Affairs</u>, 8 (1967), 63-95.

4. The Diplomacy of War

Research on Germany's diplomacy during the war shows notable gaps. The reconstruction and analysis of her relations with allies, satellite states, and non-belligerents is determined by the haphazard survival of documentary material, especially for the second half of the war. Little has been done on the policies and activities of the various agencies and emissaries that competed for power in external affairs. The whole question of peace initiatives, official and unofficial, is still largely unexplored.

For the last phase of German diplomacy, see Alfred Diefenbach, "Die Kapitulation der deutschen Wehrmacht" (<u>Jahresbibliographie der Bibliothek für Zeitgeschichte</u>, 47 [1975], pp. 615-43), a critical bibliography on the events of spring 1945.

Allies and Satellites

1108. Aspelmeier, Dieter. <u>Deutschland und Finnland während der beiden Weltkriege</u>. Hamburg, 1967.

1109. Berend, Iván, and Ránki, György. "Die deutsche wirtschaftliche Expansion und das ungarische Wirtschaftsleben zur Zeit des zweiten Weltkrieges." <u>Acta Historica</u>, 5 (1958), 313-59.

1110. Bihl, Wolfdieter. "Zur nationalsozialistischen Ungarnpolitik." <u>Österreichische Osthefte</u>, 11 (1969), 21-26.

1111.   Creveld, Martin van. "In the Shadow of Barbarossa: Germany and Albania, January-March 1941." Journal of Contemporary History, 7 (1972), 221-30.

A chapter in German-Italian relations, shaped by Hitler's plans to invade Russia and his interest in helping his ally.

1112.   ———. "25 October 1940: A Historical Puzzle." Journal of Contemporary History, 6 (1971), 87-96.

On Hitler's precipitate decision to meet Mussolini on 28 Oct., a decision reached on the 25th, which has been the subject of conflicting interpretations.

1113.   Deakin, Frederick W. The Brutal Friendship: Mussolini, Hitler, and the Fall of Italian Fascism. Rev. ed. New York, 1966.

Focuses on the last three years of Mussolini's dictatorship, and especially on the ties between Mussolini and Hitler.

1114.   Drechsler, Karl, ed. Das Bündnis der Rivalen: Der Pakt Berlin-Tokio. Berlin, 1978.

Documents on Nazi Germany's policy in East and Southeast Asia during the war.

1115.   Dress, Hans. Slowakei und faschistische Neuordnung Europas, 1939-1944. Berlin, 1972.

1116.   Erfurth, Waldemar. Der Finnische Krieg, 1941-1944. Wiesbaden, 1950.

On German-Finnish relations, by the German military attaché in Helsinki.

1117.   Fabry, Philipp Walter. Balkan-Wirren, 1940-1941: Diplomatische und militärische Vorbereitung des deutschen Donauüberganges. Darmstadt, 1966.

1118.   Fenyo, Mario D. Hitler, Horthy, and Hungary: German-Hungarian Relations, 1941-1944. New Haven, CT, 1972.

Some new information on relations between the two countries, on the German occupation, and on the abortive coup of Oct. 1944.

1119.   Förster, Jürgen. "Rumäniens Weg in die deutsche Abhängigkeit: Zur Rolle der deutschen Militärmission 1940/41." Militärgeschichtliche Mitteilungen, 28 (1979), 47-77.

1120.   Förster, Jürgen. Stalingrad: Risse im Bündnis, 1942/43. Freiburg i.B., 1975.

The impact of the Stalingrad disaster on Germany's allies.

1121. Fricke, Gert. <u>Kroatien, 1941-1944: Der "unabhängige Staat" in der Sicht des Deutschen Bevollmächtigten Generals in Agram, Glaise von Horstenau</u>. Freiburg i.B., 1972.

1122. Hehn, Paul N. "Serbia, Croatia, and Germany, 1941-1945: Civil War and Revolution in the Balkans." <u>Canadian Slavonic Papers</u>, 13 (1971), 344-73.

1123. Hillgruber, Andreas. "Das deutsch-ungarische Verhältnis im letzten Kriegsjahr." <u>Wehrwissenschaftliche Rundschau</u>, 10 (1960), 78-104.

1124. ————. "Der Einbau der verbündeten Armeen in die deutsche Ostfront, 1941-1944." <u>Wehrwissenschaftliche Rundschau</u>, 10 (1960), 659-82.

1125. ————. "Die 'Hitler-Koalition': Eine Skizze zur Geschichte und Struktur des 'Weltpolitischen Dreiecks' Berlin-Rom-Tokio, 1933-1945." In <u>Vom Staat des Ancien Regime zum Modernen Parteienstaat</u>, edited by Helmut Berding et al. Munich, 1978, pp. 467-83.

1126. ————. "Die letzten Monate der deutsch-rumänischen Waffenbrüderschaft." <u>Wehrwissenschaftliche Rundschau</u>, 7 (1957), 377-97.

An assessment of Germany's diplomatic and military relations with her client state Rumania; complements nos. 1123, 1124.

1127. ————. "Japan und der Fall 'Barbarossa'." <u>Wehrwissenschaftliche Rundschau</u>, 18 (1968), 312-36.

Documents from Japanese archives on the conversations between Ribbentrop and Oshima in 1941.

1128. Hoppe, Hans Joachim. <u>Bulgarien--Hitlers eigenwilliger Verbündeter: Eine Fallstudie zur nationalsozialistischen Südosteuropapolitik</u>. Stuttgart, 1979.

1129. Hory, Ladislaus, and Broszat, Martin. <u>Der kroatische Ustaschastaat, 1941-1945</u>. Stuttgart, 1964.

Account of the attempts by the Croatians to establish their own state while German troops occupied Yugoslavia. Hory was Hungarian press attaché in Belgrade at the time.

1130. Karsai, Elek. "Edmund Veesenmayer's Reports to Hitler on Hungary in 1943." <u>The New Hungarian Quarterly</u>, 5 (1964), 146-53.

Veesenmayer was one of Hitler's special envoys.

1131. Krimper, Ronald L. "The Diplomatic Prelude to the Destruction of Yugoslavia, January to April 1941." East European Quarterly, 7 (1973), 125-47.

1132. Krosby, H. Peter. Finland, Germany, and the Soviet Union, 1940-1941: The Petsamo Dispute. Madison, WI, 1968.

   See also, Krosby's "The Development of the Petsamo Question and Finnish-German Relations, March-December 1940," Scandia, 31 (1965), 291-330, and "The Diplomacy of the Petsamo Question and Finnish-German Relations, January-June 1941," ibid., 32 (1966), 169-211.

1133. Latour, Conrad F. Südtirol und die Achse Berlin-Rome, 1938-1945. Stuttgart, 1962.

   On one of the more troublesome issues affecting relations between Germany and Italy. For a more summary treatment, see Latour's "Germany, Italy and South Tyrol, 1938-45." Historical Journal, 8 (1965), 95-111.

1134. Loock, Hans-Dietrich. "Zur 'Grossgermanischen Politik' des Dritten Reiches." Vierteljahrshefte für Zeitgeschichte, 8 (1960), 37-63.

   On the various views and policies on the future of the Scandinavian states in the German orbit, 1940-42.

1135. Martin, Bernd. Deutschland und Japan im Zweiten Weltkrieg: Vom Angriff auf Pearl Harbor bis zur deutschen Kapitulation. Göttingen, 1969.

   Comprehensive account of German-Japanese relations during the war, particularly good in its assessment of alliance policies on both sides and the conflicts that beset these policies.

   See also, Bernd Martin, "Die 'Militärische Vereinbarung zwischen Deutschland, Italien und Japan' vom 18. Januar 1942," an excerpt from the book, in Probleme des Zweiten Weltkrieges, edited by Andreas Hillgruber (Cologne, 1967), pp. 134-44; and Bernd Martin, "Zur Vorgeschichte des deutsch-japanischen Kriegsbündnisses," Geschichte in Wissenschaft und Unterricht, 21 (1970), 606-15.

1136. Melin, Ingvar. "Die Entwicklung der deutsch-finnischen Beziehungen während des zweiten Weltkriegs." Geschichte in Wissenschaft und Unterricht, 7 (1956), 421-32.

1137. Meskill, Johanna Menzel. Hitler and Japan: The Hollow Alliance. New York, 1966.

1138. Plehwe, Friedrich-Karl von. Schicksalsstunden in Rom: Ende eines Bündnisses. Berlin, 1967. (A second edition was published as Als die Achse zerbrach: Das Ende des deutsch-italienischen Bündnisses im Zweiten Weltkrieg, Wiesbaden, 1980.)

On the events surrounding Mussolini's ouster in 1943 and on the rupture in German-Italian relations, by the German military attaché in Rome (1940-43). See also, Jens Petersen, "Deutschland und der Zusammenbruch des Faschismus in Italien im Sommer 1943," Militärgeschichtliche Mitteilungen, 34 (1985), 51-69.

1139. Pommerin, Reiner. "Rassenpolitische Differenzen im Verhältnis der Achse Berlin-Rom, 1938-1943." Vierteljahrshefte für Zeitgeschichte, 27 (1979), 646-60.

1140. Precan, Vilém. "Die nationalsozialistische Slowakeipolitik und das Tiso-Regime nach dem Ausbruch des Aufstandes 1944." In Gedenkschrift Martin Göhring, edited by Ernst Schulin. Wiesbaden, 1968, pp. 369-86.

1141. Presseisen, Ernst L. "Prelude to 'Barbarossa': Germany and the Balkans, 1940-1941." Journal of Modern History, 32 (1960), 359-70.

1142. Radandt, Hans. "Der Wirtschaftsberater der Deutschen Gesandtschaft in Bratislava." Jahrbuch für Wirtschaftsgeschichte (1972), 75-94.

On the activities of Erich Gebert, commercial attaché at the German legation in Bratislava and adviser to the Slovak ministry of economics.

1143. Salewski, Michael. "Staatsräson und Waffenbrüderschaft: Probleme der deutsch-finnischen Politik, 1941-1944." Vierteljahrshefte für Zeitgeschichte, 27 (1979), 370-91.

1144. Schramm-von Thadden, Ehrengard. Griechenland und die Grossmächte im Zweiten Weltkrieg. Wiesbaden, 1955.

An account of German-Italian relations regarding the joint invasion of Greece, 1940-41.

1145. Schröder, Josef. "Deutschland und seine Bundesgenossen im Zweiten Weltkrieg: Ein Beitrag zu Hitlers Kriegszielpolitik." Quellen und Forschungen aus italienischen Archiven und Bibliotheken, 52 (1972), 731-66.

Germany's relations with her allies, and the strains within the alliance. Special emphasis on German-Italian relations, the three-power pact (1940), and the tripartite military convention (1942).

1146. ———. Italiens Kriegsaustritt 1943: Die deutschen Gegenmassnahmen im italienischen Raum. Göttingen, 1969.

The diplomatic, political, and military relations between Germany and Italy, and their collapse in 1943. Extensive bibliography.

1147.   Sundhausen, Holm. "Südosteuropa in der nationalsozialistischen Kriegswirtschaft am Beispiel des 'Unabhängigen Staates Kroatien.' " Südost-Forschungen, 32 (1973), 233-66.

1148.   Ueberschär, Gerd R. Hitler und Finnland, 1939-1941: Die deutschfinnischen Beziehungen während des Hitler-Stalin-Paktes. Wiesbaden, 1978.

Thorough, well-researched study, on the circumstances that brought Finland into the war on the German side. Focuses on the diplomatic side without neglecting the economic interests.

Relations with Non-Belligerents

1149.   Bariéty, Jacques. "La politique extérieure allemande dans l'hiver 1939-1940." Revue Historique, 88 (1964), 141-52.

1150.   Bailey, Thomas A., and Ryan, Paul B. Hitler vs. Roosevelt: The Undeclared Naval War. Riverside, NJ, 1978.

1151.   Betten, Edith Kalmins. "German-Latvian Foreign Relations, 1939-1940." Baltic Review, 38 (1971), 42-53.

1152.   Birkenfeld, Wolfgang. "Stalin als Wirtschaftspartner Hitlers (1939-1941)." Vierteljahrshefte für Sozial- und Wirtschaftsgeschichte, 53 (1966), 477-510.

See also, Ferdinand Friedensburg, "Die sowjetischen Kriegslieferungen an das Hitlerreich," Vierteljahrshefte für Wirtschaftsforschung, (1962), 331-38.

1153.   Burdick, Charles B. Germany's Military Strategy and Spain in World War II. Syracuse, NY, 1968.

1154.   Castellan, Georges, and Jars, P.A. "La diplomatie allemande et la guerre du pacifique (sept. 1940-déc. 1941)." Revue d'histoire de la deuxième guerre mondiale, 2 (1951), 1-40.

1155.   Clauss, Manfred. "Der Besuch Ribbentrops im Vatikan." Zeitschrift für Kirchengeschichte, 87 (1976), 54-64.

The nature of German-Vatican relations as illustrated by Ribbentrop's audience with Pius XII in March 1940.

1156.   Denzler, Rudolf E. "Im Dienste fremder Interessen: Erinnerungen an meine Dienste als Delegierter der Schweizer Schutzmacht in Deutschland, 1943-1945." Wehrwissenschaftliche Rundschau, 16 (1966), 682-95.

1157.   Detwiler, Donald S. Hitler, Franco und Gibraltar: Die Frage des spanischen Eintritts in den Zweiten Weltkrieg. Wiesbaden, 1962.

On Spanish-German relations after 1939 and Germany's efforts to bring Spain into the war on the German side. See also, Detwiler's "Spain and the Axis during World War II," Review of Politics, 33 (1971), 36-53.

1158. Fleury, Antoine. "La subversion allemande en Inde à partir de l'Afghanistan pendant la deuxième guerre mondiale." Relations internationales, 3 (1975), 133-52.

1159. Friedländer, Saul. Hitler et les États-Unis, 1939-1941. Geneva, 1963. (Trl. as Prelude to Downfall [New York, 1967].)

On Germany's policy toward the United States.

1160. ———. Pius XII. und das Dritte Reich: Eine Dokumentation. Reinbek, 1965. (Trl. from the French.)

A critical review of Vatican policy, largely during the war, based on documents from the German foreign ministry.

1161. Glasneck, Johannes, and Kircheisen, Inge. Türkei und Afghanistan: Brennpunkte der Orientpolitik im Zweiten Weltkrieg. Berlin, 1968.

Policies of the major powers, 1939-45.

1162. Hauner, Milan. India in Axis Strategy: Germany, Japan, and Indian Nationalists in the Second World War. Stuttgart, 1981.

1163. Herde, Peter. "Japan, Deutschland, und die Vereinigten Staaten im Jahre 1941." In Kriegswende, Dezember 1941, edited by Jürgen Rohwer and Eberhard Jäckel. Frankfurt/M., 1984, pp. 36-54.

1164. Herwig, Holger H. Politics of Frustration: The United States in German Naval Planning, 1889-1941. Boston, 1976.

Several chapters on the period 1939-41, set in the broad context of German naval planning since the late nineteenth century. See also the same author's "Prelude to Weltblitzkrieg: Germany's Naval Policy toward the United States of America, 1939-1941," Journal of Modern History, 43 (1971), 649-68.

1165. Hill, Leonidas E. "The Vatican Embassy of Ernst von Weizsäcker, 1943-1945." Journal of Modern History, 39 (1967), 138-59.

On Weizsäcker's last diplomatic post. See also, Owen Chadwick, "Weizsäcker, the Vatican, and the Jews of Rome," Journal of Ecclesiastical History, 28 (1977), 179-99.

1166. Hillgruber, Andreas. "Der Faktor Amerika in Hitlers Strategie, 1939-1941." In Michalka (no. 656), 493-525.

More sharply delineated analysis than that in Hitlers Strategie (no. 1033).

1167. Howard, Harry N. "Germany, the Soviet Union, and Turkey during World War II." Department of State Bulletin, 19 (1948), 63-78.

Draws on German documents, but now largely superseded by Krecker (no. 1171) and Weber (no. 1182).

1168. Hubatsch, Walther. "Diplomatische Beziehungen Deutschlands zu Skandinavien unter dem Schatten des zweiten Weltkrieges." Zeitschrift für Ostforschung, 9 (1960), 161-84.

1169. Kaslas, Bronis J. "The Lithuanian Strip in Soviet-German Secret Diplomacy, 1939-1941." Journal of Baltic Studies, 4 (1973), 211-25.

On the secret protocol of 28 Sept. 1939, which amended the Nazi-Soviet pact of the previous month, and its subsequent history.

1170. Khadduri, Majid. "General Nuri's Flirtations with the Axis Powers." Middle East Journal, 16 (1962), 328-36.

1171. Krecker, Lothar. Deutschland und die Türkei im zweiten Weltkrieg. Frankfurt/M., 1964.

1172. Lutzhöft, Hans-Jürgen. Deutsche Militärpolitik und schwedische Neutralität, 1939-1942. Neumünster, 1981.

See also his "Deutschland und Schweden während des Norwegenfeldzuges (9. April-10. Juni 1940)." Vierteljahrshefte für Zeitgeschichte, 22 (1974), 382-416.

1173. Madani, S. Djalal. Iranische Politik und Drittes Reich. Frankfurt/M., 1986.

Focus on relations during World War II, with a chapter on the historical background.

1174. Pommerin, Reiner. Das Dritte Reich und Lateinamerika: Die deutsche Politik gegenüber Süd- und Mittelamerika, 1939-1942. Düsseldorf, 1977.

Mainly trade relations, because German policy toward Latin America was marked by a lack of design and planning and by conflicts between the foreign ministry and Bohle's AO.

1175. Ruhl, Klaus-Jörg. Spanien im zweiten Weltkrieg: Franco, die Falange, und das "Dritte Reich." Hamburg, 1975.

Solid study of German-Spanish relations, based on foreign ministry records and the papers of ambassador von Stohrer.

1176. Schechtman, Joseph B. The Mufti and the Fuehrer: The Rise and Fall of Haj Amin el'Husseini. New York, 1965.

Biography, somewhat one-sided, of the anti-Zionist Grand Mufti of Jerusalem. See also Anthony R. DeLuca, "'Der Grossmufti' in Berlin: The Politics of Collaboration." International Journal of Middle East Studies, 10 (1979), 125-38.

1177. Schnabel, Reimund. Tiger und Schakal: Deutsche Indienpolitik, 1941-1943. Vienna, 1968.

Rather thin account of Subhas Chandra Bose's time in Berlin, where he was in contact with the foreign ministry to seek aid in stirring up India against the British.

1178. Schröder, Bernd Philipp. Deutschland und der Mittlere Osten im Zweiten Weltkrieg. Göttingen, 1975.

Fills a gap in our knowledge of relations between Nazi Germany and the Arab powers.

1179. Sommer, Erich F. Das Memorandum: Wie der Sowjetunion der Krieg erklärt wurde. Munich, 1981.

The end of the non-aggression pact, by an eyewitness. Includes a selection of documents.

1180. Tillmann, Heinz. Deutschlands Araberpolitik im Zweiten Weltkrieg. [East] Berlin, 1965.

On Germany's expansionist policy in the Near East.

1181. Trefousse, Hans L. Germany and American Neutrality, 1939-1941. New York, 1951.

An early account, based on documents from the foreign ministry and the war crimes trials, not superseded in its essentials.

1182. Weber, Frank G. The Evasive Neutral: Germany, Britain, and the Quest for a Turkish Alliance in the Second World War. Columbia, MO, 1979.

Describes Germany's Mid-East policy in detail, and shows that it failed largely because of its inherent contradictions.

1183. Weinberg, Gerhard. "Die deutsche Politik gegenüber den Vereinigten Staaten im Jahre 1941." In Kriegswende, Dezember 1941, edited by Jürgen Rohwer and Eberhard Jäckel. Frankfurt/M., 1984, pp. 73-79.

1184. ———. Germany and the Soviet Union, 1939-1941. Leiden, 1954.

A chronological survey of the period between the non-aggression pact and Hitler's attack on Russia; has stood up fairly well.

A dramatic rendering of a dramatic story, based on published materials and interviews, is Anthony Read and David Fisher, The Deadly Embrace: Hitler, Stalin, and the Nazi-Soviet Pact, 1939-1941. London, 1988.

1185.   West, John M. "The German-Swedish Transit Agreement of 1940." Scandinavian Studies, 50 (1978), 76-99.

1186.   Wittmann, Klaus. "Deutsch-schwedische Wirtschaftsbeziehungen im Zweiten Weltkrieg." In Forstmeier and Volkmann (no. 982), 182-218.

The wartime trade agreements and trade relations, and Germany's plans to incorporate Sweden in a German-dominated economic union. Also, Martin Fritz, "Les Relations économiques Germano-Suédoises durant la seconde guerre mondiale," Revue d'histoire de la deuxième guerre mondiale, 28 (1978), 33-58.

Peace Feelers

1187.   Fieldhouse, Noel. "The Anglo-German War of 1939-42: Some Movements to End It by a Negotiated Peace." Transactions of the Royal Society of Canada, 9 (1971), 285-312.

1188.   Fischer, Alexander. Sowjetische Deutschlandpolitik im Zweiten Weltkrieg, 1941-1945. Stuttgart, 1975.

Superb study of the troubled solidarity of the two allies (1939-41), the various contacts and peace feelers (e.g., the Kleist discussions in 1943), and Stalin's plans for Germany.

1189.   Fleischhauer, Ingeborg. Die Chance des Sonderfriedens: Deutsch-sowjetische Geheimgespräche, 1941-1945. Berlin, 1986.

On the varied and rather loose contacts between Germany and the Soviet Union.

1190.   Hansen, Reimer. "Ribbentrops Friedensfühler im Frühjahr 1945." Geschichte in Wissenschaft und Unterricht, 18 (1967), 716-30.

1191.   Kleist, Peter. Die europäische Tragödie. Pr. Oldendorf, 1971.

An expanded version of The European Tragedy (London, 1965), with some dubious information on German-Soviet contacts in 1939 and again in 1943-45. See also no. 136.

1192.   Koch, H.W. "The Spectre of a Separate Peace in the East: Russo-German 'Peace Feelers,' 1942-44." Journal of Contemporary History, 10 (1975), 531-49.

Examines the Kleist mission of 1943, its antecedents and consequences.

1193. Martin, Bernd. Friedensinitiativen und Machtpolitik im zweiten Weltkrieg, 1939-1942. Düsseldorf, 1974.

A new perspective on the war: attempts by the belligerents on both sides to end hostilities, set in the context of diplomatic and military developments. Excellent at exploring motives, agendas, possibilities. The first of two volumes (the second to cover 1943-45).

See also, Martin's "Britisch-deutsche Friedenskontakte in den ersten Monaten des Zweiten Weltkrieges: Eine Dokumentation über die Vermittlungsversuche von Birger Dahlerus," Zeitschrift für Politik (1972), 206-21.

1194. ———. "Das 'Dritte Reich' und die 'Friedens'-Frage im Zweiten Weltkrieg." In Michalka (no. 656), 526-49.

Overlaps in part with his "Verhandlungen über separate Friedensschlüsse, 1942 bis 1945," Militärgeschichtliche Mitteilungen, 20 (1976), 95-113.

1195. Minuth, Karl-Heinz. "Sowjetisch-deutsche Friedenskontakte 1943." Geschichte in Wissenschaft und Unterricht, 16 (1965), 38-45.

1196. Noack, Ulrich. Norwegen zwischen Friedensvermittlung und Fremdherrschaft. Krefeld, 1952.

A German historian, who served as cultural attaché in Oslo in the early part of the war, describes his contacts with representatives of the enemy and his role in soundings for ending hostilities. His version has been challenged by Norwegians.

1197. Stehle, Hansjakob. "Deutsche Friedensfühler bei den Westmächten im Februar/März 1945." Vierteljahrshefte für Zeitgeschichte, 30 (1982), 538-55; and in Bracher, Funke, and Jacobsen (no. 260), 509-28.

1198. Viault, Bernard S. "Les démarches pour le rétablissement de la paix (septembre 1939-août 1940)." Revue d'histoire de la deuxième guerre mondiale, 17 (1967), 13-30.

Capitulation

1199. Bernadotte af Wisborg, Folke. The Curtain Falls: The Last Days of the Third Reich. New York, 1945.

On Himmler's attempts to make peace with the West (but not the East) in the spring of 1945.

1200.   Dulles, Allen W., and Gaevernitz, Gero von. The Secret Surrender. London, 1946.

The secret negotiations between the SS and the American OSS for the surrender of Germany's troops in Italy.

1201.   Hansen, Reimer. Das Ende des Dritten Reiches: Die deutsche Kapitulation 1945. Stuttgart, 1966.

The last months of Nazi Germany: Hitler's position on surrender, unofficial contacts for ending the war, Dönitz's policy and the surrender.

See also, Hansen's "Die deutsche Kapitulation, 1945," in Historisch-Politische Streiflichter, edited by Kurt Jürgensen and Reimer Hansen (Neumünster, 1971), pp. 235-56, which updates the book; and his "Aussenpolitik im Zusammenbruch des Dritten Reiches," in Funke (no. 643), 115-34.

1202.   Kimche, Jon. Spying for Peace: General Guisan and Swiss Neutrality. London, 1961.

Information on the surrender negotiations.

1203.   Lüdde-Neurath, Walter. Regierung Dönitz: Die letzten Tage des Dritten Reiches. 5th ed. Leoni, 1981 (1st ed., 1950).

Personal account by Dönitz's naval adjutant, with a selection of documents.

1204.   Smith, Bradley F., and Agarossi, Elena. Operation Sunrise: The Secret Surrender. New York, 1979.

New perspective on the surrender of German forces in Northern Italy in 1945, based on hitherto classified documents.

1205.   Steinert, Marlis G. Die 23 Tage der Regierung Dönitz. Düsseldorf, 1967.

On the final collapse, with interesting details on the capitulation.

V. INDEX

The index includes all the items in the bibliography. They are listed by author and, in the case of handbooks, journals, and collections of documents, by title. Items referring to major events and major figures are also listed by subject. The numbers refer to individual entries, not to pages.

INDEX

253

INDEX

INDEX